UNITED STATES AIR FORCE
IN BRITAIN

UNITED STATES AIR FORCE
IN BRITAIN

Its aircraft, bases and strategy since 1948

ROBERT JACKSON

Airlife
England

First published in the UK in 2000
by Airlife Publishing Ltd

British Library Cataloguing-in-Publication Data
   A catalogue record for this book
   is available from the British Library

ISBN 1 84037 075 0

Typeset by Servis Filmsetting Ltd, Manchester
Printed in China

Airlife Publishing Ltd
101 Longden Road, Shrewsbury, SY3 9EB, England
E-mail: airlife@airlifebooks.com
Website: www.airlifebooks.com

Introduction

My aim throughout this book has been to examine the fifty-year presence of the United States Air Force in Britain within the context of American military strategy and USAF activities worldwide, because I do not believe that one can be sensibly discussed without reference to the other. Therefore, if readers find themselves suddenly catapulted into France's war in what was Indo-China in the 1950s, or into Cuba in 1962, I would ask them to be patient, for there are good reasons for such digressions.

I have tried also to set the decades of nuclear confrontation between East and West in its proper perspective, sticking to the military rather than the political standpoint, and readers may be surprised to learn that the most dangerous flashpoint that might have resulted in an armed conflict in Europe belongs to much more recent history than we have been led to believe.

There is, however, a central thread that runs throughout this book. It is the quite extraordinary degree of military co-operation that existed at all levels between the USAF and the Royal Air Force during the perilous years of the Cold War. It survived all manner of political adversity and it remains firmly in place today, in a newly structured NATO that has a definite – perhaps critical – role to play in a dangerously fragmented world.

Robert Jackson
Darlington, County Durham

Contents

CHAPTER ONE

Crisis Response:
The Berlin Blockade

In the last week of March 1946, four Boeing RB-29A Superfortresses and a similar number of B-17 Flying Fortresses flew into RAF Marham, Norfolk, to take part in a series of special trials in conjunction with the RAF's Central Bomber Establishment, whose Avro Lincolns were also based at Marham. Under the code-name Project 'Ruby', the trials involved dropping VB (Vertical Bomb) series weapons on former German U-boat pens in Kiel Bay. The VB bombs were free-fall weapons to which various guidance systems were fitted; the most numerous was the VB1 Azon (a contraction of 'azimuth only') which could be guided directionally. It was based on a 1,000lb M-44 bomb fitted with a new cruciform tail incorporating a radio receiver, tracking flare, vertical gyro to stabilise the missile right side up, and rudders. An experienced bombardier could ensure that the line of the bomb's trajectory passed through the target, but he could do nothing if the weapon dropped short or overshot. Nevertheless, the bomb and a development, the 2,000lb VB-2, had enjoyed some operational success against bridge targets in the latter months of World War Two.

The Project 'Ruby' trials, which lasted six months, were a key element in the development of further VB weapons, which had range as well as azimuth guidance. These bombs, called Razon and Tarzon – the latter a 12,000lb missile with a bomb casing based on the RAF's Tallboy penetration bomb, some examples of which were also dropped experimentally by the B-29s at Marham – were subsequently used during the Korean War with some success against bridge and reservoir targets.

The Ruby deployment to the United Kingdom coincided with the formation, on 21 March 1946, of the United States Army Air Forces Strategic Air Command, whose activities were to provide the lion's share of the USAF's presence in Britain for the next twenty years and whose deployments to British bases must always be seen in the context of its operations worldwide. Its mission, as defined by General Carl Spaatz, Commanding General of the Army Air Force, would be:

> to conduct long-range offensive operations in any part of the world either independently or in co-operation with land and Naval forces; to conduct maximum-range reconnaissance over land or sea either independently or in co-operation with land and Naval forces; to provide combat units capable of intense and sustained combat operations employing the latest and most advanced weapons; to train units and personnel for the maintenance of the Strategic Force in all parts of the world; to perform such special missions as the Commanding General, Army Air Forces may direct.

Strategic Air Command would eventually become the mightiest war machine the world had ever seen. Yet when the new Command came into existence its material assets were slender, and were to become even more so before the political climate of the late 1940s dictated rapid expansion and re-equipment.

The formation of the new Command was simple enough on paper; it was achieved by the expedient of re-designating Headquarters Continental Air Forces as Headquarters Strategic Air Command. SAC HQ was established at Bolling Field, Washington DC, and was allocated the whole of the US Second Air Force, whose HQ was located at Colorado Springs. Other resources assigned to the Command from the beginning were the 311th Reconnaissance Wing, which was then equipped with 31 Beech F-2s (the photo-reconnaissance version of the Beech C-45 Expediter, later re-designated RC-45); the 4th and 56th Fighter Groups, the former with 75 P-51 Mustangs and the latter as yet with no aircraft allocated; and the 1st Air Transport Unit with 15 Douglas C-54 Skymasters. The Command was concentrated on 22 major bases and also controlled over 30 minor ones; personnel strength was about 100,000. SAC's commanding general was General George C. Kenney, but as he was at that time the senior US representative on the Military Staff Committee of the United Nations, his deputy, Major-General St Clair Streett, served as SAC's commanding general until Kenney could assume full responsibility in October 1946. Brigadier-General Frederic H. Smith Jr was Chief of Staff.

On 31 March 1946 Second Air Force was deactivated, its personnel and functions being absorbed by Fifteenth Air Force, which was activated on the same day at Colorado Springs. Second AF was assigned, still with an inactive status, to the Air Defense Command. On 7 June, in preparation for the assignment of a second numbered air force to the Strategic Air Command, Headquarters Eighth Air Force was relieved of its assignment to the US Army in the Pacific, and on 1 August Eighth Air Force HQ was attached for administrative purposes to the Fifteenth Air Force. The attachment was temporary, HQ Eighth AF moving from MacDill to Fort Worth, Texas, on 1 November. HQ Eighth AF was manned largely by personnel drawn from HQ 58th Bombardment Wing (Very Heavy) which was also established at Fort Worth. Also on 1 November, about half of the Fifteenth AF's fully equipped combat units were transferred to the Eighth AF, which was declared fully operational on the 19th.

By this time, SAC HQ had moved from Bolling to Andrews Field, Maryland. The Command's offensive strength now comprised nine very heavy bomb groups, all equipped with Boeing B-29s and each with a paper establishment of 30 aircraft. In fact, only six of the groups had been assigned aircraft, and even then they were under strength, the total number of B-29s on SAC's inventory in the autumn of 1946 standing at 148. The Command was still a conventional bombing force; only one unit, the 509th Bomb Group – the group formed specifically for dropping the first operational atomic bombs – had aircraft that were suitably modified to carry these large, bulky, first-generation nuclear weapons.

In July 1946, the 509th BG took part in Operation 'Crossroads'. Centred on Bikini Atoll, the object of this exercise was to study the effects of two nuclear explosions on a simulated naval force consisting of captured and time-expired warships. The exercise involved the efforts of some 42,000 personnel, operating under a provisional organisation known as Task Force One. Task Group 1.5, the Army Air Force contingent, consisted of about 2,200 personnel drawn mainly from SAC and commanded by Brigadier-General Roger M. Ramey, the officer commanding the 58th Bombardment Wing. Task Group 1.5 was responsible for delivering the air-dropped atomic bomb (the other, a device rather than a bomb, was to be attached to a ship and exploded under water) and for providing aircraft to photograph the explosion and collect scientific data.

On 1 July 1946, *Dave's Dream*, a 509th BG B-29 piloted by Major Woodrow P. Swancutt and temporarily based on the island of Kwajalein, dropped a Nagasaki-type (plutonium) bomb on 73 ships assembled off Bikini. The air-bursting weapon, of about 18 kilotons yield, destroyed five of the ships and severely damaged nine others. Task Group 1.5 also took part in the second phase of Operation 'Crossroads', the underwater explosion on 25 July, by providing aircraft for photographic, data collection and support functions.

In October 1946, in accordance with its stated global role, SAC despatched an entire B-29 group outside the limits of the continental United States for the first time on a period of temporary duty (TDY). The 28th Bomb Group deployed from Grand Island Army Air Field, Nebraska, to Elmendorf in Alaska for six months of combat training in arctic conditions, returning in April 1947 to a new base at Rapid City, South Dakota (see chapter three).

Meanwhile, in November 1946, SAC had despatched aircraft overseas in what was to be the first of many shows of force. The decision to do so came in the wake of the shooting down of two US Army C-47s over Yugoslavia by Soviet fighter aircraft. Colonel James C. Selser Jr, commanding the 43rd Bomb Group at Davis-Monthan Field, Arizona, led a flight of six B-29s to Rhein-Main airfield in Germany; they remained there for two weeks, during which time they made several flights along the border of Soviet-occupied territory, visited a number of European locations and surveyed several airfields for possible future use by SAC's B-29s. Quite apart from the operational value of this deployment, it served clear notice on the Soviet Union, at a time of deteriorating East–West relations, that the United States would come to the aid of western Europe in the event of Soviet aggression.

On 10 October 1946, Headquarters US Army Air Forces gave the Strategic Air Command a secondary mission: maritime reconnaissance and anti-submarine warfare. Six 509th Bomb Group B-29s deployed to Rio Hato, Panama, to participate with US Navy forces in a joint tactical exercise called Operation 'Nullus', the B-29s flying search and bombing missions against an 'enemy' task force moving north from Peru. In

December, SAC chose the 307th Bomb Group at MacDill Field, Florida, to develop the necessary tactics and requirements for this new role.

The designation of the Strategic, Tactical and Air Defense Commands in 1946 was the prelude to the inauguration, in July 1947, of the United States Air Force as a separate entity, now independent of Army control. As far as the Strategic Air Command was concerned, 1947 was a year of reorganisation and streamlining, much of it made necessary by an austere defence budget. The task of turning SAC into a muscular, combat-efficient force fell in the main to Brigadier-General Clements McMullen, who was brought in from the Eighth Air Force to be deputy commander, and he set about the job ruthlessly, pruning an unwieldy administrative machine down to manageable levels and centralising control. This process resulted in a number of SAC units being removed from the command of the Fifteenth Air Force and assigned directly to HQ SAC; they included the 311th Reconnaissance Wing, the 4th, 56th and 82nd Fighter Groups, and the 307th Bomb Group. Fifteenth Air Force was left strictly as a bomber command with three fully equipped B-29 units, the 28th, 93rd and 97th Bomb Groups. Eighth Air Force retained control of the 7th, 43rd and 33rd Fighter Groups, and the 1st Air Transport Unit.

During the year, the 311th Reconnaissance Wing was heavily involved in Operation 'Eardrum', its aircraft carrying out a complete photographic survey of Greenland and also surveying the polar route from Iceland to Alaska. So far, the 311th Wing had performed its task with a mixture of F-2 (RC-45), F-9 (RB-17) and B-29 aircraft, the latter having been fitted with temporary camera installations. In July 1947, however, the Wing received its first two fully equipped F-13A (RB-29) aircraft, and as more RB-29s were taken on strength the old F-2s were phased out. The first RB-29s were assigned to the 16th Photo Squadron (Special).

Meanwhile, the 509th Bomb Group continued to pioneer nuclear mission profiles and delivery techniques, providing SAC with the nucleus of an atomic bombing force, while the 307th Bomb Group developed the maritime function. Between May and October, the non-specialist bomber groups deployed to Yokota Air Base, Japan, for training on a rotational basis, and carried out a number of training and goodwill missions to England, West Germany, Italy, France, Holland and Belgium. The first such visit to England took place on 9 June 1947, when nine B-29s of the 340th Bomb Squadron, 97th Bomb Group (Col Charles Sommers) arrived at RAF Marham from their home base, Andrews Field in Maryland, and stayed for a week.

In the continental United States, operational training reached a new peak in the spring and summer of 1947 with a series of simulated attacks on metropolitan areas such as Los Angeles (11 April), Chicago (1 August) and New York. The latter attack took place on 16 May, when 101 B-29s filled the sky over the city with contrails in an impressive show of strength.

If the American public had any doubts about the need for such training on a large scale in peacetime, these were quickly dispelled when, in June 1948, the Russians imposed their blockade of the divided city of

Berlin. The now-famous airlift was quickly established by the western powers, and steps were taken to prevent the Russians from interfering with it. This could only be achieved by despatching modern combat aircraft to Europe with the utmost priority, and the spearhead of such a reinforcement was the B-29, which had the capability to hit the Russians hard. When the blockade began, one B-29 squadron of the 301st Bomb Group was on rotational training at Fürstenfeldbruck, Germany, and SAC immediately ordered the Group's other two B-29 squadrons to move to Goose Bay, Labrador, to reinforce Germany if necessary. Two additional B-29 groups, the 28th and 307th, were placed on alert and ordered to be ready to deploy within twelve and three hours respectively. The rest of the SAC bomber force was placed on 24-hour alert.

By early July, all three squadrons of the 301st Group were deployed at Fürstenfeldbruck, and on 16 July a joint announcement was made by the British Air Ministry and the US Air Force to the effect that two B-29 groups, totalling 60 aircraft, were flying from the USA to bases in England 'for a short period of temporary duty'; that this movement was 'part of the normal long-range flight training programme instituted over a year ago by the US Strategic Air Command'; and that the groups would be based at RAF Marham in Norfolk and RAF Waddington in Lincolnshire under the operational control of General Curtis LeMay, Commanding General of the US Air Forces in Europe (USAFE). It was also announced that C-54 aircraft would be transporting maintenance men and supplies to the UK, that each B-29 would carry a regular and a spare crew, and that about 1,500 men would be involved in the deployment.

It was the first time that the USAF would be deploying combat aircraft to another sovereign nation in peacetime, and just how this arrangement came about merits some explanation. Unlike the situation in Germany, where the United States had acquired its bases by right of occupation, the US had no bases of its own in the United Kingdom. Moreover, the two nations had no formal agreement permitting such a deployment, and six squadrons of strategic bombers constituted a sizeable military force to be deployed on British soil in peacetime without formal agreements between the host nation and visiting forces.

Setting aside the political implications, the fact that the B-29 – the West's largest strategic bomber – was able to deploy to British airfields at all was no mere accident. At the end of World War Two hundreds of military airfields remained intact in the UK, but most were Class A Standard Airfields with runways only 6,000 feet long and 150 feet wide, adequate for combat-loaded B-17s and B-24s and for the RAF's Lincolns. The B-29, however, carrying a far greater bomb load than its predecessors, required runways 8,000 feet long and 200 feet wide, and in 1948, thanks to the forward thinking of two senior officers, four such airfields were designated for American use.

In 1946, while making a final tour of air force installations in the United Kingdom, Marshal of the Royal Air Force Sir Arthur Tedder, Chief of the Air Staff, and General Carl Spaatz, Commanding General, US Army Air Forces, had discussed the uneasy peace that had followed the Allied victory in Europe. The western Allies were demobilising at a rapid rate but the Russians were not, indicating that a political and military struggle in Europe might lie ahead. Tedder and Spaatz therefore agreed that four air bases in East Anglia which already had improved runway facilities – Scampton, Marham, Waddington and Lakenheath – would be prepared for use by B-29s in the event of a forthcoming emergency in the European theatre.

To support the B-29 groups on their periods of temporary duty in England the Americans needed a supply and maintenance depot. The site selected was Burtonwood, in Cheshire, which in 1942 had been set up as a central repair depot for all American-built aircraft and engines used by the RAF and the USAAF units which had begun arriving to join the air offensive against Germany. The repair and maintenance facilities had been greatly expanded during the war years, and when the war ended a skeleton USAAF staff had remained to look after existing stocks of American equipment. Further maintenance facilities were created at Burtonwood in January 1946 with the formation of the RAF's No. 276 Maintenance Unit. Burtonwood's wartime workshops and installations were still intact, and it was logical to reactivate them. Consequently, in the summer of 1948, USAF technical personnel were moved into the base to prepare support facilities for Operation 'Looker', as the SAC deployments were to be known.

On 16 July 1948 the 3rd Air Division (Provisional) was established under General Order No. 54, issued by General LeMay, at RAF Marham under the initial command of Colonel Stanley T. Wray, a USAFE officer who was in England surveying airfields. Aligned under HQ USAFE at Wiesbaden, it was assigned operational control over the deployed B-29 units. On 17 July, 30 B-29s of the 28th Bomb Group (Col John B. Henry Jr), the first to be deployed, moved from Rapid City AFB, South Dakota, to their British base – not, as it turned out, either Marham or Waddington, but to RAF Scampton, recently vacated by the Lancasters and Wellingtons of the Bomber Command Instrument Rating and Examining Flight. The next day, the 307th Bomb Group (Col Clifford J. Heflin), comprising the 370th, 371st and 372nd Bombardment Squadrons, brought its Superfortresses to Marham and Waddington. A third group, the 2nd (Col William E. Eubank Jr), deployed to RAF Lakenheath in Suffolk between 8 and 13 August.

None of the B-29s deployed to Europe were nuclear-capable; in fact, only a relatively small number of SAC's B-29s (known as Silver Plate aircraft) were as yet equipped for the carriage and release of nuclear weapons, and these were retained on alert in the USA. In any case, no agreement existed at that time between the US and UK governments for the basing of nuclear weapons on British soil. The Russians, however, had to assume that the deployed B-29s were nuclear-capable, and the presence of even a small number of Superfortresses in Britain would, it was thought, have a considerable deterrent effect. The implementation of the informal agreement between the British Air Ministry and the USAF for the use of the designated British air bases by conventionally armed US bombers was now little more than a formality to which Clement

Strategic Air Command B-29s pictured in flight over Norfolk. (via Harry Holmes)

Attlee's Labour government readily agreed. General LeMay, meanwhile, had determined that if war should break out over the Berlin issue, he would do his utmost to stem a Soviet attack with the scant resources available. His primary concern was to protect the vital supply line between the American Zone and Bremerhaven, which was vulnerable to a sudden Russian armoured thrust, and to this end he set about organising a defence in depth by setting up a series of tactical air bases well to the west of the Rhine in France and Belgium, where they would be less vulnerable to a surprise attack. The Chiefs of Staff of the French and Belgian Air Forces, Generals Charles Lecheres and Lucien Leboutte, readily agreed to this plan and made several of their airfields available for American air reinforcement. Quietly and by devious methods the airfields were stocked with bombs, fuel and spare parts, and 200 USAF personnel in civilian clothing were assigned to each base.

The first of General LeMay's planned jet fighter reinforcements for USAFE began on 12 July 1948, when 16 Lockheed F-80A Shooting Stars of the 56th Fighter Wing (Lt-Col David Schilling), a unit then assigned to SAC, left Selfridge Field, Michigan, and flew via Dow AFB, Maine, Goose Bay in Labrador, Bluie West One in Greenland and Reykjavik in Iceland to make their UK landfall at Stornoway after a total transatlantic flight time of 5 hours and 15 minutes. On 21 July the fighters flew on to Odiham, Hampshire, where the USAF personnel visited No. 54 Squadron RAF. On 12 July, six de Havilland Vampire F3s of No. 54 Squadron had set out from Odiham to make a goodwill tour of Canada and the United States; they had taken the same route as the F-80s, though in the opposite direction, and it had taken them three hours longer, partly because of their lower cruising speed and partly because they encountered jet streams of up to 200 mph at their cruising altitude of 35,000 feet. After their Odiham visit the F-80s flew on to Fürstenfeldbruck, where they spent six weeks on exercises, including fighter affiliation with B-29s, before returning to the USA.

Early in August 72 F-80s of the 36th Fighter Wing were shipped to Glasgow in the aircraft carrier USS *Sicily* and the US Army transport vessel *Kirschbaum*, and after being offloaded and overhauled they departed for Fürstenfeldbruck between 13 and 20 August.

On 7 August 1948 Major-General Leon W. Johnson assumed command of the 3rd Air Division (Provisional), and on 23 August 1948, once it had become apparent that the tensions of the Berlin crisis were leading to a dramatic and dangerous stand-off between East and West, the term 'provisional' was dropped from 3rd Air Division's title. Later, on 8 September, the Division moved its HQ to Bushey Park near Teddington, Middlesex. It was to be a temporary move; on 15 April 1949, the Division moved to larger facilities at South Ruislip. By that time, 3rd Air Division had assumed the status of a separate major command (on 3 January 1949), and on 6 April the Strategic Air Command assumed jurisdiction over it 'for activities pertaining to Strategic Air Command units on rotational duty in the United Kingdom'.

On 25 August 1948, 3rd Air Division announced that the contingent at Burtonwood was to be expanded to 2,500 personnel under the command of Lt-Col Walter Ott. This would make Burtonwood the principal USAF base in Britain, responsible not only for supporting the B-29 deployments, but also for providing facilities for the supply and maintenance of American aircraft engaged in the rapidly expanding Operation 'Vittles', as the US contribution to the airlift was known. A few days later it was revealed that the number of US military aircraft in Europe – including the B-29s and the transports involved in the airlift – had risen to 466, and that the number of USAF personnel had risen to 18,000, about 6,000 of whom would be based in Britain before the end of the year.

At this time the principal maintenance depot for the USAF aircraft engaged in the airlift was Oberpfaffenhofen, in the American Zone, where the necessary 200-hour inspections were carried out. But facilities at this depot were primitive; aircraft were washed down with a mixture of kerosene and water on open-air ramps because there was no adequate hangarage, and with winter approaching it was clear that this would quickly become unacceptable. Top priority was therefore given to the rapid expansion of the Burtonwood facilities with the help of experienced technicians from the big USAF Air Materiel Command centre at Tinker AFB, near Oklahoma City, who arrived in England early in September and set about reactivating the wartime maintenance facilities. Gradually, they set up a three-quarter-mile-long assembly line on which eight aircraft a day could be cleaned by commercial-type vacuum cleaners and then hosed down with detergent.

The smooth operation of the facility at Burtonwood during the months that followed was crucial to the airlift operation as a whole; it is no exaggeration to say that the airlift could not have succeeded without it. All USAFE C-47s were withdrawn from the airlift at the end of September and from then on Burtonwood handled only the big four-engined C-54 Skymasters, which needed some 20 man-hours of maintenance for every flying hour. Every C-54 engaged in the airlift underwent checks after every 50, 100 and 150 hours' flying, the 100-hour check involving a change of spark plugs and oil. These checks were carried out at the aircraft's home base, but for the 200-hour inspection it was flown to Burtonwood for a six-phase check involving washing and cleaning the aircraft, running up the engines, carrying out maintenance work on engines, pipes and ignition, servicing the electrical systems, instruments, cables and rigging, and inspecting the hydraulics, wheels, brakes and tyres. Finally, each C-54 was subjected to a rigorous pre-flight check and cleared for its return to operations. Responsibility for the 200-hour inspections was assigned to the 59th Air Depot, which was under the jurisdiction of Burtonwood's 7540th Maintenance Group. The RAF, it should be mentioned, had its own Transport Command Major Servicing Unit at Honington.

The early months of the USAF deployment to Britain were characterised by a quite remarkable degree of co-operation with the Royal Air Force at all echelons. At the lower levels, the RAF made available to the USAF 385 vehicles of all types, from motorcycles to six-ton trucks, while on the financial level there was an early understanding that the British would supply the Americans with airfields, accommodation and telecommunication facilities free of charge, provided that the expenditure did not exceed the normal cost of RAF requirements and standards. This 'free of charge' aspect of the USAF presence in the United Kingdom was unique in that it never applied to the American military presence in any other country.

It was, in fact, an example of the special relationship that existed between Great Britain and the United States at a military level. The notion of such a relationship was derided many times by those of various political persuasions, but it did exist, and it continued to exist throughout the Cold War era. It was destined to withstand the passage of years, and to endure many onslaughts upon it.

Douglas C-47 transports were serviced at Burtonwood in the early stages of the Berlin Airlift.

CHAPTER TWO

The Expanding Bomber Force
and UK Air Defence

Once installed, the three B-29 groups in England began a systematic training programme designed to familiarise the crews with the European environment – although some had seen service there during the war years – and also involving simulated bombing attacks on targets around the United Kingdom and elsewhere in western Europe. In fact, simulated attacks on targets in Britain had been carried out earlier in the year by the Germany-based B-29s of the 301st Bombardment Group, but these had been *ad hoc* affairs involving small numbers of aircraft. Following the deployment of the B-29 groups to British bases, the Americans were formally invited to take part in a British air defence exercise, code-named 'Dagger', scheduled to take place between 3 and 5 September 1948. Eighteen B-29s made mock attacks on British targets on the first day and 30 on the second, the RAF's air defence fighters making 234 intercepts on the bombers during the period of the exercise.

The results of the bombing exercises over the UK, and those held in the United States, served to underline a fact that was already well known to Strategic Air Command's commanding general, George C. Kenney. Confronted with serious manning, supply and administrative problems throughout the first two years of its existence, SAC had been unable to devote much time to bombing practice, and as a consequence its bombing accuracy was far below the required standard. Hoping to stimulate interest in improving bombing accuracy, General Kenney decided to inaugurate an annual SAC bombing competition, the first of which was held at Castle FB, California, from 20 to 27 June 1948. Ten B-29 groups took part, each group represented by three crews, and although some experienced crews did well, the overall result was far from encouraging.

In October 1948 General Kenney was reassigned and command of SAC was assumed by General Curtis E. LeMay, fresh from his tour of duty with USAFE. LeMay had directed the strategic bombing offensive against Japan with great success during the last year of the Pacific war, and was horrified to discover his new Command's state of unpreparedness. To find out how bad the situation really was, he ordered a simulated bombing exercise to be mounted under realistic war conditions against the city of Denver; very few crews got within 30 miles of the target. LeMay at once ordered the training of the medium-range bomber force to be intensified; rotational training to overseas bases was stepped up, high-altitude bombing accuracy was improved, and combat crew proficiency was raised through the system of 'lead crew' training which had been proved in World War Two.

The temporary duty period of the three B-29 groups in England, originally set at 30 days, was extended to 60 days and finally to 90, setting the pattern for other SAC units that were to follow. At Scampton, the 28th Bomb Group's B-29s were replaced by those of the 301st Bomb Group from Germany; these departed in turn on 15 January 1949, whereupon Scampton reverted to RAF use. At Marham, the 307th Bomb Group was replaced in November 1948 by the 97th Bomb Group, comprising the 340th and 371st Bombardment Squadrons. Only one other SAC B-29 unit, the 22nd Bomb Group (2nd, 19th and 408th Bombardment Squadrons) was to use Marham; subsequent TDY detachments operated the more advanced Boeing B-50.

The latter aircraft was a straightforward development of the B-29, but with improvements that included more powerful engines and a taller fin and rudder. It originated as the B-29D and was in fact 75 per cent a new aircraft, with a new aluminium wing structure some 16 per cent stronger and 26 per cent more efficient than that of the B-29, while weighing 650lb less. The vertical tail surfaces were five feet higher than those of the B-29, and were hinged to fold horizontally over the starboard tailplane to enable the B-50 to be housed in existing hangars. Wings, tail unit, landing gear and other items of equipment of the B-50 were interchangeable with the Boeing C-97A transport aircraft.

The first B-50, an 'A' model (serial 46–017), was delivered to the 43rd Bomb Group at Davis-Monthan AFB, Arizona, on 20 February 1948, and further examples were delivered to the 509th Bomb Group at the same location soon afterwards. The 43rd and 509th Bomb Groups were the Strategic Air Command's nuclear strike force, and the advent of the B-50 gave a considerable boost to their operational efficiency. Powered by four Pratt & Whitney R-436055 Wasp Major engines, the B-50 had a range of 6,000 miles carrying a 10,000lb nuclear store; maximum speed was 400 mph at 25,000 feet, and operational ceiling was 40,000 feet. The aircraft could also lift up to 28,000lb of conventional bombs.

All B-50s were equipped for flight refuelling, and in July 1948 the 43rd and 509th Air Refueling Squadrons were activated at Davis-Monthan AFB and assigned to the 43rd and 509th Bomb Groups. These two squadrons were the first flight refuelling units in the USAF, and began to receive their KB-29M tanker aircraft later in the year. The KB-29M employed the British-designed probe-and-drogue refuelling system.

The story of flight refuelling in Strategic Air Command had begun in November 1946, when the USAF Air Materiel Command (AMC) asked the Boeing Company to provide a team to investigate air-to-air refuelling methods and installations. The result of their study recommended the full adoption of the 'looped hose' method, developed by the British firm Flight Refuelling Ltd, for all SAC B-29 and B-50 aircraft.

Just before Easter 1947, Mr Latimer-Needham, then chief engineer with Flight Refuelling Ltd, received a telephone call from a US general in Washington, saying that he was arriving in the UK in two days' time to negotiate a contract for FR equipment, and to take back one complete set with him. Two B-29s duly

TOP: *Photo-survey variant of the Boeing B-50.*
ABOVE: *Boeing KB-50J of the 420th Air Refueling Squadron, Sculthorpe. (Harry Holmes)*

landed at Ford in Hampshire, Flight Refuelling Ltd's base, and negotiations proceeded over the whole of Easter. By the time the US contingent left, complete with their set of equipment, a contract had been signed for the provision of a large number of looped hose sets, together with technical aid.

In March 1948, Boeing and Air Materiel Command conducted Operation 'Drip', which involved flight-testing FR equipment in two B-29s. As a result of these trials, AMC asked Boeing to undertake an accelerated programme to incorporate the British looped hose system in SAC's B-29s and B-50s; at the same time, Boeing was also asked to begin development of a superior system. By May 1948, Boeing had converted a pair of B-29s to flight refuelling tankers, and had also introduced a new boom system design at the drawing board stage, which AMC authorised them to develop further. In addition, AMC now amended the design requirement to include single-seat jet fighters, which required a different method from the looped hose

The Boeing KB-29 tanker gave SAC's bombers a greatly improved combat radius.

system. Late in 1948, while Boeing carried out the first flight tests of the 'flying boom' system, Flight Refuelling Ltd began work on a system for tanking fighter aircraft, and within four months had developed the probe-and-drogue method. The first dry contact was made in April 1949 between an Avro Lancastrian tanker and a Gloster Meteor fighter.

Meanwhile, in February 1949, B-50A *Lucky Lady II* of the 43rd BG had made a non-stop round-the-world flight using the looped hose method. The first KB-29M tankers incorporating this system had been delivered late in 1948 to the 43rd and 509th Air Refueling Squadrons at Davis-Monthan AFB and Roswell AFB, and it was the 43rd ARS that took part in this operation.

The first flying boom KB-29P tanker conversion flew in May 1949, and by the end of the following year SAC had activated 12 Medium Air Refueling Squadrons, eight

with an establishment of 20 KB-29s and four with 12. Of these, four were fully equipped, five were partially equipped, and three as yet had no aircraft assigned. SAC's first KB-29P, 44-86427, was delivered to the 97th ARS at Biggs AFB, Texas, on 1 September 1950.

The combination of B-50 and KB-29M enabled SAC to extend its operational range enormously, but an even more important step in this direction came on 26 June 1948 with the delivery of the first Convair B-36 bomber to the 7th Bomb Group at Carswell AFB, Texas. The first bomber with a truly global strategic capability to serve with any air force, the B-36 flew for the first time on 8 August 1946, powered by six Pratt & Whitney R-4630–25 'pusher' engines developing 3,000 hp each. The first XB-36 was followed by two more prototypes, the YB-36 and the YB-36A, both of which flew in 1947. Unlike the two earlier aircraft, which had

The massive Convair B-36, which gave SAC a truly global capability, was a frequent TDY visitor to the UK. (via Phil Jarrett)

conventional undercarriages, the YB-36A had a bogie-type assembly and a modified cockpit, the canopy being raised above the line of the fuselage to improve visibility. The B-36 was a massive aircraft, with a span of 230 feet and a length of 162 feet. It carried a crew of 16. Maximum speed over the target was 435 mph; service ceiling was 42,000 feet and range 8,000 miles. The aircraft carried a heavy defensive armament, with six retractable remotely controlled turrets each housing twin 20mm cannon, plus two 20mm cannon in the nose and two in the tail. Normal bomb load was a single 10,000lb nuclear store, but the aircraft could lift a maximum conventional bomb load of 84,000lb over short ranges.

An initial production batch of 22 B-36As was built, the first being delivered to Strategic Air Command in the summer of 1947. These aircraft were unarmed, and were used for crew training. The second production model, the B-36B, was powered by six Pratt & Whitney R-4630–41 engines with water injection, and was fully combat-equipped with twelve 20mm KM24A1 cannon in the six remotely controlled turrets, together with nose and tail armament. Seventy-three were built, the first flying on 8 July 1948. Thirty-five B-36A/B models had been delivered to SAC by the end of 1948.

The 43rd Bomb Group continued to operate B-29s during most of 1948, rearming gradually with the B-50, and in the course of the year undertook several long-distance flights with both types. On 22 July, three B-29s left Davis-Monthan AFB on a round-the-world record attempt; the flight was scheduled to take 14 days, but an extra day was required due to the crash of one of the B-29s in the Arabian Sea. The other two aircraft made eight en route stops and completed the 20,000-mile flight in a flying time of 103 hours and 50 minutes.

If this mission emphasised SAC's global deployment capability, it was overshadowed by a second long-range operation that took place between 7 and 9 December 1948, when a B-36B and a B-50A completed round-trip, non-stop flights from Carswell AFB to Hawaii. The B-36, assigned to the 7th Bomb Group, flew over 8,000 miles in 35 hours and 30 minutes. The B-50D, a 43rd Bomb Group aircraft, made the flight over a much longer route of 9,870 miles in 41 hours and 40 minutes, receiving three in-flight refuellings from KB-29M tankers of the 43rd and 509th Air Refueling Squadrons.

December 1948 saw the assignment of another British airfield, Sculthorpe, near Fakenham in Norfolk, to the USAF. Its runways having been lengthened and its facilities improved, it was placed on a Care and Maintenance basis by the RAF until February 1949, when the 92nd Bomb Group arrived with its B-29s.

On 6 April 1949, the Strategic Air Command assumed jurisdiction over the UK-based US 3rd Air Division for activities pertaining to SAC units on rotational duty in the United Kingdom. Major-General Leon W. Johnson, Commanding General of the 3rd Air Division, was made responsible to General Curtis E. LeMay for all matters in this respect.

Meanwhile, the Americans were expressing growing concern over the vulnerability of their East Anglian bomber bases to a Soviet surprise attack. In May 1949, Major-General Johnson wrote to the American Ambassador, Lewis Douglas, stating his desire to acquire better locations for basing the B-29s. In Johnson's opinion, Marham, Lakenheath and Sculthorpe were tactically unsuitable because of their nearness to the coast and their obvious vulnerability to enemy air attack; for adequate protection, the B-29s needed bases located behind the RAF fighter screen and behind the Greater London anti-aircraft defences.

An emergency plan called 'Double Quick' was already in place; it provided for the rapid movement of B-29s to other areas of England, preferably the Midlands, which were less vulnerable to attack and which could provide four airfields adequate for B-29 combat operations. This early requirement for bases further inland laid the foundation for the eventual procurement and rehabilitation of four RAF airfields: Brize Norton, Fairford, Upper Heyford and Greenham Common. Meanwhile, the rotational bomber units continued to come and go at Marham, Lakenheath and Sculthorpe; the USAF continued to seek more expansion of locations and facilities, but more bases required additional Congressional appropriations, and the securing of a comparable commitment from the UK government during a period of post-war austerity would be very difficult.

The USAF's concern over the vulnerability of its bases was justified, for in 1949 Britain's air defences were far from healthy. The post-war contraction of Fighter Command had actually begun before the end of the war, as the fighting in north-west Europe had moved steadily eastwards; by the end of hostilities in Europe in May 1945, of the eight Fighter Command Groups which had been responsible for the air defence of the UK, only two – Nos. 11 and 12 – were on full status, defending the country east and south of a line joining Cape Wrath at the north-west tip of Scotland, Banbury in Oxfordshire and St David's in Pembrokeshire. By December 1946, the Command's front-line strength was 192 aircraft in 18 day-fighter squadrons, each established with eight aircraft and armed with a mixture of Vampire, Meteor and Hornet aircraft, and six night-fighter squadrons armed with Mosquitos. In addition, 20 auxiliary squadrons, armed for the time being with piston-engined aircraft like the Spitfire and Mosquito, were in the process of reformation.

In December 1946, an Air Staff Directive to the AOC-in-C Fighter Command ordered that the Command's first priority during the next two years would be to concentrate on research and experimentation in air defence techniques, the main goals being to achieve the highest possible interception rate by day and night irrespective of the weather, to improve the raid reporting and fighter control organisation, and to standardise operational and training techniques to permit the rapid reinforcement of the Command in an emergency by fighter squadrons from Germany. This directive was based on the so-called Ten-Year Rule, which for defence planning purposes assumed that no threat of a major conflict would arise for at least ten years. Maximum use was to be made of existing aircraft, equipment and weapons, most of which would not be replaced until 1957 or thereabouts. There were enormous difficulties to be faced, of which a virtually bankrupt economy was only one. From a wartime air force over a million strong, the post-war

RAF was being progressively demobilised to a strength of around 300,000 all ranks; notwithstanding the reductions, manpower and aircraft still had to be spread over the whole UK commitment overseas, from Germany to the Far East.

The Air Ministry, well aware of the constraints it would have to face in the immediate post-war years, had nevertheless given much thought to the shape and organisation of the post-war air defences, as well as to the type of radars and data-processing equipment that would be required. As early as July 1945 it had issued a paper proposing a 'Defended Area' to be manned by a regular air defence force capable of expansion at short notice, and a 'Shadow Area' where a non-operational air defence network would be manned by a fully trained but non-regular reserve force; this could be brought to full operational status within two years. The Air Ministry also envisaged that the air defences would have to cope with targets flying at 600 knots at up to 100,000 feet, which meant that a future generation of early-warning radars must be able to detect high-level targets at a range of 330 miles and low-level targets at about 200 miles. A new radar system would have to incorporate secure IFF (Identification Friend/Foe) and have the capability to transmit a display of the recognised air picture to command and control centres up to 1,000 miles away.

Fighter Command worked hard to set up the Defended Area, initially from Flamborough Head in Yorkshire to Portland Bill on the Channel, but its efforts were hampered when the government called for a rapid rundown of manpower which left only 36 radars operational. The Command managed to set up four operational Master GCI (Ground Controlled Interception) stations in time for the major air exercises that took place in the autumn of 1948, after the Berlin crisis had developed, but even with a renewed interest in defence spending the best that could be done in the short term was to update the old wartime system by duplicating the radar cover, and in the meantime – as the air exercises revealed – British targets were virtually indefensible. During Exercise 'Dagger', for example, the defending fighters recorded a kill rate of only 15 per cent against the attacking B-29s.

The Berlin crisis, and subsequent events of 1949, effectively tore the Ten-Year Rule to shreds and led to a major reassessment of future air defence policy. Production of jet interceptors would now be doubled, and reconditioning of older fighter types accelerated. Air defences were to be improved with new equipment, and the auxiliary squadrons were to be brought up to strength and rearmed with jet aircraft as soon as possible. With the pace starting to quicken, a new Air Ministry Directive was issued to the AOC-in-C Fighter Command in August 1949, reflecting the urgency of the situation. In contrast to the previous one, which was concerned with research and experimentation in air defence and in the defence only of the area of the United Kingdom which could be manned effectively, the new directive stated firmly that the Command's operational commitment was the defence of the whole of the United Kingdom against air attack. Plans to strengthen Fighter Command and improve its equipment were further accelerated in the autumn of 1949, for by then the perceived threat from the Soviet Union had assumed potentially formidable proportions, as we shall see in the next chapter.

The year 1949 saw the first deployments of B-50s to the UK; in August the B-50As of the 65th Bombardment Squadron, 43rd Bomb Group, arrived on TDY with their supporting KB-29M tankers, remaining at RAF Lakenheath for 90 days. Other SAC units deploying B-50s to the UK in 1949 were the 509th Bomb Group (393rd and 715th Bombardment Squadrons) and the 2nd Bomb Group (20th Bombardment Squadron).

SAC crews also undertook more long-distance flights in 1949. On 2 March, *Lucky Lady II*, a B-50A of the 43rd Bomb Group, completed the first non-stop round-the-world flight, covering the 23,452 miles in 94 hours and one minute. Carswell AFB was the start and finishing point, and the aircraft was refuelled four times by KB-29 tankers of the 43rd Air Refueling Squadron. This was followed, on 12 March, by a long-distance record set up by a B-36 of the 7th Bomb Group, which flew 9,600 miles in 43 hours and 37 minutes without refuelling. The flight began and ended at Fort Worth, Texas, and was made as part of a series of operational trials carried out by the 7th Bomb Group's B-36s during the year, in which the speed, altitude performance, payload capacity, armament, and the ability of the aircraft to penetrate a realistic air defence system were all evaluated. Later in the year, between 3 and 7 October, B-36s took part in the second SAC Bombing Competition, the individual crew trophy going to a B-36 crew of the 28th Bomb Group, the second unit to arm with the type.

On 1 November 1949, the Second Air Force was established and assigned to SAC; HQ Second AF was activated at Barksdale AFB, Louisiana. This gave SAC three numbered air forces, each with a distinct mission. The Eighth Air Force was concerned mainly with heavy and medium bombers (the B-36 was now classed as SAC's heavy type, the B-29 and B-50 having been re-categorised as medium bombers) while the Fifteenth AF was exclusively a medium bomber force and the Second AF concentrated on reconnaissance activities. This produced a somewhat unwieldy structure, and on 1 April 1950 it was reorganised. Each numbered air force was assigned both bomber and reconnaissance aircraft, its units and bases grouped in specific geographical areas of the United States: the Second AF in the east, the Eighth in the centre, and the Fifteenth in the west.

Meanwhile, two political events had occurred in 1949 which were to have a major impact on the USAF's continued presence in the United Kingdom. The first was the signing, in April, of the North Atlantic Treaty, which was to result in the emergence of the NATO military structure; the second was the ABC (American, British, Canadian) Conference held in Washington during September, at which it was agreed that the RAF would be responsible for the air defence of Great Britain while the USAF would increase the number of bomber units operating from British bases.

The latter move was attended by considerable urgency, for while the ABC Conference was in progress an American surveillance aircraft had returned with disturbing evidence that the Russians had detonated an atomic device.

CHAPTER THREE

Probing Russia's Defences

As relations between East and West worsened, one area of particular concern to the Americans and British was the development of Soviet strategic bombers. As the Second World War drew to a close the Chief Administration of the Soviet Air Force, already mindful of changing political forces that would almost certainly lead to an East–West confrontation of some sort in the early post-war years, had plans in hand for the updating of all combat elements, and these included the formation of a modern strategic bombing force. With the wartime emphasis very much on the development of tactical bombers, assault aircraft and fighters, Soviet designers had had little time to study long-range bomber projects, and it was obvious that even if work on such projects began in 1944 there would still be a lengthy gap before a Soviet strategic bomber could be produced in series. Then, suddenly, a ready-made answer literally fell out of the sky in the shape of a Boeing B-29 Superfortress of the USAAF's 58th Bomb Wing, which made an emergency landing on Russian territory after an attack on a Japanese target in Manchuria. Before the end of 1944, the Russians had acquired three more B-29s in similar fashion.

By copying the B-29 in every detail, the Russians hoped to avoid all the technological problems associated with the development of an aircraft of this kind. The designer chosen for the task was Andrei N. Tupolev, while the job of copying the B-29's Wright R-3350 engines went to A. M. Shvetsov. The work was not easy; major snags cropped up frequently, particularly in connection with electronically controlled equipment such as the B-29's gun turrets. Despite everything, however, construction of the Russian B-29 copy – designated Tu-4 – was begun in March 1945, and the first of three prototypes would be ready for flight testing within two years.

Reports that reached US Intelligence of Russian developments in the strategic bomber field were at best vague, and although there was enough evidence to show that work was in progress the Americans would not become aware that a copy of the B-29 was involved until 1948, when the three Tu-4 prototypes were publicly revealed at the big Soviet air display at Tushino, near Moscow. What was clear in 1946, though, was that if the Russians were developing a bomber capable of launching an attack against the continental United States, such an attack would have to be made from bases in the Soviet Arctic, the aircraft relying on navigational aids positioned at forward sites in the polar regions, or from the Kamchatka Peninsula in the Far East.

Thanks to a series of well-publicised survey flights made in the 1930s, ostensibly to gather information for setting up a direct long-range air route to the United States, the Russians knew more about the Arctic than anyone else. The Americans, on the other hand, knew comparatively little, and this gap in their knowledge they were now anxious to fill. In March 1946,

therefore, the 46th Reconnaissance Squadron (Very Long Range) was deployed to Ladd Air Force Base in Alaska. Equipped with ten B-29s (including a couple of F-13s fitted out for photo-reconnaissance), the 46th RS came under the operational control of the 311th Reconnaissance Wing, which in turn was assigned to the newly established USAF Strategic Air Command. Following a series of preliminary survey flights over the Arctic by the 46th RS, which mainly involved the checking and upgrading of navigational equipment, the 28th Bomb Group, a B-29 unit stationed at Grand Island Army Air Field, Nebraska, deployed to Elmendorf in Alaska for a six-month period of training in arctic conditions. At this time, before the adoption of flight refuelling, the SAC B-29 crews knew that any missions against the USSR would be one-way, for their aircraft did not have sufficient range to recover to friendly bases.

In October 1947 the 46th RS was redesignated the 72nd Strategic Reconnaissance Squadron; this was part of a substantial reorganisation that took place following the creation of the United States Air Force in September. Within a year aircraft designations were also altered, the F-13A officially becoming the RB-29 in June 1948.

In 1948-9 the 72nd SRS carried out many photographic reconnaissance and ELINT (ELectronic INTelligence) missions over the Soviet Arctic and the Far East, its RB-29s equipped with oblique cameras that enabled them to photograph Russian territory while remaining in international air space. These long-range photographs, however, revealed little that was of use, and by the end of 1948 some RB-29s, stripped of all weapons and other unnecessary equipment to give them extra altitude, were making penetration flights into the Soviet Union on behalf of the US Central Intelligence Agency, such flights being authorised by the US president, Harry S. Truman. The first overflight was carried out on 5 August 1948 when a 72nd SRS RB-29 took off from Ladd AFB, made a surveillance flight over Siberia, and landed at Yokota AB, Japan, after a total time in the air of 19 hours and 40 minutes.

Flights of similar duration – and even on occasions of up to 30 hours – quickly became routine, the aircraft operating at 35,000 feet or more on missions that sometimes covered 5,000 miles. Before long, gaps in the Soviet radar coverage – which at this stage was quite rudimentary – were established, and RB-29 crews exploited such corridors to the full as they penetrated Russian territory. Sometimes, however, the RB-29s were detected and fighters sent up to intercept them, but until the MiG-15 entered service late in 1948 (and then only with trials units based in the western USSR) the Russians had no fighter that could touch them.

While the RB-29s carried out their photographic and electronic surveillance of the Soviet Union, officials of the US Atomic Energy Commission were expressing fears that the United States had little or no intelligence on the Soviet Union's nuclear research programme.

American concern about the development of Soviet atomic weapons led to the creation, in 1947, of a Long Range Detection Program and the establishment by the USAF of an airborne monitoring system capable of detecting and pinpointing a nuclear detonation within the main Soviet land mass or the Arctic. A number of WB-29 weather reconnaissance aircraft were equipped with air sampling boxes containing filters about the size of an eight- by ten-inch photographic plate, designed to collect radioactive particles from the atmosphere. The plates were changed every hour, and the aircraft's track during each period was recorded.

On 3 September 1949, long hours of patrol work at last paid dividends. A WB-29 flying at 18,000 feet between Japan and Alaska detected an unusual amount of radioactive debris, and the finding was confirmed by other WB-29 flights elsewhere in the world. Analysis of the particles by US atomic physicists revealed traces of the same kind of radioactive debris produced by American nuclear tests. It was clear that somewhere in the Asiatic land mass, the Russians had tested a nuclear device.

The news of the Russian test, which the Americans named 'Joe 1', was announced by President Truman on 23 September. Until about the middle of 1953, the Americans believed it had taken place on 27 August 1949; the actual date was 29 August. The apparent location of the test was in the general vicinity of the Aral Sea, although another estimate put it roughly on the north-east shore of the Caspian. The time of the test was reported as 17.00 local; plutonium was used as the fissionable material, and the US scientists deduced that it was a tower shot, indicating that it was a device rather than a finished bomb. In fact, the test had taken place a long way from the Aral and Caspian Seas, at the Semipalatinsk test site in eastern Kazakhstan, an area bounded by coordinates 49° 52′N to 50° 08′N, and 77° 42′E to 79° 06′E. It was here that most of the Soviet Union's uranium deposits were concentrated.

During the Soviet blockade of Berlin, which began in June 1948 and ended in May 1949, surveillance flights along the USSR's western frontiers were stepped up. Many ELINT missions during this period were flown by the US Navy's PB4Y-2 Privateer maritime patrol aircraft, usually deployed to Port Lyautey in French Morocco. From there, single aircraft detachments were sent to Germany for surveillance flights over the Baltic, while other Privateers monitored the Black Sea and the Adriatic.

The first post-war USAF reconnaissance deployment to the United Kingdom took place in December 1948, when four standard B-29s of the 374th Reconnaissance Squadron (308th Reconnaissance Wing) arrived at RAF Waddington and spent some weeks ostensibly flying weather recce missions. In December 1949 ten RB-29As of the 23rd Strategic Reconnaissance Squadron, 5th Strategic Reconnaissance Wing, deployed to RAF Sculthorpe on a six-month TDY, their

activities taking them as far afield as the Kola Peninsula and the Black Sea.

The numerous sorties by USAF and US Navy reconnaissance aircraft during this period enabled SAC to build up its first comprehensive target list, with Soviet airfields – in particular bomber bases – assigned the highest priority. In the event of a Soviet attack on western Europe, the UK-based B-29s also had a secondary interdiction role against enemy communications such as bridges, road and rail junctions and other choke points behind the battle area. RAF Bomber Command had a similar target list, although as yet there was no attempt to formulate a joint strike plan; that would only come much later. Because of the vulnerability of its aircraft, Bomber Command would have to be restricted to night operations.

Suddenly, the Russians decided to react against the reconnaissance aircraft that roamed through and around their air space with apparent impunity. On 8 April 1950, a Privateer of Patrol Squadron VP-26 (Captain: Lt Jack Fette) took off from Wiesbaden and headed out over the Baltic, its mission to gather intelligence on Soviet naval installations and communications on the coast of Latvia. Somewhere off the port of Libau, it was intercepted by Russian fighters – variously claimed to be La-9s, La-11s or MiG-15s – and shot down with the loss of all ten crew. The Russians stated that the aircraft (which they said was a B-29) had been destroyed after it had penetrated Soviet air space and ignored instructions to land, which was patently untrue; if it had been shot down over land it would have been identified as a Privateer, which bore no resemblance to the B-29 other than the fact that it also had four engines. In fact, the aircraft had been a good ten miles off the coast when it was shot down – a little too close for comfort, perhaps, but still over international waters.

ELINT aircraft had been intercepted before, and on one occasion fired at; that was on 22 October 1949, when an La-9, one of a pair which intercepted an RB-29 over the Sea of Japan, fired a warning burst across the Superfortress's bows. The Privateer incident was different. It was a clear warning from the Russians that in future, any ELINT aircraft that came too close to its sensitive areas might expect no mercy. A month after the loss of the Privateer, the US Joint Chiefs of Staff issued an instruction ordering surveillance aircraft to remain at least twenty miles clear of hostile territory, and the US President himself forbade any penetrations of Soviet air space.

The ink on these orders was barely dry when, in the Far East, the confrontation between East and West flared into open war. On 25 June, 1950, communist North Korean forces attacked the American-backed Republic of Korea across the 38th Parallel, placing the forces of the western alliance on their highest state of alert since the Berlin Airlift.

CHAPTER FOUR

The Jets Arrive

The news that the Russians had begun a nuclear test programme, together with intelligence indications that they were developing advanced jet and turboprop bombers, gave urgent impetus to plans for strengthening NATO's strategic air power in Europe. In October 1949 US President Harry S. Truman signed the Mutual Defense Assistance Act, providing for the supply of American military equipment and defence funding to the European NATO allies.

RAF Bomber Command was an early beneficiary, acquiring 87 B-29s to provide an interim strategic bombing capability until the advent of the first of the British V-bombers, the Vickers Valiant. Some Congressional opposition to the transfer of these aircraft to Britain soon evaporated in the wake of the Russian atomic test, and the overwhelming victory of the communists in China.

The first four B-29s, named Washingtons in RAF service, arrived at RAF Marham on 22 March 1950 amid much publicity. The deployment of the rest, however, together with all the necessary spares and supporting equipment, required much more time and effort. Initial plans called for 70 aircraft to be withdrawn from storage, refurbished and flown to England by 1 March 1951. In addition to overhauling the aircraft systems, USAF contractors were responsible for installing Norden bomb sights, C-1 autopilots, gun-laying radars, fire control computers and new Wright R-3350-57M engines. The latter were fitted with a fuel injection system, raising the operational ceiling of the aircraft to over 36,000 feet. An additional 124 bombers were to be delivered to the RAF over the following year, but in the event this number was cut to 17 following the service debut of the English Electric Canberra light jet bomber in 1951.

For a variety of reasons, not the least of which was a competing USAF demand for B-29s after the outbreak of the war in Korea, the delivery schedule slipped badly. This temporarily left Bomber Command with two squadrons short of aircraft and two squadrons trained but without aircraft. By the summer of 1951, the transfer of part of the workload to a second contractor and to two USAF Air Materiel Area Depots had eased matters considerably, and deliveries began to pick up once more.

There were problems, too, in the supply of spares. The USAF undertook initially to supply adequate flyaway spares kits to permit limited operations, but these proved insufficient to keep the bombers airworthy. To alleviate this, and to give the RAF time to establish spares and supply facilities, the USAF greatly increased its logistical support, shipping bulk quantities of ground-handling equipment, test equipment, overhaul equipment and tools to the UK. Until the RAF became self-sufficient, the USAF also made its facility at Burtonwood available for Washington maintenance. Taking everything into account, the transfer of B-29s to the RAF became the single most expensive programme (about $84 million)

managed under the Mutual Defense Assistance Program (MDAP) in the fiscal year 1950.

The initial batch of RAF Washington crews trained under a USAF Military Assistance Advisory Group training detachment; these crews formed the nucleus of the Washington Conversion Unit (WCU) at RAF Marham, where almost all RAF Washington B1 air and ground crews were subsequently trained. The exception was No. 57 Squadron's air and ground crews, who trained at Waddington.

Due to the complexity of the Washington and its anticipated brief service career with Bomber Command, the Washington squadrons adopted USAF training, maintenance and administrative procedures, right down to the reproduction of USAF spares order forms. In accordance with the MDAP agreement, the RAF established independent Washington support facilities through four Maintenance Units (Nos. 22, 23, 53 and 58). A civilian contractor, Scottish Aviation, undertook routine maintenance work and the Bristol Aeroplane Company was responsible for engine overhaul.

By July 1952, the Washington Conversion Unit had completed its task; it was then designated No. 35 Squadron and continued to operate the American bomber until April 1954, when it rearmed with Canberras.

Most of the RAF's Washingtons were assigned to eight medium bomber squadrons in No. 3 Group; these were Nos. 15, 44, 57 and 149 at Coningsby and Nos. 35, 90, 115 and 207 at Marham, all with an establishment of ten aircraft. Four more Washingtons, equipped to RB-29 standard, were used by No. 192 (Special Duties) Squadron in the electronic intelligence role until 1958, flying from RAF Watton, and three more were assigned as trials aircraft to the Ministry of Supply, operated by Vickers Armstrong Ltd. (There is speculation, as yet unconfirmed, that these three aircraft were modified in 1954 to carry Britain's first atomic bomb, the MC Mk1 Blue Danube, to provide an emergency nuclear attack capability pending the introduction of the first Vickers Valiants.)

In addition to the transfer of B-29s, it was decided to increase Strategic Air Command's UK commitment by making four more bases available to the USAF. The decision to provide the additional bases was reached without political controversy, following strong recommendations by the Air Ministry and the Air Staff, and in April 1950 an 'Ambassadors Agreement' was signed by US Ambassador Lewis Douglas and Aidan Crawley, UK Under Secretary for Air, to cover the construction plan for the bases. As mentioned in a previous chapter, the four airfields selected were Fairford, Greenham Common, Brize Norton and Upper Heyford, control of which was assumed by RAF Bomber Command on behalf of SAC early in June. USAF survey teams moved in immediately, and soon afterwards an Engineer Aviation Battalion, a Maintenance Company, an Ordnance Company, an Engineer Depot Company and a Base Support

ABOVE & OPPOSITE: *The USAF pioneered long-range escort fighter deployments with the Republic F-84 Thunderjet. (Philip Jarrett)*

Company were assigned to each location to prepare it for operational SAC units.

While the four newly assigned airfields were being made ready for use, two more RAF stations were allocated to SAC following the outbreak of the Korean War. The first of these was Mildenhall, in Suffolk, which had been vacated by RAF Bomber Command in March 1949, and at the end of June 1950 US engineers descended on the site, building a ring of anti-aircraft emplacements and a high-security fence. In July the B-50As of the 329th Bombardment Squadron, 93rd Bomb Group, arrived, and their period of temporary duty was extended until February 1951 because of the international situation. They were replaced immediately by the B-50Ds of the 509th Bombardment Group, SAC's original nuclear-capable unit. Lakenheath and Sculthorpe had already been visited by B-50Ds of the 93rd and 97th BGs during the latter half of 1950, both groups accompanied by KB-29P tankers with boom-type flight refuelling equipment. During this period, to alleviate congestion on the SAC-assigned airfields, some aircraft were temporarily deployed to RAF bases; for example, the 329th BS went to RAF Wyton, while half the strength of the 341st BS, 97th BW (eight B-50Ds), deployed to Oakington. A few 97th BW B-50Ds also deployed to RAF Lindholme in Yorkshire, which had just transferred from RAF Technical Training Command to RAF Bomber Command.

The second RAF airfield allocated to the USAF in the summer of 1950 was Bassingbourn, in Cambridgeshire. In April 1944 the first B-29 to visit Britain had landed there; now, a little over six years later, the 353rd Bombardment Squadron of the 301st Bomb Group arrived and stayed until January 1951, when it was replaced by the 38th Squadron, 55th Strategic

Reconnaissance Wing, whose RB-50s undertook electronic and photographic surveillance missions over the Baltic and off northern Russia until May, when the 97th BG moved in with its B-50Ds. The 97th remained at Bassingbourn until September 1951, when the station reverted to RAF use.

The other important development of 1950 took place at Manston, in Kent. Close to the English Channel and consequently to the continent, Manston was an important wartime fighter airfield and had been used subsequently by RAF Transport Command as a staging post for flights overseas. In July 1950 it was decided to transfer Manston to American use, although the station would remain under RAF control as part of No. 11 Group, Fighter Command. Before the end of July the airfield had been occupied by the 7512th Air Base Group, and a few days later the 20th Fighter-Bomber Wing arrived with 69 Republic F-84E Thunderjets, establishing the first permanent presence of American fighter aircraft in Britain. Their task was to provide fighter escort for the B-50s should the latter have to be used in a tactical role over a European battlefield.

The 20th FBW was not specifically designated for this role and its presence at Manston was essentially a stop-gap measure pending the arrival of the 31st Fighter Escort Wing, also with F-84Es, in January 1951; the 31st was replaced in turn by the 12th FEW in June. To provide search-and-rescue facilities a detachment of Grumman SA-16 Albatross and SB-29 Superfortress aircraft of the 9th Air Rescue Squadron deployed to Manston in April 1951.

SAC's escort fighter requirement in the immediate post-war years was in effect a hangover from wartime operations over Germany, when the USAAF had learned to its cost that bombers could not hope to

penetrate deeply into enemy territory without suffering appalling losses unless they were escorted by effective long-range fighters. The North American P-51 (later F-51) Mustang adequately filled the escort fighter requirement during the last two years of the war, and although this aircraft continued to equip most of the fighter groups assigned to SAC during the first three years of the Command's existence, the advent of jet combat types left it seriously outmoded.

In 1946, therefore, Strategic Air Command issued a requirement for a so-called 'penetration fighter', intended primarily to escort the Convair B-36, or rather to sweep ahead of the bomber force and tear gaps in the enemy's fighter defences. The Lockheed

Aircraft Corporation, whose F-80 Shooting Star was then in full production, put forward a design to meet this requirement. Bearing the company designation Model 153, and the USAF designation XF-90, it was a very graceful and highly streamlined aircraft featuring a wing swept at 35 degrees. Power was supplied by two afterburning Westinghouse J34–WE-11 turbojets. A substantial fuel load, carried internally and in jettisonable wingtip tanks, gave the fighter a combat radius of about 1,100 miles at high altitude, sufficient to penetrate as far as Kiev from bases in West Germany. The XF-90 carried a very heavy armament of four 20mm cannon and six 0.5in machine-guns. Two prototypes were built, the first flying on 4 June 1949,

The Lockheed XF-90 penetration fighter would have been based forward in the UK and western Europe, had it gone into production. Its combat radius would have taken it as far as Kiev.

but flight trials revealed that the aircraft was seriously underpowered, with a maximum speed of only 0.9M at sea level and 0.95M at 40,000 feet. This fact, together with a change in the USAF requirement, led to the project being abandoned in 1950.

North American, whose F-86A Sabre was in production in 1948, proposed a variant of this promising aircraft to meet the penetration fighter requirement. Designated F-86C, it had an increased wing span and a larger fuselage cross-section to accommodate a 6,250lb st centrifugal-type Pratt & Whitney XJ48–P-1 turbojet with reheat, fed via flush air intakes slotted into the fuselage sides beneath the cockpit. The nose section was completely redesigned and fitted with all-weather radar. The undercarriage was also redesigned, and twin-wheel main units were installed to support the fighter's 25,000lb loaded weight. The F-86C bore so little resemblance to the parent design that it was given the new designation YF-93A, the prototype flying on 25 January 1950. Flight evaluation produced good results and the USAF placed an order for 118 production F-93As, but this was cancelled following the change in requirement and the penetration fighter project was abandoned.

The third contender was the McDonnell XF-88, prototype construction of which began in 1947 under a USAF contract. The first prototype XF-88 was powered by two 3,000lb st Westinghouse XJ34-WE-13 engines, mounted side by side and exhausting just aft of the wing trailing edge under a stepped-up rear fuselage. This aircraft flew on 20 October 1948, and in 1950 it was followed by a second prototype fitted with XJ34 WE-22 engines equipped with short afterburners that could boost the thrust to 4,000lb for combat manoeuvres. The XF-88 had a very thin wing

swept at 35 degrees and spanning 38ft 8in; length was just over 54ft.

The first prototype XF-88 reached a maximum speed of 641 mph at sea level and could climb to 35,000 feet in four and a half minutes. Combat radius, however, was 850 miles, much less than the XF-90's, and the operational ceiling was only 36,000 feet. The XF-88 development programme was cancelled in August 1950, when the USAF shelved its long-range heavy fighter plans, but the first prototype – as the XF-88B – went on to have a useful life as a test bed for supersonic propellers.

In 1951, the USAF briefly resurrected its long-range escort fighter requirement as a result of the combat losses suffered in Korea by SAC's B-29s, and McDonnell used the XF-88 design as the basis for a completely new aircraft, lengthening the fuselage to accommodate two Pratt & Whitney J57-P-13 engines, giving it a top speed of over 1,000 mph and a ceiling of 52,000 feet, and increased fuel tankage. In its new guise, it became the F-101A Voodoo, an aircraft that was to serve the USAF well for many years in the tactical support and reconnaissance role, even when the penetration fighter requirement was cancelled yet again, and was to become a familiar sight in British skies.

In September and October 1950, the 27th FEW carried out a large-scale reinforcement operation called 'Fox Able Three', in which it ferried 180 Thunderjets from the United States to Germany, the F-84s following the Greenland–Iceland–UK route. This operation eclipsed a much smaller but extremely significant transatlantic flight made on 22 September 1950, when two specially modified Thunderjets of the 31st FEW, fitted with flight refuelling equipment and designated EF-84Es, staged to RAF Manston and then

The McDonnell XF-88, an unsuccessful escort fighter design, was later developed into the F-101 Voodoo.

took off on a non-stop transatlantic attempt, refuelling three times from KB-29 tankers. The leader, Colonel David Schilling, landed at Limestone, Maine, after a flight of ten hours and ten minutes, but the other pilot, Lt-Col William Ritchie, had to abandon his aircraft over Newfoundland when he suffered an engine failure; he was picked up safely by helicopter. Later, the 31st FEW was to pioneer mass non-stop flights over both the Atlantic and Pacific, using flight refuelling.

At the end of 1950 all three SAC fighter wings were equipped with the F-84E Thunderjet, 167 aircraft being on the inventory, but during 1952 this model began to give way to the F-84G, the first Thunderjet variant to be equipped for flight refuelling from the outset. It was also the first USAF fighter to have a tactical nuclear capability; atomic weapons development had advanced considerably in the USA since 1950 and the device carried by the F-84G (the Mk 7 nuclear store), although still bulky, weighed less than 2,000lb. On 1 July 1952 a fourth fighter escort wing, the 508th FEW (466th, 467th and 468th FES), was activated at Turner AFB, and by the end of the year SAC had some 230 Thunderjets on charge.

In January 1951, in accordance with proposals put forward by General Curtis E. LeMay, HQ USAF approved the reorganisation of SAC's combat forces at base level. Prior to this, each combat wing consisted of a wing headquarters, a combat group of tactical squadrons, a maintenance and supply group, an air base group and a medical group. This standard structure existed in most combat wings, including those on single- and two-wing bases. On two-wing bases, which were becoming more prevalent with the tremendous expansion brought about by the Korean War, the senior wing commander exercised control over the junior wing commander. Under the new

system, which became effective in February, each wing was reorganised to consist of a wing headquarters, a combat group of tactical squadrons (and, where applicable, air refuelling squadrons), three maintenance squadrons, and an air base group comprising administrative, supply and medical squadrons. The wing commander was also the combat group commander.

At the same time, SAC received authority from HQ USAF to organise air division headquarters on two-wing bases; these were to serve as an intermediate echelon of command between the combat wings and the numbered air force headquarters, the air division commander exercising direct control over the two wing commanders and the air base group commander. The first five air divisions, organised on 10 February 1951, were the 4th at Barksdale AFB, the 6th at MacDill, the 12th at March, the 14th at Travis and the 47th at Walker.

At a slightly earlier date, on 14 January, HQ 5th Air Division was activated at Offutt AFB, with Major-General Archie J. Old Jr nominated as commander. Major-General Old began forming a new staff and making preparations to move to French Morocco in June, but late in April he and his staff were directed to go to England to open the newly established HQ 7th Air Division at South Ruislip. This was to have been commanded by Brigadier-General Paul T. Cullen, but on 10 March he and 50 members of his staff were lost when the C-124 bringing them to the UK crashed somewhere in the North Atlantic. Major-General Old remained in England until late May, when a new 7th Air Division commander (Major-General John P. McConnell) took charge. Old and his staff then moved to Rabat, where HQ 5th AD opened on 14 June. The primary mission of the new air division HQ was to conclude negotiations for the use of bases in French Morocco, to monitor their construction and subsequently to supervise rotational training of SAC units in North Africa.

At this time, SAC's bomber fleet comprised two Heavy Bomb Wings with 38 B-36s, 12 Medium Bomb Wings and three Medium Strategic Wings with 542 B-29 and B-50 aircraft. The two B-36 units were the 7th and 11th Heavy Bomb Wings at Carswell AFB, assigned to the Eighth Air Force. In July 1951 the 92nd Bomb Wing at Fairchild AFB (Fifteenth AF) also began to rearm with the B-36. On 16 January 1951 SAC brought its B-36s to the United Kingdom for the first time when six aircraft of the 7th Bomb Wing deployed to RAF Lakenheath, returning to Carswell four days later. During their short stay, the B-36s flew a number of training sorties and practised fighter affiliation exercises with RAF Fighter Command, dwarfing the Meteors and Vampires that came up to intercept them. At the end of the year, on 3 December, B-36s made their first visit to North Africa, six aircraft of the 11th Bomb Wing flying non-stop from Carswell AFB to Sidi Slimane in French Morocco. The flight returned to the CONUS on 6 December.

The variant of the B-36 now equipping the SAC heavy bomb wings was the B-36D, which had extra power provided by four General Electric J47–GE-19 turbojets mounted in pods beneath the outer wings. The B-36D had a top speed of 406 mph at 36,200 feet, a service ceiling of 43,800 feet and a combat radius of 3,530 miles with a full fuel load of 29,995 gallons. A reduced fuel load of 19,500 gallons halved the combat radius, but enabled the aircraft to lift 72,000lb of bombs. The B-36D carried a crew of 15 (commander, two pilots, two engineers, navigator, bombardier, two radio operators, an observer and five gunners). Equipment included a K-1 (later K-3A) Bombing Navigation System, which permitted radar or visual bombing by a single crew member. By the end of 1953 the B-36 equipped six SAC Heavy Bomb Wings: the 6th BW(H) (24th, 39th and 40th BS) at Travis AFB, California; the 7th BW(H) (9th, 436th and 492nd BS) and the 11th BW(H) (26th, 42nd and 98th BS), both at Carswell AFB in Texas; the 42nd BW(H) (69th, 50th and 75th BS) at Loring AFB, Maine; the 92nd BW(H) (325th, 326th and 327th BS) at Fairchild AFB, Washington; and the 95th BW(H) (334th, 335th and 336th BS) at Biggs AFB, Texas. By this time, the B-36D had been joined in service by later variants, the B-36F, B-36H and B-36J, which featured improvements that included uprated engines and updated bombing and fire control systems. Late production aircraft had all guns except the tail armament deleted, the saving in weight boosting the top speed to over 420 mph and the ceiling to 47,000 feet.

As part of the programme to strengthen the defences of western Europe, a new agreement was signed in February 1951 between the British and United States governments covering a special airfield construction programme designed to provide a total of 23 bases in the United Kingdom from which both strategic and tactical USAF air operations could be conducted, in addition to three air depots. This jointly funded programme, which involved both new construction and modernisation, initially cost $109 million.

Because of the growing size and complexity of the 3rd Air Division's mission, it was now decided to separate its responsibilities. On 20 March 1951 Strategic Air Command activated the 7th Air Division at South Ruislip to assume operational control over deployed bomber units; on 1 May the 3rd AD was inactivated and replaced by the Third Air Force, with its headquarters also at South Ruislip. It was to be under the control of USAFE and commanded by Major-General Leon W. Johnson, who had commanded the 3rd Air Division since 1948.

The upgrading of the USAF's commitment in the United Kingdom to the status of an air force brought more changes, particularly in the concept of USAF air operations from the British base; so far, the emphasis had been exclusively on a strategic operation, but a tactical mission was now added, and preparations were made for the Third Air Force to receive tactical units to support its new mission. It was also to be responsible for the logistical support of the USAF and other US units in Britain, and to seal the foundations of the new structure a Joint Transfer Agreement, delineating the responsibilities of the two commands, was signed on 16 May 1951.

An early consequence of the new organisation was that Prestwick was reactivated to provide support for the increased volume of Military Air Transport Service aircraft now flying between the United States and Britain, and also to provide air-sea rescue coverage of the eastern Atlantic. A big new hard standing area was built, the main runway was extended, and the adjacent airfield of Ayr, which had been closed since 1946, was reopened as a USAF storage site. On 31 July 1951 two Sikorsky H-19 search-and-rescue helicopters landed at Prestwick after completing the first crossing of the Atlantic by rotorcraft; they had been escorted by a C-47 and a Grumman Albatross.

By the summer of 1951, the 7th Air Division had jurisdiction over nine bases: Bassingbourn, Lakenheath, Lindholme, Manston, Marham, Mildenhall, Sculthorpe, Wyton and Waddington. As soon as they were activated, six more bases – Brize Norton, Carnaby, Fairford, Greenham Common, Upper Heyford and Woodbridge – were added to SAC's British holdings.

The air defence of the United Kingdom still gave cause for concern, although there had been improvements in the organisation. In July 1950, for example, in response to the Korean crisis, the readiness state of Fighter Command had been increased when a number of aircraft were held on armed alert to intercept unidentified aircraft approaching British air space. But in that same month, the Air Ministry revealed alarming figures on the estimated strength of the Soviet Air Force, whose air strength was put at 19,000 aircraft, including jet fighters and long-range bombers. In August 1950, a new three-year defence plan was implemented; at £4.7 billion, it was the largest peacetime expenditure ever authorised.

By this time, Fighter Command's day fighter strength had been doubled and all squadrons were now equipped with jets, all of them inferior to the MiG-15, whose introduction in increasing numbers was viewed with mounting concern. Only one aircraft on the NATO inventory could meet the MiG-15 on equal terms, and the summer of 1951 saw its first deployment to Britain. It was the North American F-86 Sabre.

CHAPTER FIVE

Overflights and Accident Fears

The F-86A Sabres assigned to the air defence of Great Britain belonged to the 81st Fighter Interceptor Wing, which deployed from Moses Lake AFB, Washington. The first squadron to make the transatlantic crossing was the 116th FIS, a mobilised Air National Guard unit assigned to the 81st FIW, which left Moses Lake on 15 August 1951 with 25 aircraft. The Sabres flew via the now well-established route – Goose Bay, Bluie West One, Keflavik, Stornoway – before proceeding to their operational base at Shepherd's Grove, Suffolk. The 81st

FIW's other two squadrons, the 92nd and 91st, arrived on 5 and 26 September respectively, the former deploying to Shepherd's Grove and the latter to Bentwaters.

Britain's air defences received a further boost with the formation of No. 1 Fighter Wing RCAF at RAF North Luffenham on 1 November 1951. The Wing was armed with the Canadair-built Sabre Mk 2; its three squadrons, Nos. 410, 419 and 441, had all served in the United Kingdom during World War Two. The Canadians

TOP: *F-86A Sabres of the 92nd FIS, 81st FIW, photographed at Dunsfold in June 1952. (Harry Holmes)*
ABOVE: *F-86A Sabre of the 81st FIW flying near Shepherd's Grove, June 1953. (via Harry Holmes)*

were to remain at North Luffenham for the next three years, departing to join the NATO-assigned 1 Air Division RCAF only when the UK air defence role could be adequately assumed by the Hawker Hunters of RAF Fighter Command. The latter's regular day fighter strength at the end of 1951 comprised 20 squadrons of Meteor Mk 8s and three of Vampire Mk 5s, although the Vampires were being swiftly phased out of first-line service; added to these were the 20 auxiliary squadrons, all with a unit establishment of eight aircraft and armed with a mixture of Vampire 3s and 5s with the exception of No. 600 Squadron, which had Meteor 4s and 8s. There were also six night all-weather fighter squadrons armed variously with Meteor NF11s, Vampire NF10s and Venom NF3s, all with an establishment of 16 or 22 aircraft.

The defensive thinking was that if hostilities broke out within the next two or three years the Russian medium bomber force, which would probably be jet-equipped from about 1954, would be in a position to launch heavy attacks on UK targets, but tactical bombers such as the Ilyushin Il-28, which was starting to be deployed in 1951, would not have the range to reach targets in Britain unless a Soviet land offensive reached the Rhine, which would enable the air squadrons to use bases in western Germany. In that event it was assumed that the UK air defences would also have to contend with Russian jet fighters, although their restricted combat radius would impose severe limitations on their offensive operations. If the Russians reached the Channel coast, however, the picture would be very different. In the summer of 1951, United Nations aircrews in Korea had occasionally observed MiG-15s fitted with long-range tanks penetrating almost as far as the 38th Parallel, a distance of about 200 miles from their Manchurian bases, which meant that similarly equipped MiGs operating from captured airfields in the English Channel area would be able to range as far afield as East Anglia and the East Midlands.

The losses sustained by its B-29s on daylight operations over Korea, meanwhile, had left Strategic Air Command under no illusion about the survival chances of its piston-engined bomber fleet, and although its UK-based B-29s and B-50s continued to participate in Fighter Command's daytime exercises, there was a growing emphasis on night flying. The RAF's Washingtons, on the other hand, operated mostly at night, in accordance with Bomber Command's policy, routine training being interspersed with live bombing in the Heligoland Bight and long-range sorties to the Filfla range off Malta with practice bombs, requiring a flight time of 16 to 18 hours.

Since the end of the Second World War there had been no formal detailed strategic bombing planning between the USAF and RAF. Indeed, the USAF made it clear that it preferred strategic bombing to be left to Strategic Air Command. The RAF, therefore, did not know what targets SAC would attack in the event of war, and the Americans did not know what progress the British were making with their atomic weapons programme, because at this stage there was no interchange of information on nuclear research between the two nations. The creation of NATO in 1949 made the Americans realise the inevitability of

joint strategic planning, but to complicate matters the USAF and the US Navy were locked in a bitter battle over strategic roles – in other words, long-range bombers v. aircraft carriers – and the Navy, reluctant to endorse a strategic role for any air force, wanted to limit the RAF's Washingtons to a tactical role. In a memorandum to the Joint Chiefs of Staff, Vice-Admiral Arthur C. Struble, Deputy Chief of Naval Operations, had stated that he approved the transfer of B-29s to the RAF 'subject to such employment for tactical purposes'.

Bomber Command, however, had other ideas. The Washington restored the RAF's strategic capability, and the Command made it clear that it wished to retain a strategic role. Although it could not launch a campaign against Russian cities and industries with a mere eight squadrons of B-29s, it could attack Soviet airfields and naval facilities. As to whether any of the Washingtons were made nuclear-capable, the question was addressed by Dr William Suit, Historian of the US Air Materiel Command History Office, speaking at a 1993 symposium on Anglo-American air power co-operation during the Cold War:

> Not surprisingly, historians disagree on whether the RAF's B-29s played an atomic role. Margaret Gowing (*Independence and Deterrence: Britain and Atomic Energy, 1945-52*, St Martin's Press, New York, 1974) states that 'the British received American B-29 (Washington) bombers, but these did not carry atomic bombs'. Peter Malone (*The British Nuclear Deterrent*, St Martin's Press, New York, 1984), while discussing the atomic-capable USAF B-29s stationed in England, noted that 'there is no evidence the RAF's Washingtons were similarly modified'. C. J. Bartlett (*The Long Retreat*, Macmillan, London, 1972) takes a position similar to Gowing's, concluding the RAF used the B-29s 'only to train future Valiant bomber crews'. R. N. Rosencrance (*Defence of the Realm: British Strategy in the Nuclear Epoch*, Columbia University Press, New York, 1968) concludes, 'British acquisition of B-29s under MDAP, then, is probably largely to be explained by British needs from the period 1952 through 1954 when UK bombs would begin to be available.' John Baylis (*Anglo-American Defense Relations, 1939-1984*, St Martin's Press, New York, 1984) is of the opinion that 'quite apart from the information on atomic energy from 1958 onwards, the United States also contributed to the British delivery systems throughout the 1950s. American B-29s had filled the gap until the V-bomber force was ready'. Michael A. Fopp (*The Washington File*, Air Britain, Tonbridge, 1983) remarked that 'on occasions, large covered objects were wheeled out on bomb trolleys, under heavy guard, from ordnance stores at Washington bases. These same objects were quietly removed when the Washingtons were dispensed with and taken away by US air force aircraft.'

If Fopp's remark is correct, it may mean that at least some Washingtons were armed with American nuclear weapons. If this is so, it indicates an unprecedented degree of collusion between SAC and Bomber Command at a time when no such collusion was supposed to exist, and that in turn indicates agreement at the highest level – although not necessarily governmental level. It is quite possible that a secret deal was struck, and that the man behind it was General LeMay, who was not above acting on his own initiative, and without recourse to his political superiors, on matters of strategic air policy.

In 1950, inspired by a study of the RAF's experiences between the wars – when aircraft had been used to intimidate dissident tribesmen on the Northwest Frontier of India and in Iraq by threat of attack from the air – LeMay and his staff devised a scheme known as Project 'Control', whereby strategic air power would be used to intimidate the Soviet Union by constant displays of force. The end result, it was hoped, was that the Communist bloc would collapse in the face of the threat of nuclear annihilation. Project 'Control' also envisaged a second phase, which involved pre-emptive attacks on targets whose destruction would eliminate Russia's capability to wage nuclear war.

Project 'Control', in fact, was based on the premise that if the Americans demonstrated their capability to fly over Soviet territory with impunity – and, by implication, to drop bombs if they wanted to – the Russians would virtually capitulate. Further communist

expansion would be halted, and the 'captive' satellite states of eastern Europe would be freed.

Regular reconnaissance overflights of Soviet territory would provide the necessary tool. Not only would overflying the Soviet Union give an active demonstration of the overall determination of the United States to stand up to the Russians; it would also provide a very substantial amount of intelligence with respect to target systems should it be decided to launch a pre-emptive attack on the USSR. The whole policy was highly dangerous and provocative, taking little or no account of the often unpredictable nature of the Russian psyche and the perils attendant in throwing down such a gauntlet, but it was nevertheless implemented, and it led to some extraordinary escapades, some of which were to demonstrate, yet again, the degree of collusion that existed between the Americans and their British allies during this period.

In July 1951 Squadron Leader John Crampton, then commanding No. 97 (Lincoln) Squadron at RAF Hemswell, was summoned to HQ Bomber Command at RAF High Wycombe to be told by the AOC-in-C, Air

Two of the first USAF jet types in Britain, the North American B-45 Tornado and the F-86A Sabre.

North American B-45 undergoing trials with rocket-assisted take-off gear (RATOG).

Chief Marshal Sir Hugh P. Lloyd, that he was to assume command of a Special Duty Flight whose operations would be conducted in conditions of utmost secrecy. The Flight would be equipped with the North American RB-45C, the reconnaissance version of America's first operational multijet bomber, and the aircrew involved – nine in all, including Crampton – were to assemble at RAF Sculthorpe in Norfolk, one of the UK bases used by Strategic Air Command, before proceeding to the USA for a 60–day period of training. On 3 August 1951 the RAF personnel flew to Barksdale AFB, Louisiana, and spent ten days familiarising themselves with the B-45 bomber before flying to Lockbourne AFB, Ohio, to become acquainted with the RB-45C variant. Lockbourne was the home base of the three RB-45C squadrons of the 91st Strategic Reconnaissance Wing; two were absent on overseas deployments and the RAF crews converted with the 323rd SRS, which had returned to the USA in May after a five-month TDY to Manston and Sculthorpe.

One of the RAF pilots was returned to the UK after writing off an aircraft in a heavy night landing, luckily with no damage to his crew, and his place was taken by another RAF pilot already on secondment to a B-45 squadron. After successfully completing their conversion course, the crews returned to Sculthorpe

and were attached to the RB-45C unit already in residence there. Neither the British nor their American hosts had any inkling about what was in the offing, and it was not until early 1952 that Sqn Ldr Crampton and his navigator, Flt Lt Rex Sanders, were summoned to Bomber Command HQ to be told about their mission, which was to carry out night radar photography of routes over which RAF and USAF bombers would fly to targets in the Baltic states, the Moscow area and central southern Russia. One of the principal concerns was to detect surface-to-air missile (SAM) sites (the Russians were known to be developing a SAM system, although in fact this, based on the SA-1 Guild, would not be operational until at least 1954) and to try to establish evidence of the deployment of surface-to-surface missiles.

Four RB-45Cs (three operational aircraft and one spare) were allocated to the Special Duty Flight; these were stripped of all USAF markings at RAF West Raynham and repainted in RAF insignia before returning to Sculthorpe. Before the first mission, Sqn Ldr Crampton and his crew made a 30-minute flight over the Soviet Zone of Germany while ground stations listened for unusual Russian radio and radar activity that might indicate the flight was being tracked, but nothing untoward was noted and it was decided to proceed with the principal mission.

All three routes were to be flown simultaneously, the three aircraft departing Sculthorpe in rapid succession and heading for a point north of Denmark, where they were to make rendezvous with USAF KB-29 tankers. After taking on the maximum possible fuel load they were to climb at maximum continuous power at 0.68M until they reached the highest attainable altitude the prevailing conditions would permit. As they made their penetrations, the intelligence agencies would again be listening for signs of a Russian reaction. Radio silence would be broken only in the direst emergency. When the crews were briefed they received three separate weather forecasts for each route: a genuine one and two bogus ones. One of the latter was to uphold their Sculthorpe 'cover story' and the other was for the benefit of Russian interrogators if they were forced down and captured; the crews were to maintain that they had been involved in a weather reconnaissance of the Black Sea in the case of the southern route and of the Gulf of Bothnia in the case of the northern ones, and that they had strayed off course.

The first sortie was flown in April 1952, the aircraft taking off from Sculthorpe in the late afternoon. The three crews were: Sqn Ldr John Crampton, Flt Lt Rex Sanders and Sgt Lindsay; Fl Lt Gordon Cremer, Flt Sgt Bob Anstee and Sgt Don Greenslade; Flt Lt Bill Blair, Flt Lt John Hill and Flt Sgt Joe Acklam. The aircraft made rendezvous with their tankers and then headed into Soviet air space, all lights extinguished. Sqn Ldr Crampton's crew had the longest haul, south-east across Russia, and he later recalled that his most

enduring memory of the route was the apparent wilderness over which he was flying. There were no lights on the ground and no apparent sign of human habitation, a scene quite different from the rest of Europe.

All the target photographs were taken as planned, the navigators taking 35mm photographs of the radar displays, and all three aircraft returned to base safely, though not without incident; about 20 minutes before the first aircraft (Flt Lt Blair) was due to arrive at Sculthorpe low stratus started to roll in from the North Sea, so he had to divert to Manston. Sqn Ldr Crampton arrived during a temporary break in the weather and got in successfully, but Flt Lt Cremer, who had had to land at Copenhagen because of iced-up fuel filters, had to divert into Prestwick.

A few days later the RB-45Cs, still bearing RAF markings, were returned to Lockbourne AFB and the crews returned to other duties, Sqn Ldr Crampton being given command of No. 101 Squadron at Binbrook, the first to rearm with Canberras. In October 1952 the Special Duty Flight was reactivated, with Crampton once again in command, but with some changes of personnel. His previous co-pilot, Sgt Lindsay, had been involved in a B-29 crash and his place was taken by Flt Lt McAlistair Furze, a flight commander on No. 101 Sqn. The crews embarked on a period of intensive training, only to have the forthcoming operation cancelled early in December. It was not the end of the Special Duty Flight's activities, however, as we shall see later.

Meanwhile, the USAF presence in Britain continued to grow. In November 1951 the 123rd Fighter Escort

Republic F-84E Thunderjet armed with high-velocity aircraft rockets. (via Harry Holmes)

Wing (156th, 165th and 167th FS) of the Kentucky Air National Guard arrived at Manston to replace the 12th Fighter Escort Wing, whose aircraft it took over. It was the first ANG wing to be deployed to Britain, its personnel having been mobilised as a consequence of the Korean War. ANG personnel were rotated to Manston until July 1952, when the 123rd Fighter-Bomber Wing, as it was now designated, was inactivated and its aircraft used to form the 406th FBW (512th, 513th and 514th FBS). The 406th was armed with Thunderjets until November 1953, when it received Sabres and the new designation Fighter Interceptor Wing. Also in 1952, the air-sea rescue detachment at Manston was upgraded to squadron status, becoming the 66th Air Rescue Squadron.

By June 1952 HQ Third Air Force controlled an Air Division, a Light Tactical Bomb Wing, and three Tactical Fighter Wings. The Air Division was the 49th, of which the 20th FBW and the 47th BW were the component parts.

The 20th FBW returned to the UK in May 1952, now armed with F-84G Thunderjets and nuclear-capable; two of its squadrons, the 55th and 77th, went to Wethersfield in Essex, while the third, the 79th, deployed to Woodbridge. The 20th FBW had a flight refuelling capability and its tanker aircraft were based at Sculthorpe to support the other component of the 49th Air Division, the 47th Bombardment Wing, whose two squadrons – the 84th and 85th – arrived early in June 1952 with their B-45 Tornados. Later, in March 1954, the 86th BS was added to the 47th BW's strength, giving a total complement of 75 aircraft. The deployment of these units, with their associated support organisations, brought the number of USAF personnel in Britain to more than 45,000 by the autumn of 1952.

Meanwhile, the number of British bases available to Strategic Air Command had also increased. By the closing weeks of 1951 Upper Heyford's main runway had been lengthened to 10,000 feet and most of the planned expansion had been completed (under the control of the 7509th Air Base Squadron), permitting the arrival of the KB-29P tankers of the 93rd Air Refueling Squadron from Castle AFB, California, early in December to begin their 90-day TDY. Upper Heyford saw further construction work during 1952 and the airfield defences were substantially strengthened; during the year the Oxfordshire base was host to the KB-29P tankers that supported the 97th, 509th and 2nd Bombardment Wings, as well as the KB-29Ms responsible for flight refuelling the 301st BW.

Greenham Common, which was to be the subject of much controversy in later years, was formally handed over to the Strategic Air Command's 7th Air Division on 18 June 1951, and US engineers set about the systematic destruction of the airfield's wartime hangars and buildings to make room for a new 10,000ft runway, together with taxiways and hard standings. Not only the old airfield buildings were destroyed; 44 local families had to be rehoused when their homes became the victims of a government compulsory purchase order, and two local pubs were bulldozed. Such was the scale of the reconstruction work that the airfield would not be ready for SAC use until the autumn of 1953.

Work on a lesser scale also went ahead at the Oxfordshire airfield of Brize Norton, and the first SAC deployment to this base took place in the last days of June 1952, when 21 B-36D and B-36F bombers of the 11th Bombardment Wing arrived from Carswell AFB in Texas. Other SAC units to visit Brize Norton in 1952 were the 43rd and 301st Bombardment Wings, with B-50As.

Inevitably, the increased tempo of air operations arising from the USAF build-up in the United Kingdom brought about a rise in air accidents, and consequent civilian fears of a catastrophe. Unlike the RAF, the Americans seemed to have few qualms about flying over densely populated areas at all altitudes. For example, there was an outcry following an incident on 7 February 1953, when a B-36 – one of 17 making a dawn arrival at Fairford after flying from Carswell – got into difficulties in the airfield circuit. The captain, Lieutenant-Colonel Herman Gerick, ordered his crew of 15 to bale out, which they did successfully. The problem was that the massive bomber flew on for 30 miles before crashing near the village of Laycock, some four miles from Chippenham, fortunately without hurting anyone. Prior to this, there had been four crashes involving SAC bombers deployed to the UK: on 13 October 1949 all 12 crew were killed when a B-50 developed a serious engine fire shortly after taking off from Lakenheath and crashed near Isleham; on 7 June 1950 an RB-29A of the 5th SRW was forced to ditch 20 miles off Cromer, also as a result of engine fire, eight crew members baling out safely and one being picked up from the sea; on 10 October 1950 a B-50 suffered a landing accident at Mildenhall, all the crew escaping from the blazing wreck; and on 25 June 1952 a B-50 of the 509th BW crashed at Stallode Fen near Lakenheath with the loss of all on board, the cause being loss of control while taking avoiding action in formation. What might have been a fifth serious accident was narrowly averted on 26 January 1951 when a B-36 of the 7th BW undershot the runway at Boscombe Down in a heavy snowstorm, bounced for 200 yards and then skidded across country for half a mile before coming to rest almost on the runway threshold, its 15-man crew unscathed.

Incidents such as these enhanced fears that an accident might one day involve a UK-based bomber carrying nuclear weapons, and it was perhaps just as well that the British public were unaware that accidents of this kind had already occurred, although none so far on British territory. There were five accidents in 1950. The first of these, on 13 February, occurred when a Convair B-36, en route from Eielson AFB in Alaska to Carswell AFB in Texas, developed engine trouble and descended into icing conditions at 8,000 feet after three engines were shut down. The weapon, containing a dummy nuclear capsule, was jettisoned into the Pacific off British Columbia and the HE element detonated. The B-36 crashed on Vancouver Island after the crew abandoned it over Prince Royal Island.

The second accident occurred on 11 April 1950, when a Boeing B-29 left Kirtland AFB, New Mexico, at 21.30 hours and crashed into a mountain at Manzano Base three minutes later, killing the crew. The bomb case was demolished and the HE burned in the post-crash fire, but no nuclear capsule was fitted and there was consequently no contamination.

Three months later, on 13 July, a B-50 on a training flight from Biggs AFB, Texas, was flying at 7,000 feet on a clear day near Lebanon, Ohio, when the aicraft inexplicably went into a steep dive and flew into the ground, killing the 16-man crew. The aircraft carried a bomb shape with its HE element, which exploded, but no nuclear capsule was present. Then, on 5 August 1950, a B-29 carrying a weapon but no capsule suffered two runaway propellers on take-off from Fairchild-Suisun AFB, California. The pilot was unable to retract the undercarriage and the aircraft crashed and burned. Nineteen crew and rescue personnel were killed when the weapon's HE element exploded 12 minutes after the crash; they included General Travis, after whom the base was subsequently renamed.

In the last such accident of 1950, on 10 November, a B-50 on an overwater flight outside the area of the United States got into difficulties and the crew had to jettison the special weapon from 10,500 feet. The HE element was seen to detonate on impact with the sea, but no nuclear capsule was fitted.

During all the years of the Cold War era in which British and American airborne nuclear deterrent forces were maintained in the United Kingdom, there were widespread fears – often inflamed by uninformed (and sometimes deliberate) media comment – that the carriage and storage of nuclear weapons must eventually result in a catastrophic nuclear accident. Although there were in fact a number of accidents involving nuclear weapons – or, more usually, nuclear weapon components – the possibility of an accidental nuclear explosion was always remote. To understand why, it is useful at this juncture to provide a brief description of how nuclear weapons work, and why they will not work under certain circumstances.

An atomic (i.e. nuclear, as distinct from thermonuclear) explosion is caused by the fission of heavy elements such as the U-235 isotope of uranium and the P-239 isotope of plutonium. To trigger a fission reaction it is necessary to assemble a large enough mass of U-235 or P-239 to ensure that a sufficient number of the high-energy neutron particles that are generated by the normal steady fission process taking place in the raw material do not escape from the surface of the mass, but collide with other atoms, causing these to break up in turn and release more neutrons. If the process creates more neutrons than can be consumed, a chain reaction of ever-increasing intensity is set up. Since each fission of a U-235 or P-239 atom liberates huge amounts of energy, the result is a powerful explosion.

The minimum amount of fissile material required to sustain a chain reaction is known as the critical mass, and is around 25lb of P-239 or 100lb of U-235. The mere creation of a critical mass, however, is not enough to produce a nuclear explosion sufficient for military purposes, because the sheer magnitude of the reaction will tend to blow the assembly apart before a large amount of its material has been consumed by the energies liberated in the fission process. In early atomic weapons, this problem was overcome by using the so-called 'gun' principle, in which a sub-critical mass of fissile material was fired at a target made of the same material. Their combined mass exceeded the critical value, while the energy imparted by the gun to the moving mass was sufficient to keep the two sections in contact while the reaction built up. In the late 1940s, however, following a further series of nuclear tests by the US government, the more sophisticated 'implosion' system was brought into use. In this case, a spherical fissile mass of sub-critical size is surrounded by a layer of high-explosive 'lenses'; when the latter are fired at precisely the same instant, the fissile mass is compressed to produce a super-critical mass in which the chain reaction can begin. No explosion is possible, therefore, unless the nuclear capsule is married to the HE component and the weapon is fully armed, a process that would not be completed unless an actual war situation existed and the bomber was en route to its target.

Thermonuclear weapons present a different problem, requiring a different set of safety precautions. The only method of initiating a thermonuclear (fusion) explosion is by using a fission trigger, because only a nuclear explosion can produce the required combination of temperature and pressure. The deuterium and tritium isotopes of hydrogen (hence the popular term 'H-bomb') then combine to produce the minimum temperature of about 80,000,000° C that is needed to kindle the thermonuclear reaction. However, tritium is a cryogenic material which has to be stored within a few degrees of absolute zero, and this gave scientists some headaches when it came to devising a thermonuclear weapon that could be air-delivered.

The solution was to surround the fission trigger with a blanket of lithium-6, creating what was essentially a tritium factory at the heart of a nuclear explosion. Lithium-6 was converted into tritium when bombarded by the neutrons released by the nuclear trigger, and had the advantage of being relatively easy to handle and store. But the problems were by no means over. Although the basic device was fairly small – the amount of lithium-6 required to create a thermonuclear weapon is in the region of 200lb – the safety precautions that were necessary to produce an operational weapon that could safely be handled by non-scientific personnel were so exhaustive that they resulted in a much larger and bulkier assembly than had been envisaged at first. These factors contributed to making the development of a deliverable thermonuclear weapon a protracted affair.

In all cases, the main risk associated with accidents to nuclear weapons is that the HE element might detonate, destroying the nuclear capsule if the latter is fitted to the bomb shape and scattering poisonous radioactive material over the immediate area. Unless the conventional explosive charges detonate in precisely the correct sequence and time interval, which cannot happen unless the weapon is armed – that is, its firing circuit activated – there can be no nuclear reaction and therefore no nuclear explosion. Even the risk of the HE element detonating accidentally was virtually eliminated after the Los Alamos Scientific Laboratory in New Mexico developed an Insensitive High Explosive, which was highly insensitive to temperature and shock and which was subsequently used in all US nuclear warheads.

CHAPTER SIX

B-47 Stratojet:
The New Dimension

By the beginning of 1953, the UK air defences were facing realistic opposition following the deployment in numbers of the English Electric Canberra B2 jet bomber. In May 1953, for example, Canberras of the Binbrook Wing took the part of the enemy in Exercise 'Rat/Terrier', carrying out low-level attacks on the USAF bases at Lakenheath and Sculthorpe to test the defences against this kind of strike. The best performance was put up by Sgt B. D. Platt, who took the Lakenheath defences completely by surprise and obligingly made a second run at the request of the US air defence observers so that they could have another go at shooting him down. Earlier, on 19 March, during Exercise 'Jungle King', the Binbrook Canberras had penetrated deep into Germany to attack the US airfields at Fürstenfeldbruck near Munich and Rhein-Main, Frankfurt. The scenario was that 45 enemy swept-wing jet fighters were refuelling at the first target and that an enemy general, in a four-engined jet transport with a 45-strong fighter escort, was calling at the second. The Canberras made a high-level G-H attack and successfully completed their mission.

USAF and RCAF Sabre pilots found the Canberra a very difficult aircraft to intercept, for it was very manoeuvrable at low and medium altitudes and at high altitudes it could outclimb the F-86. For RAF Fighter Command, armed with the Meteor F8, it was a particularly frustrating time. The diary of No. 43 Squadron (RAF Leuchars, Scotland) recorded that 'It was most disconcerting to find Canberras out-turning us at 40,000 feet and converting their mild evasive-action-only tactics into perfect quarter attacks on our exposed bottoms . . .' Fighter Command could only eagerly await the introduction of the Hawker Hunter and Supermarine Swift, scheduled for early in 1954; even then an unforeseen disappointment was in store, for the Swift was to show characteristics that made it unacceptable as a fighter.

There was no slackening in the tension between East and West during the early months of 1953. On 10 March two Czechoslovak Air Force MiG-15s attacked a pair of USAF F-84 Thunderjets near Regensburg, inside Federal German territory, and shot one of them down; the pilot, Lt W. G. Brown, baled out safely. Two days later an Avro Lincoln of RAF Bomber Command, on a routine training sortie, strayed into the Soviet Zone as the result of a navigational error and was also shot down, with the loss of all its crew.

It was clearly time for a further demonstration of the USAF's offensive capability, and it was to be done by the deployment to the United Kingdom of SAC's latest asset, the Boeing B-47 Stratojet. The development of this remarkable aircraft had begun in September 1945, when the Boeing aircraft company commenced design of a strategic jet bomber project designated Model 450. The aircraft, which was a radical departure from conventional design, featured a thin, flexible wing – based on wartime research data – with 35 degrees of sweep and carrying six turbojets in underwing pods,

the main undercarriage being housed in the fuselage. Basic design studies were completed in June 1946, and the first of two XB-47 Stratojet prototypes flew on 17 December 1947, powered by six 3,750lb st Allison J35 turbojets. On 8 February 1949 one of the Allison-powered XB-47s made a coast-to-coast flight over the United States, covering 2,289 miles in 3 hours and 46 minutes at an average speed of 607.8 mph. Later, the J35s were replaced by General Electric J47-GE-3 turbojets, the XB-47 flying with these in October 1949.

Meanwhile, Boeing had received a contract for ten B-47A Stratojets in November 1948, and the first of this pre-production batch flew on 25 June 1950. The B-47A was used for trials and evaluation and, to some extent, for crew conversion. The first production model was the B-47B, which was powered by J47-GE-23 engines and which featured a number of structural modifications, including a strengthened wing. It carried underwing fuel tanks, and was fitted with 18 JATO solid fuel rockets to give an emergency take-off thrust of up to 20,000lb. These were not used during normal operational training, but would have been necessary in a real combat situation to get the B-47, carrying a full fuel load and a 10,000lb bomb load, off the ground, for the aircraft needed a very long take-off run and was tricky to handle during the take-off phase.

The B-47's undercarriage consisted of two pairs of main wheels mounted in tandem under the fuselage and outrigger wheels under each wing; the main gear folded up into the fuselage, while the outriggers retracted into the inboard engine nacelles. The arrangement was light and space-saving but gave the B-47 a tendency to roll on take-off, so that in a strong crosswind the pilot had to hold the control column right over to one side. Steering on the ground was accomplished by the nosewheel, which was adjusted to prevent the aircraft swinging more than six degrees either way. However, the aircraft's optimum attitude for take-off was the one it assumed as it sat on the ground, and at about 140 knots, depending on its weight, the Stratojet literally flew itself off the runway with no need for backward pressure on the control column. Once off the ground, with flaps up and the aircraft automatically trimmed, the technique was to hold it down until safe flying speed had been reached and then climb at a shallow angle until 310 knots showed on the airspeed indicator, after which the rate of climb was increased to 4,000 or 5,000 feet per minute, depending on the aircraft's configuration.

At its operating altitude of around 40,000 feet the B-47 handled lightly and could easily be trimmed to fly hands off. The quietness of the cockpit, the lack of vibration and the smoothness of the flight were noticeable, the only exception being when turbulence was encountered at high altitude in jet streams. Then, looking out of the cockpit, the crew could see the B-47's long, flexible wings bending up and down – a rather unnerving phenomenon when experienced for the first time.

The Boeing B-47 Stratojet brought a new dimension to Strategic Air Command operations. (Phil Jarrett)

The B-47 had a spectacular landing technique that began with a long, straight-in approach from high altitude when the pilot lowered his undercarriage to act as an air brake; with landing gear down the Stratojet was capable of losing 20,000 feet in four minutes. Flaps were not lowered until final approach, which started several miles from the end of the runway and demanded great concentration. The bomber must not be allowed to stall, yet its speed had to be kept as low as was safely possible to prevent it from running off the far end of the runway. Each additional knot above the crucial landing speed added another 500 feet to the landing run, so the pilot had to fly to an accuracy of within two knots of the landing speed, which was usually about 130 knots for a light B-47 at the end of a sortie.

Ideally, the Stratojet aimed to touch down on both tandem mainwheel units together, because if one or the other made contact with the runway first the

aircraft bounced back into the air. With the wheels firmly down the pilot used his ailerons to keep the wings level, much as a glider pilot does after touchdown, and as the ailerons were moved the flaps automatically adjusted their position to help counteract roll; rudder had to be used very cautiously and sparingly or the aircraft might turn over. To slow the fast-rolling B-47 a brake parachute was deployed immediately on touchdown, and the pilot applied heavy braking. In addition, the aircraft was fitted with an anti-skid device which automatically released the brakes and then reapplied them to give fresh 'bite'. On average, the B-47's landing roll used up 7,000 feet of runway.

On 23 October 1951, Colonel Michael N. W. McCoy accepted the first operational B-47B from the Boeing Company at Wichita, Kansas, and flew it to MacDill AFB, Florida, for delivery to the 306th Bomb Wing. Eleven more B-47s had been delivered by the end of

The B-47's undercarriage configuration required a very precise landing technique, and was the cause of numerous accidents. (Phil Jarrett)

1951, replacing the Wing's B-50s on a one-for-one basis, but production was fairly slow and by the end of 1952 the number of B-47s on SAC charge was still only 62. Most of these went to the 306th BW (367th, 368th and 369th BS) which, like the other B-47 Wings then in the process of forming, had a planned establishment of 45 aircraft. The 305th BW (364th, 365th and 366th BS) at MacDill and the 22nd Bomb Wing (2nd, 19th and 33rd BS) at March AFB, California – both B-29 units – also received a number of B-47s before the end of 1952 to enable them to begin conversion training, and delivery of their full complement of B-47s continued during January and February 1953.

Meanwhile, the 306th BW had been given the task of evaluating the B-47 under realistic operational conditions and formulating appropriate tactics; this culminated in an exhaustive exercise known as 'Sky Try', which lasted from 22 January to 20 February 1953, during which all operational procedures were tested. These included the carriage and release of dummy bomb shapes, having the exact configuration of the Mk 7 atomic bomb which the B-47 was to carry initially. This weapon, with a yield of 30 to 40 kilotons,

weighed 1,700lb and was 15½ft long, with a diameter of 30 inches. Its casing was streamlined, with three stabilising fins. The Mk 7 was the result of a crash programme, initiated by President Truman in 1948 at the time of the Berlin crisis and designed to give the United States a substantial stockpile of atomic weapons; the programme was continued under President Eisenhower's administration, and in 1952 Mk 7 bombs were being produced at the rate of one a day. By early 1953 the stockpile stood at about 1,500.

Later in the 1950s, SAC's B-47 fleet standardised on the Mk 28 thermonuclear weapon, two of which could be carried by the Stratojet. This weapon could be assembled in five different configurations, with yields controllable between 1.1 and 20 megatons. Depending on the chosen yield, its length varied between 9 and 14 feet. Its diameter was 20 inches, and weight varied with the selected yield. It could be dropped in free fall, or retarded by a parachute.

Soon after completing Exercise 'Sky Try' the 306th BW was declared combat-ready, and SAC HQ decided that the entire Wing should deploy to the United Kingdom on a 90–day TDY. On 6 April, Colonel McCoy led two 306th BW Stratojets on a proving flight from MacDill AFB via Limestone AFB, Maine, to RAF Fairford in Gloucestershire, and established a record for the transatlantic crossing by covering the 3,120 miles from Limestone to Fairford in 5 hours and 38 minutes; the rest of the 306th BW staged to Fairford by the same route on 4, 5 and 6 June, all 45 aircraft in place by the end of the third day. During the deployment McCoy's record was broken nine times. The best time was recorded by a B-47 which landed on 6 June; it completed the trip in 5 hours and 22 minutes, at an average speed of 575 mph. The 306th Air Refueling Squadron's KC-97s, crammed with support personnel, deployed on the same dates as the B-47s. They made a night stop at Ernest Harmon AFB, Newfoundland, and then flew on to RAF Mildenhall.

At the end of its TDY, the 306th BW was replaced in the UK by the 305th BW, whose B-47s went to RAF Brize Norton and its tankers to RAF Mildenhall. The 306th departed, flight for flight, as the 305th arrived, the B-47s flying non-stop to MacDill with one in-flight refuelling. The 305th was in turn replaced by the 22nd BW, and the policy of retaining at least one B-47 Wing on TDY in England at all times was to continue until early in 1958, when the RAF's V-Force became combat-ready.

By the end of 1953 five more B-29 medium bomber wings had armed, or were in the process of arming, with the B-47. These were the 44th BW (66th, 67th and

68th BS) and the 68th BW (51st, 52nd and 656th BS), both at Lake Charles AFB, Louisiana (later to be renamed Chennault AFB); the 301st BW (32nd, 352nd and 353rd BS) at Barksdale AFB, Louisiana; the 303rd BW (358th, 359th and 360th BS) at Davis-Monthan AFB, Arizona; and the 320th BW (445th, 446th and 447th BS) at March AFB, California. For the first time, B-47s took part in the SAC Bombing Competition of 1953, all Wings except the 68th – which was still converting – sending two crews to Davis-Monthan AFB between 25 and 31 October. Mainly through lack of experience on the type, the B-47's showing fell below expectations on several counts, particularly navigation; of the seven Wings competing, one was placed ninth, one tenth, and the other five brought up the rear. The trophy was won by the 92nd Bomb Wing, a B-36 unit, with B-50D Wings taking the next four places, a situation that caused the 'jet jockeys' not a little embarrassment.

During the course of 1954 the number of SAC units armed with the B-47 more than doubled, with seven more B-29 units and two newly established Wings receiving the Stratojet. The B-29 units were the 9th BW (Mountain Home AFB, Idaho), the 19th BW (Pinecastle AFB, Florida), the 40th BW (Smoky Hill AFB, Kansas), the 98th BW (Lincoln AFB, Nebraska), the 308th BW (Hunter AFB, Georgia), the 310th BW (Smoky Hill AFB) and the 376th BW (Barksdale AFB). The two new Wings were the 321st BW (Pinecastle AFB) and the 340th BW

B-47 undergoing RATOG trials. UK-based B-47s were fitted with RATO gear, but this would only have been used under war conditions to assist rapid take-off. (Phil Jarrett)

TOP & ABOVE: *B-47Es of the 380th BW at Brize Norton. (Phil Jarrett)*

(Sedalia AFB, Missouri). Both had been activated some time earlier, but did not receive their equipment until 1954. With this expansion of B-47 Wings, SAC was able to retire the last B-29s in its fleet. The last operational Superfortress on the Command's inventory, B-29A serial 42-94032, which had been assigned to the 307th BW at Kadena AB, Okinawa, returned to the USA on 4 November 1954 to be stored at Davis-Monthan AFB in the facility's 'desert boneyard'.

Prior to 1954, SAC's concept of war operations had been based on the deployment of its bombers to forward bases outside the continental United States (CONUS). The combination of B-47 and KC-97 now made it feasible for SAC's bomber Wings to strike

directly at targets inside the Soviet Union from the USA, afterwards recovering to bases in Europe or North Africa. On 6 and 7 August 1954, to demonstrate the feasibility of this new concept, the 2nd and 308th Bomb Wings flew from Hunter AFB, Georgia, carried out a simulated bombing mission, and then recovered to a North African base. During this exercise, two 308th BW Stratojets made a 10,000-mile non-stop flight from Hunter AFB to French Morocco and back, each aircraft refuelled four times by KC-97s. One aircraft made the flight in 24 hours, the other in 25 hours and 23 minutes.

Impressive though it was, this achievement was overshadowed by a real marathon of a flight that took place on 17 November 1954, when Colonel David A. Burchinal, commanding the 43rd Bomb Wing, took off from Sidi Slimane in French Morocco to fly to RAF Fairford, where his Wing was on a 90–day TDY. Bad weather prevented him from landing at Fairford, so he returned to Sidi Slimane only to find that the weather had clamped there too. With the assistance of nine in-flight refuellings by KC-97s, Colonel Burchinal kept going until the weather finally cleared on 19 November, he and his co-pilot/gunner taking it in turns to fly and rest. In the meantime, he had established a distance and endurance record for a jet aircraft, flying 21,163 miles in 47 hours and 35 minutes. More important than the record was the fact that everything on board the B-47 had functioned well throughout the two-day flight.

The B-47 would, ultimately, provide SAC with a much-needed strategic reconnaissance capability, its high speed and operational ceiling once again making overflights of the USSR feasible without undue risk. In the meantime, General LeMay once more prevailed upon the RAF to carry out another clandestine mission. The Special Duty Flight was again activated in March 1954. The crews were briefed to cover three routes, north, central and southern; the latter was a long and potentially dangerous trip that would require refuelling inbound as well as outbound, and Sqn Ldr Crampton selected this one for himself. There was some comfort to be derived from the Intelligence briefing, at which he had been told that although his aircraft might be tracked by Soviet GCI, he was not likely to encounter radar-equipped night fighters and he need not worry about flak, as he would be flying too high and too fast.

Late in April, the three RB-45Cs once again refuelled off northern Denmark and set off on their respective routes. Apart from the replacement of Sgt Lindsay by Flt Lt Furze, already mentioned, the only other crew

TOP: *The Boeing KC-97 was the mainstay of SAC's tanker fleet during the 1950s.*
ABOVE: *Symbolic of SAC's striking power in the 1950s, a formation of B-47 Stratojets.*

change was in Crew 3, where Flt Lt Bill Blair was replaced by Flt Lt Harry Currell.

The first leg of Sqn Ldr Crampton's flight took him towards Kiev, and as he flew on at 36,000 feet and a steady 0.7M he noticed what looked like lightning flashes twinkling on the ground far below. Then, as he approached the area north-east of Kiev, the sky ahead erupted with what he later described as a 'veritable flare path of exploding golden anti-aircraft fire', at the same height as the RB-45C and a few hundred yards in front. His reaction was instinctive: he pushed the throttles wide open and turned west, heading for Germany, a good 1,000 miles away. His destination was Fürstenfeldbruck, the planned air refuelling rendezvous and emergency alternative airfield.

Contact was made with the KB-29 tanker as scheduled, but because of a refuelling malfunction Crampton decided to land at Fürstenfeldbruck and top up there before returning to Sculthorpe, where the other two aircraft had already landed. Their flights had been without incident, but the results obtained on this mission were analysed as only partially successful. It is quite possible that the operation was compromised; for a year beforehand, letters had been appearing in various UK aviation publications, questioning the presence at Sculthorpe of mysterious RB-45Cs bearing RAF markings, and the British Intelligence system itself – although this was not known at the time – had been infiltrated at senior levels by communist sympathisers.

In fact, the intelligence material gathered during the whole series of overflights was far less than had been hoped or anticipated. This was due in part to the fact that the special cameras fitted to the aircraft had been wrongly focused prior to the first series of flights prompting Air Chief Marshal Sir Hugh P. Lloyd to write on 16 December 1952 to Major-General John P. McConnell, commanding the British-based USAF 7th Air Division, to express his regrets that the operation had not provided the required answers. Nevertheless, these were the highest and fastest missions flown by RAF crews up to that time, and they were undertaken at considerable risk. All the crew members received decorations.

There may have been a political motive behind the operation, probably involving the release by the Americans of information that was needed by the British to accelerate their nuclear research programme. There is some evidence that such information was released in exchange for the RAF's cooperation. The man in charge of development of the British thermonuclear bomb was W. R. J. Cook (later Sir William Cook), the Deputy Director of the Atomic Weapons Research Establishment, who began active work on the project at Aldermaston on 1 September 1954, forming a Weapons Development Committee to plan the work and the necessary tests. Cook and his scientists cut a number of corners in developing a workable two-stage thermonuclear bomb in less than three years, and a lot of mystery still surrounds the precise way in which they achieved it. At least part of the solution may lie in the fact that there was now growing collusion in nuclear affairs between the British and Americans.

Early in 1954 the Americans carried out a series of six tests (Operation 'Castle'), the overall aim being to prove the feasibility of producing lightweight thermonuclear weapons. It may have been no coincidence that, just weeks before the Special Duty Flight's last overflight of the USSR, RAF Canberras were permitted to carry out radiation sampling flights in connection with these US nuclear tests in the Pacific.

The RAF unit involved was No. 1323 Flight at RAF Wyton, which in February 1954 deployed two Canberra B2 aircraft (WH701 and WH738), each equipped with wingtip samplers and a small sampler attached to the underside of the fuselage, to the Pacific. All RAF insignia were deleted from the aircraft during the operation. The deployment was dogged by misfortune: on 23 February 1954 WH738 vanished without trace on a transit flight from Momote to Kwajalein, in the Marshall Islands, and on 11 March a replacement aircraft, WH679, lost its radio compass and had to make a forced landing on Ailinglapalap atoll, also in the Marshalls. The aircraft could not be salvaged, so its engines were removed and the airframe destroyed.

These mishaps left only WH701 to carry out the sampling task, which it did on shots Bravo (28 February), Romeo (26 March) and Koon (6 April). An engine failure just prior to take-off prevented its participation in Union on 25 April, but together with another replacement Canberra – WJ573, which arrived at Kwajalein on 27 May – it participated in test shots Yankee (4 May) and Nectar (13 May). Prior to each shot the RAF task force was given notice of the date and time of detonation, meteorological data, and vectoring information that enabled the Canberras to track and intercept the clouds. The radio call sign Eager Beaver was used on each operational sortie. Because the RAF operation was impaired by the loss of some of its aircraft, the Americans obligingly provided filter papers containing radiation samples collected by their own aircraft. All samples were flown back to the UK by Hastings aircraft the day after each event.

Scientific analysis of the samples almost certainly provided British scientists with valuable clues as to the nature of the American devices under test in the 'Castle' series, and may have contributed to a series of British tests, code-named 'Mosaic', which were held two years later. The first of these, Mosaic G1 (16 May 1956), was designed to provide scientific data on thermonuclear reactions in light elements, and required small quantities of thermonuclear material – lithium deuteride – to be incorporated in the fission device to see if it could be ignited. This test produced a yield of 10 kilotons, but the second test, Mosaic G2, gave a yield of 98 kilotons, and was probably a 'layer cake' assembly, with a layer of U-238 surrounding a layer of lithium deuteride, which in turn surrounded the fissile core.

The Mosaic results were to be crucial to the planning for the series of British thermonuclear tests which were to begin just under a year later. In the meantime, other tests had proved the British Blue Danube atomic bomb as a viable nuclear system, and the Valiant squadrons could now go ahead with defining operational procedures. A British deterrent was at last in place, but it was still the bombers of Strategic Air Command which remained the western world's primary insurance against hostile attack.

CHAPTER SEVEN

The Threat:
Russia's Strategic Bomber Force

By 1954, the perceived threat of nuclear attack on the British Isles, and to a lesser extent on the United States, had increased substantially with the deployment of of the Soviet Union's first strategic jet bombers and first-generation atomic weapons. Since the late 1940s the Tupolev design team had been turning its attention to improving the basic Tu-4 design, the principal object being to increase the bomber's range. Retaining the basic structure of the Tu-4, Tupolev's engineers set about streamlining the fuselage, increasing its length by several feet and redesigning the nose section, replacing the Tu-4's rather bulbous cockpit with a more aerodynamically refined stepped-up configuration. The area of the tail fin was also increased and the fin made more angular in design. To reduce drag, the nacelles of the Ash-73TK engines (the Wright R-3350 copies) were redesigned. The outer wing sections were also redesigned and the span increased slightly, allowing for an increase in fuel tankage of 15 per cent.

The redesigned aircraft, designated Tu-80, flew early in 1949. Two prototypes were built, and the operational version, while carrying a similar payload to that of the Tu-4, was to have had a defensive armament of ten 23mm cannon or ten 12.7mm machine-guns in remotely controlled barbettes. By this time, however, the Soviet Air Force had begun to think in terms of an aircraft that would compare with the Convair B-36, which was beginning to enter service with Strategic Air Command, and the Tu-80 was not ordered into production. Another Tu-4 derivative, the DVB-202, designed by Vladimir Myasishchev, suffered the same fate.

In mid-1949, in response to the new specification, Tupolev embarked on the design of the biggest aircraft so far constructed in the Soviet Union, and the last Russian bomber type to be powered by piston engines. At this time, several engine design bureaux in the USSR were working on powerful jet and turboprop engines that would power the next generation of Soviet combat aircraft, but it would be some time before these became operational, and in the meantime – with relations between East and West deteriorating rapidly, particularly as a result of the Russian blockade of Berlin – the race to achieve parity with the United States assumed a high degree of urgency. This was especially true in the strategic bombing field; it was of little use if the Russians broke the American nuclear weapons monopoly by building up their own stockpile of atomic bombs, only to lack the means of delivering them to their targets. The B-36 had given Strategic Air Command the capability to deliver nuclear bombs deep into the heart of the Soviet Union, but in 1949 the Russians had no comparable bomber. The Tu-4 had the capacity to lift Russia's early, cumbersome atomic weapons, but only over limited ranges; it could theoretically strike at targets in North America across the Arctic regions, but such a mission would be strictly one-way.

The new specification called for an intercontinental bomber capable of carrying an 11,500lb bomb-load over a combat radius of 4,375 miles and then returning to base without refuelling. Tupolev's answer was to produce a scaled-up version of the Tu-80 powered by new 4,000 hp piston engines. In this way, Tupolev succeeded not only in retaining the proven aerodynamic and technical qualities of the Tu-80 and its predecessor, the Tu-4, but also saved time: only two years elapsed between the start of the intercontinental bomber programme and the first flight of a prototype. By way of comparison, it took the Americans five years to produce the B-36, although the latter was somewhat more revolutionary in concept.

The new bomber, designated Tu-85, began flight testing at the beginning of 1951, powered by four Dobronin VD-4K engines producing 4,300 hp on take-off. The structure was light, employing a number of special alloys (although for some reason magnesium, which was used in the structure of the B-36, was not incorporated) and the long, slender, semi-monocoque fuselage was split into five compartments, three of which were pressurised and housed the 16-man crew. Defensive armament was the same as the Tu-4's, comprising four remotely controlled turrets each with a pair of 23mm cannon. The roomy weapons bay could accommodate up to 44,000lb of bombs. With an 11,000lb bomb-load, the Tu-85 had a range of 7,500 miles at 340 mph and 33,000 feet; normal range was 5,530 miles. Maximum speed over the target was 406 mph.

Several Tu-85 prototypes were built and test-flown in 1951–52, but the aircraft was not ordered into production. Times were changing fast. In February 1951, before the Tu-85 began its flight test programme, the US Air Force had decided to order the Boeing B-52 Stratofortress, which was capable of attacking targets in the USSR from bases in the continental USA, and it was clear that the day of the piston-engined bomber was over. The Russians therefore decided to abandon further development of the Tu-85 in favour of turbojet-powered strategic bombers, although they fostered the impression that it was in service by showing the prototypes, escorted by jet fighters, at Aviation Day flypasts.

The production of a strategic jet bomber was entrusted to Tupolev and also to the Myasishchev design bureau; the latter's efforts were to culminate in the four-engined Mya-4, which first appeared at Tushino in 1954 and received the NATO code-name of 'Bison'. Although never an outstanding success in the long-range strategic bombing role for which it was intended, the 'Bison' was nevertheless the Soviet Union's first operational four-engined jet bomber, and was roughly comparable with early versions of the B-52. Its main operational role in later years was maritime and electronic reconnaissance, and some were converted as flight refuelling tankers.

Tupolev's strategic jet bomber design was much

TOP & ABOVE: *The Myasishchev Mya-4 'Bison', not a success as a strategic bomber, served subsequently in the ELINT and tanker roles.*

more successful. Designated Tu-88, it flew for the first time in 1952 and entered service three years later as the Tu-16, receiving the NATO code-name 'Badger'. Owing much, in fuselage design at least, to the Tu-80, the Tu-16 was destined to become the most important bomber type on the inventories of the Soviet Air Force and Soviet Naval Air Arm for over a decade, about 2,000 examples being produced.

Tupolev also adopted the Tu-85's basic fuselage structure in the design of a new turbojet-powered strategic bomber, the Tu-95. To bring the project to fruition as quickly as possible, the Tupolev team married swept flying surfaces to what was basically a Tu-85 fuselage. Development of the Tu-95 and Mya-4 proceeded in parallel, and it was intended that both types should be ready in time to take part in the

Tushino flypast of May 1954. However, some delay was experienced with the Tu-95's engines, and in the event only the Mya-4 was test-flown in time. Flight testing of the Tu-95 began in the summer of 1954, and seven pre-series aircraft made an appearance at Tushino on 3 July 1955, the type being allocated the NATO code-name 'Bear'.

By this time the importance of the turboprop-powered bomber was growing, for the performance of the Mya-4 had fallen short of expectations and as a result production orders were cut back drastically. Even though the Tu-95's massive Kuznetsov NK-12 engines were still causing problems, it was realised that the Tupolev design would form the mainstay of

the Dalnaya Aviatsiya's strategic air divisions for at least the next decade; an ironic turn of events, for in the beginning emphasis had been placed on the production of the Mya-4 in the mistaken belief that the turboprop-powered Tu-95 would be limited to 0.76M.

Russia's new strategic bomber assets were divided in the main between three formations: the 30th Air Army (HQ Irkutsk), the 36th Air Army (HQ Moscow) and the 46th Air Army (HQ Smolensk). The 46th Air Army, forming the Western Theatre Strike Force, was numerically the most important, being eventually expanded to a strength of four bomber divisions of 12 bomber regiments. (The other Soviet air armies of the Cold War era, the 4th at Legnica in Poland and the 24th

TOP: *The Tupolev Tu-16 'Badger' was the most successful Russian jet bomber design of the 1950s.*
ABOVE: *Maritime reconnaissance variant of the Tu-95 'Bear'.*

at Vinnitsa, were essentially tactical formations. The other tactical air army, the 16th, which was also the largest, was based in East Germany.)

The bomber regiments were dispersed at 22 principal airfields around the perimeter of the USSR: Murmansk North-east and Olenegorsk on the Murmansk peninsula; Vorkuta in the Soviet Arctic; Soltsy near Leningrad; Tartu and Chernyakhovsk on the Baltic; Lvov, close to the Polish border; Bobruisk, Bykhov and Zhitomir in the Kiev region; Saki, Oktyabrskoye and Adler on the Black Sea; Engels and Voronezh south of Moscow; Dolon, Belaya and Belogersk near the China/Mongolia border; and Alekseyevka, Mys, Shmidta and Anadyr in the Far East. Some of these bases were expanded wartime airfields, while others were newly built.

While the build-up of the strategic bomber force was progressing, so was the development of Russia's nuclear weapons. On 12 August 1953, the Russians exploded their first thermonuclear device; this was a fusion reaction with a boosted configuration involving the use of lithium deuteride, and produced a yield in the 200 to 300 kiloton range. At about this time the Soviet Air Force received its first issue of atomic bombs, and in September 1954 the Russians conducted their first large-scale exercise involving an atomic bomb detonation. By 1955 small numbers of nuclear weapons were being produced for the Army and Navy as well as the Air Force, and in 1955 a series of tests took place involving the delivery of nuclear weapons by aircraft. These culminated in two significant shots, both occurring in November. The first, on the 6th, was apparently a thermonuclear bomb reduced in size to fit the bomb bays of Russia's new generation of jet bombers; it produced a yield of 215 kilotons. The second, which took place on the 22nd, was the first Soviet high-yield (1.6 megaton) weapon test and the detonation occurred at an elevation of several thousand feet. Subsequent analysis by the US Atomic Energy Commission showed that it was a two-stage bomb using both U-235 and U-233, as well as U-238 and lithium deuteride. It was Russia's nineteenth atomic test since 1949.

By the end of 1955, then, the Russians had an effective nuclear strike force in place, and were about to deploy thermonuclear weapons. But the manned bomber was to have only a secondary place in Russia's military strategy. At the end of 1945 the Russians had taken the decision to build their own versions of the German V-2 rocket, one produced by captured German scientists, the other by a Soviet group under the leadership of Sergei Korolev, a noted rocket scientist. Both missiles were tested in 1947 and the Russian version proved to have a better performance than its German-designed counterpart; designated R-1, it formed the basis of all subsequent Soviet rocket development.

The relative success of the R-1 prompted a decision, taken in principle in 1947, to begin development of a weapon that could serve as an intercontinental ballistic missile (ICBM). According to one source, Stalin himself stated in 1947 that 'Such a rocket could change the face of war . . .The problem of the creation of transatlantic rockets is of extreme importance to us.'

The firm decision to throw massive funding into the development of an operational ICBM was taken in 1953, the year of Stalin's death. The decision pushed Soviet strategic planning along a road that was to be beset with technical difficulties and which, for a critical period in the early 1960s, was to hand undisputed superiority in the dangerous world of nuclear confrontation to the Western Alliance.

In the meantime, the surveillance of the Soviet Union's strategic bomber bases and nuclear test sites assumed cosmic importance. The expansion of Strategic Air Command's reconnaissance assets had really got underway in the summer of 1950 with the delivery of three new aircraft types, beginning with the Convair RB-36D. This strategic reconnaissance version of the massive global bomber had 14 cameras weighing 3,309lb in the forward bomb bay, the second bay containing up to 80 T86 flash bulbs. An extra 3,000-gallon fuel tank could be installed in the third bay, and ECM equipment in the fourth. The RB-36D carried standard gun armament, together with an AN/APQ-24 radar navigation system for locating targets. The aircraft carried a crew of 18, later rising to 22 with the addition of four more specialist crewmen.

The first RB-36D (44–92091) was delivered on 2 June 1950 to the 28th Strategic Reconnaissance Wing at Rapid City AFB, South Dakota, which became operational in the following year. In December 1950 the 5th SRW at Travis AFB also began to rearm with the RB-36D, the establishment of the two Wings being 18 and 22 aircraft respectively. In fact only 31 RB-36Ds were built, so re-equipment of the 5th SRW was completed with the RB-36E version. This was a converted B-36A, and the last of 22 examples was delivered in July 1951.

The next strategic reconnaissance aircraft was the RB-50B, the first of which (47–123) was delivered to the 91st SRW at Barksdale AFB, Louisiana, on 12 July 1950. A few weeks later, on 26 August, the 91st SRW also took delivery of its first RB-45C. From April 1951 the RB-50Bs were redesignated according to their specific tasks: RB-50E for photographic reconnaissance, RB-50F for photo-mapping, and RB-50G for electronic reconnaissance.

From 1951 surveillance of Soviet arctic bases was undertaken by RB-36s operating from British bases, mostly Sculthorpe, the main area of interest being the island of Novaya Zemlya, where the Russians were building what appeared to be a large nuclear weapons test complex. (It was; most Russian nuclear testing took place there from 1958 to 1964.) These excursions resulted, in November 1951, in the Soviet Aviation Ministry issuing an urgent specification for an all-weather fighter fitted with a long-range search radar, the Izumrud (Emerald) AI radar then carried by existing Soviet fighter types being quite inadequate for the interception of the American reconnaissance aircraft. It was not until 1956 that such an aircraft – the Yakovlev Yak-25 'Flashlight' – entered service with the Soviet Air Force's fighter squadrons, and until then the reconnaissance flights continued with impunity.

Successful 'ferret' missions depended on locating gaps or 'dead spots' in the Russian radar defences, which was done initially by monitoring Soviet radio and radar traffic from ground stations in Europe, the

Middle East and Far East. When such a dead spot was found, a penetration of some 25 or 30 miles would be made – often longer in the case of eastern and southern areas, where radar coverage was poorer – the ferret aircraft staging out of bases such as Rhein-Main in Germany; Mildenhall, Lakenheath and Sculthorpe in the United Kingdom; Atsugi, Misawa and Iwakuni in Japan; Kadena on Okinawa; Sangley Point in the Philippines; and other locations in Norway and Libya.

Ferret crews were left under no illusions by their briefing officers about their chances of being rescued if they were forced down in hostile territory. There were none. Their only hope of survival, if they sighted enemy fighters, was to find a cloud formation large enough to conceal them before they were intercepted. Clear skies were anathema to them, and yet many operations were flown in clear weather. It was quite amazing that no USAF aircraft was shot down over the Soviet Union during this dangerous period of the early 1950s.

In 1953 SAC began to receive the first reconnaissance version of the Boeing B-47 Stratojet. The first new-build variant that was specifically dedicated to the reconnaissance role was the RB-47E, but delays in production during 1952 led to the choice of an interim conversion. Camera pods were fitted to 90 B-47Bs, which were then designated YRB-47B. In fact, the first batch of YRB-47Bs, minus reconnaissance equipment, was delivered to the 20th Bomb Wing at Mather AFB for use in bombardment training, and it was not until 25 April 1953 that the first YRB-47B with its full eight-camera bomb bay pod was delivered to the 91st SRW at Lockbourne AFB. In September the

26th SRW, also at Lockbourne, became the second unit to arm with the YRB-47B.

Both Wings began to re-equip with the RB-47E during 1954, two more units also receiving this variant in the course of the year. These were the 55th SRW, a former RB-50 unit, and the 90th SRW, which had operated RB-29s. Both were located at Forbes AFB, Kansas. The fifth and last unit to equip with the RB-47E was the 70th SRW, which was activated at Little Rock AFB in 1955. In all, 240 RB-47Es were delivered to SAC.

Two more reconnaissance variants of the Stratojet were produced. These were the RB-47H and RB-47K, which were modified for the ELINT role and had a pressurised compartment containing three electronics warfare specialists in the bomb bay. Thirty-five RB-47Hs and 15 RB-47Ks were built, the former being delivered to the 38th and 346th SRS and the latter to the 338th SRS of the 55th SRW in 1955–56.

In the RB-47H the specialist signals operators – known popularly as 'Crows', although officially called Ravens – were crammed into a compartment only four feet high, forcing them to move about on their knees. All three Crows had to cram themselves into the cockpit before take-off, then crawl down into the compartment, where they sat facing aft, strapped into ejection seats and with solid banks of equipment – scopes, analysers, receivers, recorders and controls – in front and on one side. Raven One was the commander and sat in the right forward corner of the compartment. As well as the banks of equipment in front of him and on his left, there was an array of video, digital and analogue recorders along the wall to his right and behind him. Ravens Two and Three sat

Boeing RB-47H 53–4280 of the 55th SRW at Upper Heyford. (Harry Holmes)

side by side at the rear of the compartment, with just enough room between their seats for someone to squeeze through.

On the day before a sortie into a sensitive area, specialist crews were given a very comprehensive briefing covering the route, timing, up-to-date intelligence on likely defences, and specific tasking. To perform a mission successfully required a great deal of experience, but a Crow who was good at his job could

identify an intercepted signal from its various characteristics – frequency, pulse shape, pulse rate, type of modulation, type of scan and so on – displayed on his equipment. These functions determined the radar's function, be it early warning, search or fire control. Variations were what the specialists were seeking; emitters were constantly being modified to increase their capability or to defeat surveillance and countermeasures techniques.

Nose detail of RB-47H 53-4280, showing the Strategic Air Command insignia. (Harry Holmes)

At a predetermined point during the mission the Crows began processing signals, keeping each other constantly informed about activity on their assigned bands. If, for example, an SA-2 surface-to-air missile radar was activated, one Crow would track it while another looked for the missile guidance signal. It was difficult work, for there might be a couple of dozen signals in the narrow band to which each receiver was tuned. As well as audio recordings, signals appearing on oscilloscopes and other visual equipment were filmed and photographed. By switching to one of the direction-finding antennae, which rotated at 300 rpm, the Crows could log a number of bearings to obtain a position fix on a transmitter.

RB-47H 0-34280 of the 55th SRW at RAF Brize Norton. This aircraft was the last reconnaissance Stratojet to operate from the UK.

On some sorties, RB-47 crews logged several interceptions by Soviet fighters. Detecting an approach was the responsibility of Raven One, who would identify the aircraft from the signals emitted by its AI radars and weapon systems and alert the pilots to its presence. Sometimes, if the Russians showed signs of aggression, the mission had to be aborted and Raven One used chaff and jammers while the RB-47 got clear of the danger area. Even though overflights were still banned in the mid-1950s, flights along the frontiers of the Soviet Union were dangerous enough, and Soviet air defence technology was becoming increasingly sophisticated.

In the face of the American strategic threat, Soviet planners had given a very high priority to the creation of an effective air defence system in the late 1940s, which in practice meant the co-ordinated development of jet interceptors, anti-aircraft artillery and radar networks, with surface-to-air missile deployment envisaged in the not too distant future. These elements were the responsibility of the Air Defence Command, the Protivo-Vozdushnaya Oborona (PVO), which was rapidly bringing new aircraft types into its inventory. By the end of 1952 the successor to the well-tried and combat-proven MiG-15, the MiG-17 (NATO reporting name 'Fresco') had completed its State Acceptance Trials and the type went into production immediately, entering service in 1953. The Fresco-B, or MiG-17P (P for *Poiskoviy*, meaning search radar) was equipped with the Izumrud AI kit; the Fresco-C, or MiG-17F (*Forsazh*, meaning afterburner), was fitted with reheat, boosting the performance of its Klimov VK-1 engine to 7,500lb; and a later model, the MiG-17PF Fresco-D, was equipped, as its suffix

denoted, with both AI radar and afterburner.

The 'Fresco', as RB-47 crews soon learned, had a performance that matched that of their own aircraft, which was now outstripped in terms of both maximum speed and operational ceiling. This fact had serious implications for Strategic Air Command's main striking force, which in 1953 was in the process of rearming with the B-47. The ability of the B-47 to penetrate Russia's air defences was in serious doubt, and on 8 May 1954 the Americans felt justified in taking an appalling risk by sending an RB-47 of the 91st SRW on a photographic mission over northern USSR, with fighter airfields as its main objectives. The flight appears to have been authorised by General Curtis LeMay, SAC's commander; in all probability, neither the State Department nor President Eisenhower had any knowledge of it. The RB-47, flown by Colonel Hal Austin, took off from RAF Fairford and was supported by two others, which flew a feint mission towards the Kola peninsula before turning back, leaving the photographic aircraft to penetrate in the Murmansk area and continue to Archangel'sk before turning south-west to fly over Finland, the Gulf of Bothnia and Sweden before making a timely refuelling rendezvous with a KC-97 tanker over Norway. The RB-47 was intercepted by MiG-17s and took some hits, but at the altitude at which the interceptions took place the MiGs' cannon recoil gave them some stability problems and they were unable to sustain their attacks. The RB-47 crew replied with their twin 20mm tail cannon, which helped to keep the MiGs at bay, but they were extremely lucky to get away with it.

Perhaps, though, it was not only the Americans who

took extraordinary risks. In the meantime, an RAF Canberra had become the focus of a rather odd story, one which remains uncorroborated to this day. It first came to light in a book, published in 1968, about the activities of the Central Intelligence Agency (*The Centre*, Steward Alsop, New York: Popular Library, p. 194) in which it was stated that a modified Mk 2 Canberra 'flew at its maximum altitude from a base in West Germany, photographed the missile launch site at Kapustin Yar in the Soviet Union, and landed at a base in Iran. The Soviets – possibly forewarned by Kim Philby, the life-long Soviet spy then in charge of British intelligence's anti-Soviet operations – very nearly succeeded in shooting down the Canberra, which took several hits.'

The background to this story is that towards the end of 1952 the CIA became aware, through interrogation of German scientists and other personnel who were slowly being repatriated from the Soviet Union, that a missile test facility had been set up at Kapustin Yar, north of the Caspian Sea (48° 35´N, 46° 18´E). In fact, testing had been in progress there since 1947, with the launching of captured German V-2 rockets and derivatives of them. The first Soviet serial production version of the V-2 was known to NATO as the SS-1a 'Scunner', which was followed, in 1950, by a longer-range variant, the SS-2 'Sibling'. Neither of these weapons was deployed operationally, and at the end of 1952 there were indications that the emphasis was shifting towards the development of surface-to-air missiles and very-long-range strategic rockets.

It therefore became a matter of the highest priority to establish exactly what was going on at Kapustin Yar, and that meant clandestine photo-reconnaissance. Robert Amory Jr, who at that time was the CIA's deputy director for intelligence, later stated in an Oral History interview that the CIA requested photographic coverage of the site, but was told by General Nathan F. Twining, the US Air Force Chief of Staff, that Kapustin Yar was outside effective reconnaissance range (in other words, it was beyond the range of any camera operating outside Soviet air space, as overflights were still officially vetoed) and that the USAF could not undertake the mission.

One of the RAF's PR Canberras, however, was capable of making a daylight sortie to Kapustin Yar, and the subsequent scenario is as follows. The CIA, presumably through clandestine diplomatic channels (which probably meant the Secret Intelligence Service), approached the RAF and asked them to do the job. A Canberra was specially modified with a 100–inch focal length camera of American design and provided with extra fuel tankage, and some time in the early summer of 1953 it took off from Giebelstadt in Germany, flew over eastern Europe at altitude, turned south along the Volga to Kapustin Yar, and landed in Iran. Somewhere along its route it was intercepted, shot at, and damaged. According to some sources, the Canberra involved was B2 WH726, the only B2 allocated to the RAF's No. 540 (PR) Squadron, which had begun arming with the Canberra PR3 in December 1952. If the story is true, and there is no real reason to doubt that the flight took place, it is indicative yet again of the extraordinary degree of collusion that existed between the British and Americans.

The Kapustin Yar and Kola missions showed that, once again, the Western Allies had a critical strategic reconnaissance gap to fill, and it could not have opened up at a worse time. On 12 August 1953, the Russians exploded their first thermonuclear device, and before the end of the year they had tested three more, at least one of which was thought to be an air drop. The Americans had to assume that the Russians had already deployed operational atomic bombs (in fact, they were only just doing so in late 1953) and were on the verge of deploying operational thermonuclear weapons. Constant surveillance of nuclear test sites, bomber airfields and missile development centres was now no longer just a question of strategic importance; it was a question of survival.

CHAPTER EIGHT

Nuclear Alert

Although Soviet nuclear capability was growing fast, the USA still held most of the atomic cards. The policy of the nuclear deterrent had already been clearly defined by President Eisenhower as the need 'to be constantly ready, on an instantaneous basis, to inflict greater loss upon the enemy than he could reasonably hope to inflict upon us'. This view matched the opinion of US Secretary of State John Foster Dulles, although the two did not agree on how the deterrent force should be implemented.

In the summer of 1953, during a discussion with Eisenhower on post-Korea foreign policy, Dulles had advocated that the United States increase its weapons production and withdraw its troops from Asia and Europe on the basis that the nuclear threat would be enough to ensure East–West stability. Eisenhower had rejected this, believing that the first task was to educate the American people about the horrors of nuclear war, 'otherwise we will drift aimlessly, probably to our own eventual destruction'. At the same time, he continued in a memorandum to Dulles, 'We should patiently point out that any group of people, such as the men in the Kremlin, who are aware of the great destructiveness of these weapons – and who still decline to make any honest effort towards international control by collective action – must be fairly assumed to be contemplating their aggressive use.' Only then, Eisenhower thought, would the average citizen recognise the need for a nuclear deterrent.

Responding to Dulles's recommendation for a defence policy based on a massive overkill capacity, Eisenhower agreed that such a capacity would constitute a deterrent, but warned that 'if the contest to maintain this relative position should have to continue indefinitely, the cost would either drive us to war or into some form of dictatorial government. In such circumstances, we should be forced to consider whether or not our duty to future generations did not require us to *initiate* war at the most propitious moment that we could designate.' In short, Eisenhower was considering whether the best way to deal with the Soviet nuclear threat might be to eliminate it while it was still in its embryo stage by means of a preemptive atomic attack. It was exactly the philosophy that was being increasingly voiced among his peers by General LeMay. Fortunately, at the highest political level it remained no more than a consideration, and Eisenhower did not advocate such a step. Nevertheless, the possibility remained in his mind, and he was to voice it again in the summer of 1954, when the French were being beaten by the communist Viet Minh forces in Indo-China.

In May 1954, the French came to believe that the Viet Minh were about to receive massive aid from communist China in the shape of squadrons of jet aircraft, which the French completely lacked in that theatre, and sought assurances that the United States would intervene with its military forces if such a thing occurred. The options for such intervention were studied in depth by the Joint Chiefs of Staff, the National Security Council, the State Department and the White House. The Joint Chiefs of Staff, who had made a set of unauthorised promises to the French, had already worked out a war plan and were ready to take action – not in Indo-China, but in China itself. The National Security Council's view, expressed by Robert Cutler, the chairman of its planning board, was that 'there was little use discussing any "defense" of Southeast Asia; that US power should be directed at the source of the peril, which was, at least in the first instance, China, and that in this connection atomic weapons should be used'.

Secretary of State Dulles, who viewed any Chinese intervention in Indo-China as tantamount to a declaration of war against the United States, urged the President to get a resolution through Congress immediately, authorising him to respond to such intervention as he saw fit. Eisenhower, Robert Cutler recorded, told Dulles that if he were to go to Congress for authority he would not ask for halfway measures. If the situation warranted it, there would be declared a state of war with China, and there might be a strike on Russia. The President watered down his statement somewhat by commenting that he would never permit the United States to act unilaterally in Indo-China, but if the occasion arose to act in concert with Allies 'there should be no halfway measures or frittering around. The Navy and Air Force should go in with full power, using new weapons, and strike at air bases and ports in mainland China.'

The main problem with the punitive strike policy, however, was that American strategists underestimated China's reaction to the threat of nuclear attack, and had done since the beginning of the war in Korea. Once they had decided to intervene in that conflict in October 1950, China's leaders were under no illusions. They knew that the coming offensive by their armies in Korea would bring with it the possibility of an all-out war with the United States. It was a risk they were prepared to accept, including the awesome threat of an atomic strike against Chinese targets by Strategic Air Command. By the beginning of November 1950, in preparation for such an eventuality, the whole of north-east China was placed on a war footing. Air raid drill was carried out in every town and village, and deep air raid shelters were being built in and around major targets. These activities were accompanied by a rapid expansion of the Chinese communist air defence system, which was being brought up to date with Soviet help.

With Chinese armies flooding into Korea, serious thought was indeed given by the US Joint Chiefs of Staff to the possibility of using nuclear weapons against the massed Chinese ground forces. Later estimates indicated that a 40-kiloton airburst weapon exploded over a dense enemy concentration at Taechon on the night of 4/25 November would have destroyed about 15,000 of the 22,000 Chinese troops assembled there; six 40-kiloton airbursts over the Chinese troop assembly area in the Pyongyang–Chorwon–Kumhwa triangle between 27 and 29 December 1950 would have destroyed half of an estimated force of 95,000 men; while six 30-kiloton airbursts laid along enemy lines north of the Imjin River on the night of 31 December 1950 would have wiped out between 28,000 and 40,000 of an enemy force numbering 70,000 to 100,000.

The idea, however, was politically untenable, and in any case there were major technical obstacles. At the end of 1950 only a small part of SAC's bomber force was nuclear-capable, and that was based in the United States; it would have taken time to deploy the aircraft (which would have been drawn from the 509th Bomb Group) and their special weapons to the Far East, and by that time the enemy troop concentrations would have long since dispersed. Temporary deployments of SAC's nuclear strike force were made to the Far East later in the war, but although the aircraft brought the bomb cases and HE elements with them, nuclear capsules were not fitted and would have had to have been flown out at short notice. Up to the end of 1950 the US stockpile of atomic weapons was small, and was wholly assigned to strategic use. Also, the use of nuclear weapons in a tactical situation in Korea, close to the front line, would have inflicted casualties on friendly forces as well as on the enemy.

It was not until the spring of 1953, when the Americans made it clear they were prepared to extend the war into China, using nuclear weapons if necessary, that they fully realised the power of the atomic bomb as a political weapon in forcing the communists to conclude an armistice. Later, Admiral C. Turner Joy, C-in-C Naval Forces Far East, wrote that 'The threat of atomic bombs was posed. Defeat for Red China became a possibility. In understandable prudence they took the only step open to them to remove the growing threat of a holocaust. It was as simple as that. It had always been as simple as that.'

But it was not as simple as that. The real factor that persuaded China to review her stance at the negotiating table was the death, on 5 March 1953, of Soviet Premier Josef Stalin, an event rapidly followed by a full reappraisal of Soviet policy towards the Korean conflict and the withdrawal of Russian combat units and advisers from Manchuria. Faced with the swift withdrawal of Soviet support for the continuation of the war – and that included the elimination of any possibility that the Russians might be persuaded to carry out retaliatory nuclear attacks on UN targets – the Chinese and North Korean negotiators immediately began to make concessions at Panmunjom.

Now, faced with the nuclear attack option a year later, President Eisenhower was convinced that an atomic attack on China would inevitably draw the Soviet Union into the conflict, so if there were to be an American first strike Russia and China would have to be attacked simultaneously. To the Joint Chiefs he had this to say: 'I want you to carry this question home with you. Gain such a victory, and what do you do with it? Here would be a great area from the Elbe to Vladivostok torn up and destroyed, without

government, without its communications, just an area of starvation and disaster. I ask you what would the civilised world do about it? I repeat there is no victory except through our imaginations.'

As it turned out, there was no Chinese communist intervention in Indo-China; there was no need of it, for the Viet Minh under Ho Chi Minh and the redoubtable General Giap were doing all that was necessary to drive the French into a corner from which there was no escape. But in the summer of 1954, a year that saw the destruction of two US reconnaissance aircraft by Chinese fighters, the threat of Chinese – and possibly joint Sino-Soviet – action in south-east Asia seemed very real, and during this tense period the USAF was placed on a high alert state.

In Britain, Third Air Force and SAC units trained by day and night with an increased intensity that brought strong protests from local communities adjacent to the major bases. At Greenham Common the base commander was inundated with more than 1,000 letters from the residents of nearby Newbury, who complained that the constant B-47 operations made life seem like 'hell with the lid off'. At Upper Heyford, members of the local populace voiced fears that there might be a repetition, with more disastrous consequences, of an accident that occurred on 5 February 1954, when a B-47 crashed in Stoke Wood, a mile and a half from the end of the main runway.

The first atomic weapons were introduced to USAF bases in Britain during 1954, mainly as a result of intelligence that the Soviet Union was starting to deploy its own weapons and would soon have a modern strategic air force to deliver them. To some extent, the emphasis was on building up a stockpile of tactical, rather than strategic, nuclear weapons in Britain. By mid-1954 nuclear weapons components were under secure storage at Sculthorpe, where the B-45s of the 47th Bomb Wing were based, at Woodbridge and Wethersfield, homes of the 20th FBW's F-84Gs, and at Bentwaters, as well as at the SAC bases.

On 1 April 1954 the 81st Fighter Interceptor Wing at Bentwaters changed its designation to the 81st Fighter-Bomber Wing, and later in the year its Sabres were replaced by F-84F Thunderstreaks. The F-84F was essentially a swept-wing version of the Thunderjet, but it could carry up to three times its predecessor's weapons load, and at higher speeds. In addition to its conventional war load of bombs and 5-inch High Velocity Aircraft Rockets (HVAR), it could carry the 2,000lb Mk 7 nuclear store. The 20th FBW at Wethersfield also rearmed with the F-84F during 1955.

Following the deployment of the Hawker Hunter Mk1 day fighter to the squadrons of RAF Fighter Command in 1954, the Sabres of No 1 (RCAF) Fighter Wing began moving from North Luffenham to the Continent, the redeployment completed in March 1955. Two UK air defence squadrons, Nos. 66 and 92, were also armed with the Canadair Sabre in December 1953 and February 1954 respectively, operating the type from RAF Linton-on-Ouse in Yorkshire until receiving the Hunter F4 in the spring of 1956. The two squadrons suffered a spectacular accident rate, losing 18 aircraft in two years, about half the accidents the result of engine flameouts or sudden power loss.

TOP: *F-86D Sabre. (Philip Jarrett)*
ABOVE: *F-86D discharging a salvo of FFAR rockets from its ventral pack.*

To further augment the UK air defences, the 406th Fighter-Bomber Wing at Manston changed its designation to the 406th Fighter Interceptor Wing on 1 April 1954, and its three Manston-based squadrons, the 512th, 513th and 514th, rearmed with the F-86F Sabre. On 1 November 1954 the 512th FIS moved to Soesterberg in Holland, and on 21 December a fourth squadron, the 87th FIS, arrived at Bentwaters from Sioux City, Iowa. This squadron was armed with the North American F-86D Sabre night/all-weather fighter, which was equipped with a Hughes AN/APG-36 search radar, an E-3 fire control system, and carried 24 2.75in folding fin aircraft rockets (FFAR) in a ventral pack. The two Manston squadrons also re-equipped with the F-86D early in 1955 and all three came under the control of No. 11 (Air Defence) Group RAF.

The F-86D was an important asset to the round-the-clock air defence of the UK. On a typical air defence mission beginning with a cold start, the F-86D would be off the ground in about four minutes, which included warming-up time, and would then take 11 minutes to climb to 45,000 feet at full power. The pilot would then initiate the search phase, the AN/APG-36 (AN/APG-37 in later models) radar antenna sweeping an area 68.5 degrees left and right of the centreline in a three-and-a-half-second cycle and also, if required, 33.5 degrees up and 13.5 degrees down. When a target was acquired at a range of up to 30 miles the radar locked on to it and the AN/APA-84 computer then worked out a lead collision course, which the pilot followed by keeping the 'blip' on his radar scope inside a one-inch circle.

When the automatic tracking system indicated twenty seconds to go, the system instructed the pilot to turn on to a 90-degree collision course, at which point he elected to launch 6, 12 or all 24 rockets and pressed the trigger switch. The computer controlled the actual firing, extending the rocket pack in half a second and initiating the firing sequence when the target was about 500 yards away. It took only one fifth of a second to fire the full salvo of rockets, each weighing 18 pounds, the missiles fanning out like a charge of shotgun pellets to make sure of a hit. The rocket pack retracted in just over three seconds, and a symbol on the radar scope, which illuminated at a range of 250 yards, warned the pilot to break off.

As the quality of the aircraft assigned to UK air defence improved, strenuous efforts were being made to update the warning radar system, but the best that could be done in the short term was to update the existing system by duplicating the radar cover, making some of it mobile, going underground for protection where possible, making the radars more reliable and easier to maintain and improving the readiness by deploying more manpower on watch. This led to the so-called ROTOR programme, in which immediate steps were taken to modify the old wartime radars pending the introduction of new ones from 1957. In fact, technological progress made it possible to begin installing the new radars by the end of 1954.

The new TRE Type 80 radar provided good long-range coverage, being able to track targets down to the horizon, which in practice meant 22,000 feet at 200nm. However, the deployment of thermonuclear weapons in both East and West led to the concept of a short three-day war in which Britain could not hope to survive unless high-speed, high-altitude enemy aircraft carrying H-bombs were destroyed, and in its early stages ROTOR could not be relied upon to give sufficient early warning.

Everything depended on speeding up the elapsed time between the detection of a hostile target by the ground radar warning system and passing the relevant information to the interceptor force. In this respect the Americans had made a considerable advance in 1953 with the USAF's acceptance of SAGE, a semi-automatic ground environment system developed by the Massachusetts Institute of Technology. This was an early datalink system in which all information received from surveillance radars was processed by a high-speed digital computer and transmitted to a receiver installed in the interceptor, where it was converted into factors such as heading, speed, altitude, target bearing and range. This information was displayed in the cockpit and the interceptor automatically positioned for a lead-collision attack with its fire control system, eliminating the need for any voice communication.

By the end of 1955 the USAF in Britain was concentrating overwhelmingly on tactical operations, following a change in Strategic Air Command's policy that saw the end of 90-day spells of overseas temporary duty. SAC's overseas bases, including those in the United Kingdom, would now be used as post-strike facilities. The policy switch, a result both of economic considerations and a desire to reduce overcrowding on overseas bases that were becoming increasingly vulnerable to attack by Soviet weaponry, enabled the 7th Air Division to reduce its strength by almost half in the early part of 1956. The 49th Air Division was also inactivated on 21 March 1956 and its two Wings were assigned as direct reporting units to HQ Third Air Force. Later in the year the US Army anti-aircraft and smoke-generating units that had deployed to Britain for the protection of the bomber bases were withdrawn as part of the planned reduction in the US combat force.

Defence policy in the European context had changed radically between 1954 and 1956. In 1954 the thinking was that any all-out war would begin with a massive nuclear attack, followed by a period of 'broken-backed' warfare that would continue in desultory fashion while both sides marshalled their strategic forces for round two. By 1956, however, the western nuclear deterrent was a credible force, and the launching of all-out nuclear war was becoming unthinkable; defensive policy now rested on a European 'shield' of strong conventional forces backed up by massive tactical air support. On 5 May 1956 the United States initiated a series of nuclear tests in the Pacific; 12 bombs were exploded, and the purpose of most of the shots was to produce the prototypes of small, lightweight bombs that could be carried by tactical aircraft. In the words of President Eisenhower, the tests, known collectively as Operation 'Redwing', were designed 'not to cause more destruction, but to find out ways and means in which you can limit it, make it useful in defensive purposes . . . reduce fallout, make it more of a military weapon and less one just of mass destruction. We know that we can make them big

[but] we are not interested in that anymore.'

The B-47 force reached its peak during 1956, with the activation of three more Wings: the 341st BW at Dyess AFB, Texas; the 379th BW at Homestead AFB, Florida; and the 100th BW at Portsmouth AFB, New Hampshire. The latter was actually in the process of equipping at the end of the year, and received its full complement of 45 Stratojets in February 1957. SAC now had 1,260 B-47B and B-47E Stratojets on strength, the latter variant the most numerous. The B-47E was powered by six General Electric J47–GE-25A turbojets, each rated at 6,000lb st dry and 7,200lb st with water methanol injection. Like previous variants it carried a crew of three: pilot, co-pilot/gunner and navigator/bombardier. Armament comprised two M24A1 cannon in a radar-controlled tail barbette, with 350 rounds of ammunition. Maximum bomb-load was 20,000lb, and the aircraft could carry four Mk 28 bombs. The B-47E was capable of a speed of 606 mph (0.84M) at 16,300 feet, and 557 mph (0.82M) at 38,550 feet; maximum cruising speed was 495 mph (0.75M) at 38,550 feet. Service ceiling was 40,500 feet, and maximum unrefuelled range with a 10,000lb weapons load was 4,000 miles. The last production B-47E (53–6244) was delivered to the 40th BW at Schilling AFB, Kansas, on 24 October 1956.

In October 1956, the whole of SAC came to readiness in response to the Hungarian uprising, which was closely followed by the Suez Crisis. As a first step, KC-97 tankers were concentrated into tanker task forces at key bases in the northern part of the United States, and also in Greenland, Newfoundland and Labrador, on rotational training assignments. The tactical air forces in the UK and on the Continent also stood alert during this period. These moves were followed by two closely related exercises that were held over a two-week period ending on 11 December. In these exercises, code-named 'Power House' and 'Road Block', more than 1,000 B-47s and KC-97s flew massive simulated combat missions over North America and the Arctic. Although the US Government strongly opposed the Anglo-French military intervention in Egypt, it was nevertheless prepared to use SAC's awesome striking power in a visible show of strength as a means of deterring the Russians from taking sides.

The exercises were also a reaction to the Soviet Union's growing offensive power. In the spring of 1956 Nikita Khrushchev had boasted that the USSR would soon have guided missiles with H-bomb warheads capable of hitting any point in the world. The Americans took the boast seriously; it was known that the Russians were testing long-range rockets, and US Intelligence wrongly asserted that an operational ICBM, the SS-6, was rolling off the production line like cars in Detroit. In fact the SS-6 – which was to be used as the basis of the booster rocket that would launch the world's first artificial earth satellite, Sputnik 1, 18 months later – was completely ineffective as a long-range military missile (it was later established that only six were ever deployed) but the vision of giant Soviet rockets delivering enough H-bombs to burn America from coast to coast was enough to send a shudder of panic through even the most hard-headed members of the US Joint Chiefs of Staff.

In the light of this, SAC had for some time been taking steps to ensure that it would survive any surprise Soviet ICBM attack, and remain in a condition to launch a massive retaliatory strike. One important step, taken in November 1956, was to begin the relocation of SAC HQ at Offutt AFB, Nebraska, from a cluster of buildings that had once housed the Glenn L.

The F-84F Thunderstreak was the mainstay of the Third Air Force's tactical fighter-bomber units in the 1950s, until the arrival of the F-101 Voodoo.

An F-84F launching a salvo of HVAR high-velocity rockets.

Martin bomber plant in World War Two to a brand-new control centre, built at a cost of nine million dollars. The new facility consisted of two inter-connected structures: an administration building, comprising three storeys above ground and a basement, and an underground three-storey command post. Access from one facility to the other was provided by a tunnel. The underground facility, which was designed to survive anything other than a direct hit by a high-yield nuclear weapon, housed the control room and related communications equipment and computers installed

to maintain close contact with SAC forces throughout the world. Giant map and board displays were used to depict the exact disposition and operational status of the entire force.

Another step was the inauguration of the One-Third Ground Alert Programme, which was based on the premise that SAC would have only 15 minutes in which to get its bombers airborne after incoming ICBMs were first detected. In order to provide an effective and immediate retaliatory strike force, SAC devised the ground alert concept, whereby it would

TOP: *Boeing KC-97L refuelling F-84Fs. (via Harry Holmes)*
ABOVE: *A Boeing C-97 Stratofreighter. As a cargo transport it carried a maximum load of 68,500 lb. (Philip Jarrett)*

maintain about one third of its aircraft on ground alert, with weapons loaded and crews standing by for immediate take-off. SAC's combat wings were neither manned nor organised to support this new concept, and so the Command conducted three extensive tests to determine what was needed to develop and maintain the one-third alert force. The first test, code-named Operation 'Try Out', was conducted by the 38th Air Division (the 2nd and 308th BW and their associated KC-97 tanker squadrons) at Hunter AFB between November 1956 and April 1957; this proved that the scheme was feasible, but pinpointed

numerous areas where changes would be required to make it fully practical. To perfect these areas, SAC conducted two additional tests, Operation 'Watch Tower' by the 825th Air Division at Little Rock AFB between April and November 1957, and Operation 'Fresh Approach' by the 9th Bomb Wing at Mountain Home AFB in September 1957. Convinced that the concept was workable, although many organisational and operational details were still to be worked out, SAC's commander, General Thomas S. Power, authorised ground alert operations to begin at several CONUS and overseas bases from 1 October 1957.

CHAPTER NINE

Reflex Action

Ever since General Dwight D. Eisenhower became President of the United States in 1953, the US military hierarchy and the various intelligence agencies had been making determined efforts to persuade him that overflights of the Soviet Union could be undertaken without seriously jeopardising US–Soviet relations or, at worst, starting a war. One of the key arguments used was that the aircraft performing the mission would be virtually undetectable, and on 24 November 1954 Eisenhower was persuaded by two very influential and well-trusted advisers, James Killian and Edwin Land, that an aircraft could overfly the USSR without being detected. They did not pretend that it would be invisible, simply that it would evade detection. The theory was that if it could reach an altitude significantly greater than 40,000 feet while still outside the 200–mile range of the Russians' SCR-270 early warning radar, the SCR-585 anti-aircraft, automatic tracking radars would not be alerted to the presence of an intruder and would not be activated. At this time, Killian was chairman and Land a member of the Technological Capabilities Panel, empowered by Eisenhower to advise him on the Soviet threat; he accepted their recommendations, although with some reservations that an aircraft flying straight and level for long distances over hostile territory might still be vulnerable to interception.

The pro-overflight lobby received some useful ammunition when, at the May 1955 Red Air Force Day at Tushino, Moscow, western observers – including Colonel Charles E. Taylor, the US Air Attaché in Moscow – witnessed what appeared to be a whole Wing of 'Bison' strategic bombers in the flypast. It was a clever ruse; what the observers had seen was the same formation, deliberately varied in size, flying past several times. The inference, though, was that the 'Bison' outnumbered its American counterpart, the Boeing B-52, by about four to one, so the position seemed grim. Two months later, in July, President Eisenhower proposed his famous 'Open Skies' policy, which envisaged frequent inspection flights by US and Soviet reconnaissance aircraft over one another's territory and an exchange of information about military installations. When the Soviet leadership, now under Nikita Khrushchev, rejected the 'Open Skies' proposal out of hand, Eisenhower and his close advisers decided irrevocably that Operation 'Overflight' would be set in motion, and that the aircraft to undertake the mission would be the Lockheed U-2, then under development with funding provided by the Central Intelligence Agency.

By April 1956 the first group of U-2 pilots had completed their flight training and CIA indoctrination course, a rigorous procedure that included resistance to interrogation, survival techniques and personal endurance tests. Some pilots were ex-military; others were serving military personnel who had volunteered for special duties and were attached to the CIA in a temporary duty basis. The civilian pilots were 'employed' by Lockheed as 'flight test consultants', and various other cover stories were invented for the military participants. The first four U-2 pilots to be declared operationally ready, together with the first two production U-2As, were deployed by Globemaster to RAF Lakenheath in Suffolk, the necessary approval having been given earlier in the year by senior RAF officers, senior officials of the British intelligence services, and Prime Minister Anthony Eden himself. For the benefit of curious aircraft spotters, who were bound to notice the U-2s when they carried out pre-mission test flights, the task of the Lockheed aircraft was stated to be high-altitude weather reconnaissance, and the Lakenheath-based unit was given the cover designation of Weather Squadron (Provisional) One (WRSP-1).

The spotters lived up to their reputation, and from the moment the strange, unmarked aircraft made an appearance in British skies the country's aviation periodicals were deluged with letters from enthusiasts avid to know its identity and mission. For some time the USAF refused to comment, but it finally issued a statement to the effect that the machine was a Lockheed U-2 and that it was engaged in gathering information 'relating to clear air turbulence, convective clouds, wind shear and the jet stream . . . cosmic rays and the concentration of certain elements in the atmosphere, including ozone and water vapour'.

The spotters were not fooled. As the months passed there was a growing realisation that the mysterious U-2's activities might not be concerned solely with research, and that in some respects this strange machine, with its black anti-corrosion paint finish and total lack of identification markings, might be the proverbial wolf in sheep's clothing. In June 1957 the journal *Flying Review* ventured the opinion that 'it is possible that U-2s are flying across the Iron Curtain taking aerial photographs or probing radar defences'.

Flying Review's supposition was entirely correct, although by that time the U-2 detachment was no longer British-based and the overflights had been going on for a year. In June 1956, Anthony Eden had decided that U-2 operations from Britain would not be politically acceptable after all, and so WRSP-1 moved to Wiesbaden, Germany. Eden's decision was made in the light of a series of disastrous covert operations by the British Secret Intelligence Service, culminating in the mysterious death of the frogman Commander Lionel Crabbe in what was apparently an underwater mission to investigate sonar and other equipment on the Soviet cruiser *Sverdlov*, which was on a goodwill visit to Britain.

On 5 July 1956, after some preliminary high-altitude flights over East Germany, U-2A Article 347 (USAF serial No 56-6680) took off from Giebelstadt, a small airfield near the East–West German border, and headed for Moscow, where it photographed the Russian capital's defences and the nearby test airfield of Ramenskoye before turning north for Leningrad. A second mission to Leningrad was flown on 8 July. Both sorties were detected by the Russians' Token warning radars, but subsequent tracking was intermittent and inaccurate. On 9 July the Russians protested about the first flight, omitting to mention that the U-2 had overflown Moscow as well as Leningrad, and they made no reference at all to the 8 July mission. The protest note also described the aircraft that flew over Leningrad as 'twin-engined', which was probably a shot in the dark on the assumption that it was a PR Canberra. The US State Department naturally denied that a twin-engined American aircraft had been anywhere near Leningrad, but President Eisenhower was unhappy that the overflight had been picked up. While he understood that the U-2s were safe from interception, he saw the need for a future reconnaissance aircraft that would be truly 'invisible' to enemy defence systems. His awareness was to result in the launching of a research and development programme that would ultimately lead to a true 'stealth' aircraft.

The U-2, whose overflights ended abruptly with the shooting down of Francis Gary Powers by an SA-2 missile battery near Sverdlovsk on 1 May 1960, was not a permanent resident in the UK until the latter years of the Cold War and therefore does not play a significant part in this history. In one respect, however, it was the focus of a very significant area of USAF/RAF joint operations.

In 1958, the Royal Air Force became involved in the U-2 overflight programme. This move resulted from the adoption of a joint targeting policy by SAC and RAF Bomber Command; the RAF's V-bomber force now had a formidable nuclear attack capability in its own right, and the testing of British thermonuclear weapons in 1957 had helped to convince the USAF that Bomber Command would be a viable partner in a nuclear war.

The first batch of four RAF pilots assigned to the U-2 programme (Sqn Ldr Christopher Walker, and Flt Lts Michael Bradley, David Dowling and John MacArthur) were sent to Laughlin AFB, Texas, to undergo training in May 1958. Laughlin was a Strategic Air Command Base; SAC had taken delivery of its first U-2 (56-6696) there on 11 June 1957, the aircraft being assigned to the 4028th SRS of the 4080th SRW. The declared mission of SAC's U-2s was weather reconnaissance and atmospheric sampling, although they had a far more perilous role to play.

The RAF pilots went through the same stringent CIA indoctrination procedure as their American counterparts before beginning flight training. On 8 July 1958, Sqn Ldr Walker was killed when his U-2 broke up at high altitude, probably after going out of control, and crashed near Wayside, Texas; his place was taken by Flt Lt Robert Robinson, fresh from the British H-bomb trials at Christmas Island.

The RAF's U-2 operations were held to be a matter of the highest security and very few people, certainly on the UK side, knew about them. The programme on the RAF side was run by the Assistant Chief of Air Staff (Operations) in the Ministry of Defence. It was a subject that came up occasionally during the Vice Chief to Vice Chief talks. It was a subject known to have been discussed between the respective chiefs at that level and, of course, the Central Intelligence

Agency and the Joint Intelligence Committee in London were involved. In London, details of the programme were certainly known to the Defence Committee at Cabinet level.

For a number of years, the RAF sent detachments of four pilots on regular rotation to Edwards AFB, from where they would deploy singly to operating locations in Europe. RAF-manned U-2s appear to have operated mainly from Cyprus, although in 1959–60, before the Powers incident, a U-2 was occasionally seen departing RAF Watton in Norfolk, the home base of No. 192 (Special Duties) Squadron, whose function was to gather electronic intelligence.

Some American sources maintain that the RAF pilots were responsible for 'between two and four' of the 24 overflights that were made over the Soviet Union. Whatever the truth, it remains classified as this book is being written in the summer of 1998, and until the relevant documents are declassified it is quite useless to speculate. The official history of the U-2's operations has already been written by a US historian, but it cannot be released without the agreement of the British Government. If overflights conducted by RAF pilots had involved penetrations into Russia, it is hard to understand this attitude. But what if the RAF flights were made not over Russia, but over targets in other countries, particularly in the Middle East, which had been within the British sphere of influence but which were now leaning more and more towards the USSR and its doctrines? In some quarters, that might still cause political embarrassment.

Meanwhile, in 1957, the revised system of Strategic Air Command overseas deployment known as 'Reflex Action' had come into effect. Each wing would now deploy a small number of aircraft in rotation to an overseas base for a period of 21 days, instead of a whole Wing being deployed overseas for a 90–day TDY. Reflex Action was pioneered in July 1957 by the 2nd, 305th, 306th and 308th BW, each of which deployed five B-47s to Sidi Slimane in French Morocco. The same four Bomb Wings – all Twentieth AF units – continued to evaluate the concept for the remainder of the year, the aircraft at Sidi Slimane going over to ground alert with the rest of SAC on 1 October.

Reflex Action deployments to the United Kingdom began on 7 January 1958, the 98th, 307th and 310th BW sending B-47s to RAF Greenham Common while the 2nd, 308th and 384th BW deployed aircraft to RAF Fairford. B-47s on nuclear alert did not fly in an armed configuration, although nuclear weapon components were ferried to their Reflex Action destinations in separate aircraft. In January 1958, B-47s deploying to the UK took part in two major air defence exercises, 'Buckboard' and 'Grabhook', the incoming bombers being intercepted by Hawker Hunter F6s of RAF Fighter Command. The B-47s approached Scotland from the north-west, although one group in Exercise 'Grabhook' was routed to approach from the north via the Shetland Islands to provide a realistic threat. As usual, the B-47s flew at 35,000 to 40,000 feet, and the Hunters registered some good claims against them. The Stratojet's vulnerability was increasing.

By this time, however, SAC's deterrent posture was devolving more and more on the Boeing B-52 Stratofortress. This aircraft was the product of a USAAF requirement, issued in April 1946, for a new jet heavy bomber to replace the B-36 in Strategic Air Command. Two prototypes were ordered in September 1949, the YB-52 flying for the first time on 15 April 1952 powered by eight Pratt & Whitney J57–P-3 turbojets. On 2 October 1952 the XB-52 also made its first flight, both aircraft having the same powerplants, carrying a crew of five and armed with four tail-mounted 0.50in calibre machine-guns. Basically, the B-52 used the same configuration as the B-47, and in many respects was Boeing's ultimate show of confidence in the thin, swept wing with cantilevered and podded engine installations.

The two B-52 prototypes were followed by three B-52As, the first of which flew on 5 August 1954. These aircraft featured a number of modifications and were used for extensive trials, which were still in progress when the first production B-52B was accepted by SAC. This aircraft, 52–8711, was flown from the Boeing factory at Seattle to Castle AFB, California, by Brigadier-General William E. Eubank Jr, on 29 June 1955 for

delivery to the 93rd Bomb Wing, which he commanded. By the end of March the 93rd BW was fully equipped with 30 B-52Bs (the strength was later expanded to 45 aircraft), and soon afterwards the Wing's 4017th Combat Crew Training Squadron, which had been activated on 8 January 1955, began training personnel for additional B-52 Wings.

The 42nd BW at Loring AFB, Maine, was the second Wing to rearm with the B-52, its first aircraft being delivered in June 1956; this was the first B-36 unit to convert to the Stratofortress, the 93rd BW having operated B-47s prior to conversion. The 99th BW at Westover AFB, Massachusetts, also began receiving B-52s in December 1956. The B-52B, which carried a six-man crew, was powered by eight Pratt & Whitney J57–P-19W engines and had a gross weight of 360,000lb. Fifty examples were produced for SAC (including ten of the thirteen B-52As originally ordered, which were converted to B-52B standard) and it was followed on the production line by the B-52C, 35 of which were built and which had a 50,000lb

Boeing B-52H of the 19th BW at RAF Marham for participation in the annual RAF Bombing Competition. Note the legend on the nose, the brainchild of Lt Gen. David Wade, commanding general, US Eighth Air Force. (Phil Jarrett)

greater gross weight. The focus of B-52 production then shifted to Wichita with the appearance of the B-52D, the first of which flew on 14 May 1956; 170 were eventually built.

The early service life of the B-52 was plagued by many problems. Turbos had a tendency to explode, causing fires or wrecking sections of the fuselage, and the main undercarriage units were a constant source of trouble. On the ground the bomber rested on four twin-wheel units, all of which were steerable and which could be slewed in unison to allow crosswind landings to be made with the wings level and the aircraft crabbing diagonally on to the runway; the trouble was that the main gear trucks had a habit of trying to slew in two different directions at the same time, or of jamming in the maximum 20-degree slewed position. The bomber's big Fowler-type flaps also had a tendency to crack and break under the tremendous sonic buffeting set up by full-power take-offs. Problems such as these caused the B-52 fleet to be grounded on several occasions before they were eventually solved, a process that took more than two years.

These troubles attracted little attention simply because SAC, in the interests of security, took great pains not to publicise them. Instead, the Command placed great emphasis on a number of notable flights which took place during 1956–57 and which appeared to indicate that the B-52 was well suited to its role of long-range strategic bombing. On 24 and 25 November 1956, in a spectacular operation called 'Quick Kick', four B-52s of the 93rd BW and four of the 42nd BW carried out a non-stop flight around the

perimeter of North America. The most publicised individual flight was that of a 93rd BW aircraft captained by Lt-Col Marcus L. Hill Jr, which started at Castle AFB and ended at Baltimore, Maryland, after covering approximately 13,500 nautical miles in 31 hours and 30 minutes. This flight demonstrated the value of in-flight refuelling, but also the limitations of the KC-97. The B-52 was refuelled four times, but if a jet tanker had been used, according to Colonel Hill's estimate, at least three hours could have been cut off the total flying time. (The Boeing KC-135 was, at that time, still undergoing trials.)

The second long-distance flight by B-52s took place from 16 to 18 January 1957, when three B-52Bs of the 93rd BW under the command of Major-General Archie B. Old Jr flew non-stop around the world. General Old, who was then commanding the Fifteenth Air Force, flew in the lead aircraft, *Lucky Lady III*, which was commanded by Lt-Col James H. Morris; the latter had flown as co-pilot in *Lucky Lady II*, a 43rd Bomb Group B-50A which had made a round-the-world non-stop flight in 1949. Five aircraft, including two spares, started the flight from Castle AFB. One of these, unable to take on fuel at the first rendezvous with KC-97 tankers, landed at Goose Bay, Labrador; the second spare continued with the main flight until after the second refuelling over Casablanca, when it left the flight and flew to RAF Brize Norton, arriving at the British base on 16 January. It remained for a few days before flying on to Castle AFB. Local fears that it might herald the influx of a fleet of similar aircraft were unfounded; Stratofortresses were never based in Britain except on temporary deployment to take part

B-52F 70039 of the 93rd BW at RAF Marham. (Phil Jarrett)

B-52H 00049 of the 449th BW at RAF Marham. (Phil Jarrett)

in exercises and bombing competitions.

The round-the-world flight went smoothly, with the aid of three more in-flight refuellings; the only deviation came at the end of the trip when, instead of the lead aircraft landing at March AFB and the other two at Castle, according to plan, fog at Castle compelled all three aircraft to land at March, having flown 24,325 miles in 45 hours and 19 minutes.

By the end of 1957 the B-52 equipped five Wings, the original three – the 93rd, 42nd and 99th – having been joined by the 92nd BW at Fairchild AFB and the 28th BW at Ellsworth AFB. Two more, the 6th BW at Walker AFB and the 11th BW at Altus AFB, were in the process of rearming. All except the 93rd BW were former B-36 units. Strategic Air Command now had a weapon which, flying at more than 600 mph at altitudes in excess of 50,000 feet from bases in the continental United States, was capable of delivering nuclear weapons to any point in the world. But the B-52, formidable though it was, would represent only a proportion of SAC's growing deterrent power in the years to come.

In the meantime, there had been some organisational changes in the Third Air Force's UK establishment. RAF Burtonwood, which in 1957 employed 10,000 people, was relinquished as a result of a new streamlined supply system enabling support to be given direct from depots in the USA; the Military Air Transport Service terminal remained until 1958, when it moved to Mildenhall. Full Sutton in Yorkshire, which had been designated as a reserve site for the USAF and was occupied by the 3930th Air Base Squadron from 1955 to 1957, was returned to the Air Ministry in February 1957, while East Kirkby in Lincolnshire, another reserve airfield, was relinquished by the USAF in 1958. In all, ten UK bases reverted to Air Ministry control during this period. The majority

had hosted non-flying units, but Manston and Shepherd's Grove were two important exceptions.

By 1957, the night/all-weather squadrons of RAF Fighter Command were rearming with the Gloster Javelin, and in May 1958 the 406th Fighter Wing at Manston was deactivated, its role as part of Britain's air defences at an end. Manston reverted to Air Ministry control in June. The other operational Third Air Force base, Shepherd's Grove, remained the home of the 78th Fighter-Bomber Squadron's F-84Fs until December 1958, when it too reverted to the Air Ministry. At the same time, work ceased on two airfields – Elvington and Stansted – which had been earmarked for use by 7th Air Division's bombers under the expansion scheme of 1954. Both were subsequently designated as dispersal airfields for the RAF's V-bombers.

In June 1957 the Third Air Force's tactical strike capability received a considerable boost when the 20th TFW at Wethersfield began to rearm with the North American F-100D Super Sabre. The F-100D was the major production version, a total of 1,274 being built for the USAF Tactical Air Command and various NATO air forces. The F-100D had a maximum speed of 924 mph at 36,000 feet; its service ceiling was 51,000 feet, and a combat radius of 700 miles with external fuel meant that from bases in the eastern United Kingdom it could hit targets in East Germany and Czechoslovakia. It could carry six 1,000lb bombs, twenty-four HVARs, or a single Mk 7, Mk 28 or Mk 43 nuclear store. Two squadrons were positioned at Wethersfield and a third at Woodbridge.

The second new type to arrive, in January 1958, was the Douglas RB-66 all-weather reconnaissance aircraft, which replaced the RB-45Cs of the 19th TRS at Sculthorpe. Soon afterwards the 47th BW also began to exchange its B-45s for B-66s, giving it a much

TOP: *F-100 Super Sabre 63319 of the 20th TFW at Middleton St George, September 1963, flanked by a Vickers Valiant B1 of No. 207 Squadron RAF. (Ken Mason)*
ABOVE: *F-100D Super Sabre 56–3239 of the 492nd TFS, 48th TFW, Lakenheath. (Harry Holmes)*

enhanced tactical strike capability. The twin-jet B-66, a land-based development of the US Navy's A3D Skywarrior, had a maximum speed of 620 mph at 10,000 feet, a combat radius of 800 miles on internal fuel and a bomb-load of 12,000lb. The 47th BW was to continue operating B-66s until June 1962, when it was deactivated.

On 10 August 1958 there was great excitement at Bentwaters when seven McDonnell F-101 Voodoos,

then the world's most powerful operational fighters, arrived over the airfield with an upward bomb-burst; breaking into the circuit for a stream landing, they taxied up to the flight line to be greeted by a welcoming committee of senior Third Air Force officers, wives and civilian base employees. They had completed a transatlantic flight of 5,199 miles in eleven hours and one minute, refuelling twice from KC-135 tankers. There should have been eight

Voodoos, but one had been forced to turn back with technical trouble. One of the pilots, Major Adrian Drew, had captured the world air speed record from Britain's Fairey Delta 2 in December 1956, logging an average speed of 1,207.6 mph in his F-101.

The Voodoo, developed from McDonnell's abandoned XF-88 long-range escort fighter, and first flown in September 1954, had been taken over as a project by Tactical Air Command. Three squadrons were equipped with the first production version, the F-101A, while the RF-101A equipped the 63rd Tactical Reconnaissance Wing. The next variant, the F-101B all-weather interceptor armed with high explosive or nuclear AAMs, eventually equipped sixteen squadrons in the USAF Air Defense Command, while the F-101C – the type deployed to Bentwaters – was a single-seat fighter-bomber version for Tactical Air Command. It had entered service in May 1957 with the 523rd TFS of the 27th FBW.

The deployment of the seven 27th FBW Voodoos to Bentwaters, apart from testing the aircraft's capacity for rapid overseas reinforcement, was intended to

TOP: *F-100D 56–2977 of the 48th TFW landing at Lakenheath, May 1970. (Harry Holmes)*
ABOVE: *Douglas RB-66B 54–0523 of the 10th Tactical Reconnaissance Wing pictured at Alconbury in May 1960. (Harry Holmes)*

TOP & ABOVE: *Douglas RB-66 30453 of the 10th TRW seen at RAF Middleton St George, September 1963. (Ken Mason)*

familiarise base personnel with the new aircraft prior to the re-equipment of the 81st TFW. The first of the 81st's own Voodoos arrived on 4 December 1958 and re-equipment thereafter was rapid, enabling 41 F-84F Thunderstreaks to be released for transfer to the Federal German Luftwaffe. The Wing's 91st and 92nd Squadrons were based on Bentwaters, with the 78th at nearby Woodbridge.

Meanwhile, Strategic Air Command's 7th Air Division continued to make use of six UK bases, TDY operations at Lakenheath having ceased in 1956. Detachments of B-47s still visited Fairford, but the use of that base by SAC had seen a steady decline since the end of 1955. Brize Norton continued to receive detachments of B-47s and RB-47s, together with their supporting KC-97G tankers, and Greenham Common

TOP: *A 10th TRW RB-66 making a fast run over RAF Middleton St George in September 1963, with the Cleveland Hills in the background. (Ken Mason)*
ABOVE: *McDonnell F-101C Voodoo of the 81st TFW, Bentwaters, pictured at the Battle of Britain air display, RAF Finningley, in September 1961. (Harry Holmes)*
BELOW: *RF-101C Voodoo in natural metal finish, prior to the application of camouflage. (Ken Mason)*

TOP: *McDonnell RF-101C Voodoo 56–199 of the 66th TRW at Upper Heyford, May 1967. (Harry Holmes)*
ABOVE: *McDonnell RF-101C Voodoo of the 66th TRW at Lakenheath, May 1967. (Harry Holmes)*
BELOW: *RF-101C Voodoo 56–126 of the 66th TRW at Bentwaters, June 1969. All RF-101Cs were camouflaged from March 1968. (Harry Holmes)*

TOP: *Allied line-up: C-124 Globemaster, RB-66, Hunter FGA9 and F-86D at Middleton St George, 1963. (Ken Mason)*
ABOVE: *Boeing KB-50 tanker flight refuelling an F-100 and F-101. (Ken Mason)*

Lockheed T-33 70536 on display at Middleton St George, September 1963. (Ken Mason)

remained busy but not so noisy as before, since B-47s on their Reflex Action deployments did not fly continuously.

There was a nasty incident at Greenham Common in February 1958 when a B-47 experienced engine trouble on take-off and the crew had to jettison two full 1,700-gallon underwing fuel tanks. These missed the designated safe area on the base, one hitting a B-47 in its dispersal and the other crashing through a hangar roof to explode inside. The resulting fire blazed for 16 hours, despite great efforts to bring it under control with the help of fire crews from RAF Odiham; the final toll was two dead, eight injured, two B-47s totally destroyed and the hangar wrecked. The B-47 that had caused all the trouble landed safely at Brize Norton.

The other regular 7th Air Division base, Upper Heyford, continued to host Reflex Action B-47s, and early in 1959 two other British airfields were temporarily added to SAC's list. Bruntingthorpe, in Leicestershire, had been reactivated for USAF use in February 1957, with a new 10,000-foot runway laid for use by B-47s; while this work was in progress the base was occupied by the 3912th Air Base Squadron and later by the 3912th Combat Support Group. In January 1959 a B-47 detachment of the 100th BW arrived and stayed until April; then, in August, the 19th TRS came over from Sculthorpe with its RB-66s. This unit formed part of the 10th TRW, the rest of which

was then based at Spangdahlem in Germany; in the summer of 1959, when the 10th TRW was relocated at Alconbury, Bruntingthorpe became a satellite of that airfield. The other airfield was Chelveston, which had been under USAF control since the beginning of 1953. After substantial reconstruction work, including the building of a new runway, the airfield was ready for use by SAC B-47s, which occupied it during the first six months of 1959 and were followed by a squadron of 10th TRW RB-66s.

Strategic Air Command's continuous airborne alert function had now been taken over by the B-52 Stratofortress Wings, operating from the United States, and Reflex Action B-47 medium bombers deployed on UK bases maintained a flight, usually of four aircraft, on 15 minutes' readiness. This procedure was also followed by RAF Bomber Command's V-Force, which never maintained an airborne alert force; instead, it depended on the dispersal of its bombers in clutches of two to four aircraft to more than thirty airfields around the United Kingdom during periods of alert, and on quick-reaction scramble times of two minutes or less.

By this time, the nuclear alert forces of Strategic Air Command and RAF Bomber Command were no longer functioning as two separate entities. As a consequence of what was undoubtedly the most important cooperative effort of the Cold War, they now formed a single, jointly coordinated deterrent force.

CHAPTER TEN

Joint Strike Force

Throughout the late 1940s and early 1950s, the British Government constantly sought to re-establish the spirit of wartime collaboration and to gain a greater degree of participation within the American nuclear programme, while at the same time pursuing its policy of developing an independent nuclear deterrent force. The approach eventually brought success; in 1952, Prime Minister Winston Churchill was given a personal briefing on the US Strategic Air Plan. Further steps in strengthening the Anglo-American nuclear relationship were taken in 1954, when the US Congress approved amendments to the Atomic Energy Act which permitted the exchange of data on nuclear weapons in terms of size, weight, shape, yield and effects; and in September 1955, after further contacts at senior political level, Marshal of the Royal Air Force Sir William Dickson, the then Chief of Air Staff, was able to begin discussions with his opposite number in the USAF, General Nathan F. Twining, on the planning requirements for an atomic counter-attack on the Soviet Air Force's long-range bomber bases in the event of general war.

MRAF Dickson was armed with a written brief that set out clearly what it was hoped to achieve. Its opening paragraph stated that 'the primary aim of the defence policy of the United Kingdom is to prevent war' and that 'the main instrument for achieving this aim lies in the nuclear capability, together with the means of delivery, which is possessed by the United Kingdom and the United States alone. We should achieve a closer association with the United States world-wide in the field of defence strategy. This is particularly important in strategic air operations, where Bomber Command and the Strategic Air Command will be attacking components of the same vast target complex. It follows that unless there is a full exchange of information and a coordinated plan of attack, wasteful overlapping and dangerous omissions will result.'

A further step along the road of full collaboration was taken in 1956, when senior British and American officers were invited to take part as observers in one another's nuclear tests. By December 1956, it was becoming clear to the Americans that RAF Bomber Command had an increasingly viable nuclear attack force through the combination of the Valiant and Blue Danube, and in that month Air Chief Marshal Sir Dermot Boyle, now Chief of Air Staff, received proposals from General Twining to provide the RAF with nuclear weapons in the event of general war and to coordinate the nuclear strike plans of the USAF and RAF. These proposals were later ratified in an exchange of letters between the British Minister of Defence, Duncan Sandys, and the American Secretary of Defense, Charles E. Wilson, during a meeting held in January 1957.

In August 1951, for the first time, RAF Bomber Command had taken part in SAC's annual bombing

The Americans were impressed by the Vickers Valiant, mainstay of the British nuclear deterrent in the 1950s.

competition, sending two Washingtons to MacDill AFB in Florida. SAC had also participated in the first RAF bombing competition which took place in December that year, entering two B-29s, two B-50Ds and two B-36s, all deployed to Sculthorpe for the event. In 1952, Bomber Command's entrants in the SAC competition had been two Washingtons and two Lincolns, while SAC had taken part in two RAF bombing contests, the Visual Bombing Competition held in July and the Blind Bombing Competition conducted in December.

Since then there had been no further RAF participation in SAC's annual event, but now, in October 1957, two Vickers Valiants – both from No. 138 Squadron, but with one crew from No. 214, together with two Avro Vulcans from No. 83 Squadron – deployed to Pinecastle AFB in Florida to represent Bomber Command once more. The competition lasted for six nights and involved 45 SAC Bomb Wings, each one represented by two aircraft and two crews, flying on three alternate nights. The route, flown at level cruise, was more than 2,700nm long and included an astro navigation leg of over 800nm and three widely spaced simulated bombing attacks. There were strict limitations, including a take-off 'window' of five minutes and an *en route* tolerance of plus or minus three minutes; failure to meet these automatically disqualified a crew, as did the failure to achieve a competition total of six scored bomb runs and two scored astro runs.

The two Valiants that took part were among the first to be delivered to the RAF with underwing fuel tanks, and were resplendent in their new white anti-flash finish. The competition began on 30 October and ended on 5 November, the RAF crews arriving three weeks early in order to familiarise themselves with SAC procedures and target data. The three targets were very precise. The first was the base of the north-east corner of the Columbian Steel Tank Company building in Kansas City; the second the centre of the turntable in the railway marshalling yards at St Louis; and the third the top of the north-west corner of the General Services warehouse in Atlanta. Despite some initial difficulty with the navigation bombing system in one of the Valiants, their final placing was 27th out of a total of 45 teams involved, one of the Valiant crews from No. 214 Squadron (Sqn Ldr Ronald Payne) being placed eleventh out of a total of 90 in the individual crew scoring part of the contest. Considering the quality and quantity of the SAC crews, it was a very satisfactory result for the Valiant crews, although the Vulcans did not do so well, placed 44th overall. Some of the Vulcans' electronic equipment was affected by the high humidity, and the bombing altitude of 36,000 feet was well below that at which their crews had been practising. Nevertheless, Bomber Command's participation yielded some valuable lessons, and it was to be an annual event from then on, with only an occasional break for operational or technical reasons.

The Americans were impressed by both the Valiant and Vulcan. The former, though not as fast as the B-47, had a considerably higher ceiling, while the Vulcan had a higher ceiling than either the B-47 or B-52 and was faster than the latter at altitude. There was no longer any doubt that these aircraft, together with the Handley Page Victor, which was about to enter RAF service, would have a formidable attack capability, and the realisation almost certainly accelerated the convening of a series of meetings in November 1957 between representatives of SAC and Bomber Command, with the aim of establishing a combined

BELOW: *Vulcan B1s at RAF Scampton.*
OPPOSITE: *Vulcan B2s on their Operational Readiness Platform at RAF Waddington.*

strike plan.

The meetings revealed that all Bomber Command's targets were also covered by SAC. In the early days, following the introduction of Blue Danube, the RAF Medium Bomber Force had been primarily concerned with attacking targets that presented a direct offensive threat to the UK and western Europe; in other words, Soviet bomber and naval bases. Following the 1957 consultations, it was decided that the total strategic air forces at the Allies' disposal were sufficient to cover all Soviet targets, including airfields and air defence systems. On the assumption that Bomber Command's assets would be 92 aircraft by October 1958, rising to 108 aircraft by June 1959, the Command was allocated as its targets 69 cities which were centres of government or had other military significance, 17 long-range air force airfields which formed part of the Soviet nuclear threat, and 20 elements of the Soviet air defence system. In the event of the UK being forced to take unilateral action against the Soviet Union, the target policy of Bomber Command would be to attack centres of administration and population, which was seen as the most effective system for the Command's limited resources.

In 1958, the unilateral action plan was revised to include 98 Russian cities, all of which had a population exceeding 100,000 and which lay within 2,100nm of the UK. This meant, in effect, that from its earlier policy of selective attacks on military targets, Bomber Command had reverted to its wartime policy of area bombing.

The supply of US nuclear weapons to the RAF, known as Project 'E', initially involved the provision of enough 6,000lb Mk 5 free-fall atomic bombs to arm 72 aircraft at Honington, Marham and Waddington. Some modifications were necessary to permit the carriage of the American weapon, but the scheme was in place by 1 October 1958, the date when the first fully coordinated strike plan was implemented. It caused complications insofar as the warheads themselves had to remain in American custody at the principal bases or in secure storage depots, which meant that they could not be flown to the V-Force dispersal airfields in time of emergency and that there was no guarantee the Americans would release the weapons in time for the V-bombers to get airborne; moreover, British nuclear weapons could not be stored in secure storage areas occupied by their American counterparts. There was little alternative, however, but to continue with Project 'E' until such time as British weapons became available in sufficient quantity to allow the phasing out of the 'E' weapons.

In the event, Project 'E' weapons were to remain on the Bomber Command inventory until early 1963, and with the Command's nuclear strike Canberra squadrons in Germany until 1969. The Canberras used the 1,650lb Mk 7. Other American weapons assigned to Bomber Command, for use principally by the Valiant, were the Mk 15/39 multi-megaton bomb (7,500lb), reducing to 6,700lb and 6,600lb in subsequent modifications, the Mk 28 (1,900lb) and the Mk 43 (2,100lb).

The second component of the joint nuclear strike plan was the Thor Intermediate Range Ballistic Missile (IRBM), the possible deployment of which to the UK – together with the provision of US atomic weapons – had been discussed in March 1957, when Prime Minister Harold Macmillan met President Eisenhower for talks in Bermuda and in June 1958 the AOC-in-C Bomber Command, Air Chief Marshal Sir Harry Broadhurst, went to SAC HQ at Omaha to confer with the Commanding General, Thomas S. Power. As a result

Douglas C-124C Globemaster II 52–950 of the 63rd Troop Carrier Wing at Lakenheath in May 1965. The massive Globemaster was a vital component of the Third Air Force's support assets. (Harry Holmes)

Lockheed C-130E Hercules 62–7889 of the 1611th Air Transport Wing at Prestwick, June 1965. (Harry Holmes)

of this meeting, Broadhurst was able to report to the Vice Chief of Air Staff on 25 June 1958 that the purpose of his meeting with Power had been:

> to prepare a co-ordinated nuclear strike plan, based on the target directive contained in COS(57)244 dated 16 October 1957, which could be put into effect should combined nuclear retaliation by Bomber Command and Strategic Air Command ever be required. The plan, approved by C-in-C SAC and myself, is applicable to the period 1 July 1958 to 30 June 1959, is targeted to utilise stocks of British, and after October 1958 USAF, nuclear weapons for the Medium Bomber Force, and includes targets for the first Thor squadron expected to be operational in January 1959 . . .

Throughout the early 1950s, Strategic Air Command had become increasingly involved in the development of missiles as a means of increasing its long-range striking power. The actual development and testing of missiles remained in the hands of the various contractors and the Air Research and Development Command (ARDC), but SAC maintained close liaison with the missile development programmes. In 1955, after President Eisenhower had placed the highest national priority on the development of ballistic missiles, Headquarters USAF accelerated the development of several promising missile types, and on 18 November that year HQ USAF instructed SAC to work closely with the ARDC in establishing an initial operational capability (IOC) for ICBMs, after which they would be turned over to SAC for operational use.

On 18 March 1956, HQ USAF gave SAC and the

ARDC the responsibility for developing an initial operational capability (IOC) with the Thor intermediate-range ballistic missile, and assigned SAC the responsibility of deploying this missile to the United Kingdom and bringing it to a combat-ready status, after which it would be turned over to the Royal Air Force. In July, HQ SAC announced that the missile programme was entering the planning phase, with interest centred primarily on the Thor IRBM, the Navaho and Snark subsonic intercontinental cruise missiles, and the Atlas and Titan ICBMs.

On 26 November 1956, US Secretary of Defense Charles E. Wilson gave the USAF the sole responsibility for the operational deployment and control of all land-based IRBMs and ICBMs. At the same time, the US Army was made responsible for land-based surface-to-air defensive missiles and surface-to-surface tactical missiles with a range of less than 200 miles. In simple terms, this meant that the US Army was debarred from operating missiles with a range greater than 200 miles.

The USAF's IRBM contract went to the Douglas Aircraft Corporation, which by prodigious feats of design and engineering delivered the first SM-75 Thor in October 1956, and despite an inauspicious start to the flight test programme – the first four launches ended in failure – the system was declared operational in 1959. The missile itself carried the same 1.1 megaton warhead over the same 1,900–mile range as the US Army's Jupiter, but unlike the latter missile it was designed for fixed-base deployment. Both Thor and Jupiter were liquid-fuelled, but because it was not mobile Thor was far more vulnerable to surprise attack.

73

Boeing WC-135B 61–2667 of the 55th Weather Reconnaissance Squadron on the approach to Mildenhall, May 1966. A regular visitor to Britain, this aircraft was assigned to the 10th Airborne Command and Control Squadron as a crew trainer in the late 1980s. (Harry Holmes)

From the beginning, it had been the intention of the United States Government to deploy Thor missiles to Britain. The proposal had first been put forward in January 1957 to the British Defence Minister, Duncan Sandys, who was a firm advocate of ballistic missiles and who was deeply involved in the development of Britain's own IRBM, Blue Streak. The latter weapon, however, was not expected to be ready for deployment for some years (in fact it was never to be deployed at all) and the prospect of an interim deterrent in the form of Thor seemed attractive. Thor, the Americans emphasised, would cost Britain nothing except the outlay of funds necessary for site preparation, and to avoid political complications the missiles would be manned by the Royal Air Force, though the warheads would remain under American control.

Despite considerable opposition from various quarters in Britain, plans for the deployment of Thor went ahead, and in February 1958 a joint government agreement was signed. It provided for the US Third Air Force to assist in the construction of the Thor sites and deliver the missiles to the RAF, which would maintain and control them, while targeting was to be a matter of joint operational policy, relying on the close liaison already established between SAC and RAF Bomber Command. On 20 February, the 705th Strategic Missile Wing was activated at RAF Lakenheath and assigned to the 7th Air Division, moving to South Ruislip shortly afterwards to merge with the Divisional HQ. Prior to

this, the 392nd Missile Training Squadron had been activated at Vandenberg AFB on 15 September 1957 for the training of RAF Thor crews.

The original plan was for four RAF Bomber Command squadrons to operate a total of 60 Thors at four specially constructed sites, but because of the system's vulnerability and the consequent need for dispersal this was quickly revised. The Thors would now be operated by 20 squadrons, each with its own site and three missiles. After its number, each squadron would carry the initials SM (Strategic Missile) – the only RAF squadrons ever to bear this designation.

The first of the designated squadrons, No. 77(SM), was re-formed at RAF Feltwell in Norfolk on 1 September 1958. As yet without missiles, its task was to establish training techniques and procedures with SAC. Prior to April 1959 the US research and production facilities had been directed mainly towards proving the Thor weapon system at White Sands, New Mexico and Cape Canaveral, Florida, and to setting up the first two missile sites in the United Kingdom. Very little equipment was dedicated to training, and it was not until 16 April 1959 that an RAF crew of No. 98(SM) Squadron, having received formal Integrated Weapon System training, became the first to launch a Thor.

Royal Air Force launch crews, consisting of a General Duties officer (usually a squadron leader) as Launch Control Officer, three aircrew NCOs as Launch Control Console Operators, and three technicians as Missile Maintenance Technicians, were initially trained at the Douglas Aircraft Company school at Tucson, Arizona. Training comprised missile theory, construction and operation, and an introduction to the necessary ground support equipment. A realistic simulator was used for instruction in countdown sequences, and malfunctions could also be incorporated for emergency training. On graduating from Tucson, the crews went to the 392nd MTS at Vandenberg AFB, where they received more detailed training using operational equipment.

On 19 September 1958 No. 77(SM) Squadron received its first Thor, which was flown to RAF Feltwell aboard a C-124 Globemaster, and all subsequent missiles were delivered by this means, along with their ancillary equipment. The missile was still being operationally proved as a weapon system, however, and nearly a year was to elapse before the next batch of RAF squadrons was declared operational with the Thor in July 1959. All 20 squadrons were operational by the end of the year.

The three missiles at each site were not readily visible to the casual onlooker. For much of the time they lay prone and invisible in their shelters, behind heavily guarded perimeters, erected only for practice countdowns. Any launch order, simulated or otherwise, had to be authenticated by RAF and USAF officers at HQ Bomber Command and HQ 7th Air Division using a special and highly secret code. Operation of the Thor required a lengthy countdown procedure, so in time of crisis the system required plenty of warning of impending hostile activity; on average, the sequence required something like 105 minutes from receipt of the positive launch order. At that point the RAF

Launch Control Officer turned a phase sequence key to initiate a fully automatic sequence of events: the guidance system was aligned and checked, the shelter moved back and the missile raised slowly to the upright position, while the liquid propellants were pumped into the missile at a high rate. They had to be pumped out again after a simulated launch, because the Thor could only remain fuelled for a limited period before it had to be stood down.

The liquid-fuel rocket motor was the Thor's principal disadvantage, but there were others. Further time would have been needed to fit the nuclear warheads, which were not kept on site but stored with other nuclear weaponry under extreme security at Faldingworth, an old wartime airfield near Scampton, Lincolnshire. Such was the secrecy surrounding Faldingworth that, from 1957 to 1980, the airfield was not shown on Ordnance Survey maps. Spare parts for the Thors in the UK were held in the United States; RAF squadron supply officers could indent directly for spares by radio link and receive them immediately by air, as all equipment could be carried in the C-124 Globemaster.

The Thor deployment to the United Kingdom was designed to be nothing more than an interim measure, aimed at closing what was then believed to be a dangerous and expanding missile gap until SAC's ICBM force became fully operational. Few could have foreseen that it was to have a valuable and real deterrent effect during the dangerous crisis that developed in October 1962, when the Americans discovered that Soviet missiles and jet bombers were clandestinely being supplied to Cuba.

Douglas HC-54D 42–72456 of the 67th Air Rescue Squadron, Prestwick, March 1966. (Harry Holmes)

TOP: *Douglas HC-54D 42–72696, 67th ARS, at Prestwick in March 1966. (Harry Holmes)*
ABOVE: *Douglas C-118A 53–3266, 1611th Air Transport Wing, at Prestwick in March 1966. (Harry Holmes)*
BELOW: *Boeing EC-135H 61–293 of the 55th SRW on the Mildenhall approach, July 1966. (Harry Holmes)*

CHAPTER ELEVEN

Crisis Response: Cuba

During 1958, with the process of building up SAC's ground alert force to the one-third level well under way, the Command was taking other action to ensure that a high proportion of its bomber force would survive a surprise attack and be in a position to launch a massive retaliatory strike. The main problem that had to be overcome was one of overcrowding; because of the tremendous expansion that had taken place during the 1950s some bases were supporting as many as 90 B-47 bombers and 40 KC-97 tankers. The first B-52 wings were also very large, consisting of 45 bombers and 15 or 20 KC-135 tankers, all located on one base.

As the Soviet missile threat became more pronounced and warning time less, the SAC bases, with their massive concentrations of aircraft, became increasingly attractive targets. The obvious answer was dispersal, and as a first step several KC-97 squadrons were separated from their parent B-47 Wings and relocated on northern bases, which in fact were strategically better placed to support the B-47s' Arctic operations. The B-47 dispersal programme itself was a long-term one, and was to be achieved mainly through the phasing out of B-47 Wings in the late 1950s and early 1960s.

The B-52 force, on the other hand, was still growing, and in this case the dispersal programme called for the larger B-52 Wings to be broken up into three equally sized units of 15 aircraft each. Two of these units, which were re-designated Strategic Wings and given full supporting services, including an attached KC-135 squadron of 10 or 15 aircraft, were relocated, normally to bases of other commands. The remainder of the B-52 force was also to be organised on these lines.

SAC was subjected to two major alerts during 1958, both affecting the alert states of Reflex B-47s in the United Kingdom. The first occurred in August and September, when President Eisenhower sent US naval, air and ground forces to the Middle East in response to a plea from the President of the Lebanon, who feared that a Russian invasion was imminent. SAC was also ordered to place its bomber force on alert, and within a few hours over 1,100 aircraft were armed and ready for take-off, additional ground alert forces having been generated. SAC maintained this alert posture for several days, the units involved stood down only when it became clear that the Russians did not intend to invade the Lebanon. This crisis was followed almost immediately by another, when Chinese communist artillery began a heavy bombardment of the nationalist-held islands of Quemoy and Matsu, off the mainland. Fearing that this was part of preparations for a full-scale invasion of Taiwan, the US Seventh Fleet was despatched to the Formosa Strait and the B-47 ground alert force at Andersen AFB on Guam was

Boeing EC-135H 61–285 of the 55th SRW at Mildenhall, May 1967. (Harry Holmes)

TOP: *The Convair T-29A, seen here approaching to land at Mildenhall in June 1967, was used as a navigational trainer by the 47th Bomb Wing. (Harry Holmes)*

ABOVE: *The large red cross on the fin of this Convair MC-131A Samaritan (52–5787), seen taxying at Ringway, Manchester, in October 1967, clearly identifies it as an Airevac aircraft. (Harry Holmes)*

Boeing B-52G 59–2583 of the 2nd Bomb Wing at RAF Marham in April 1971. The aircraft was taking part in the annual RAF Strike Command Bombing Competition. (Harry Holmes)

increased in strength. Several CONUS Bomb Wings were also alerted for possible contingency duty in the Far East, but these were soon stood down when the Commander-in-Chief, Pacific Command indicated that he did not think the use of SAC forces would be necessary.

In addition to dispersal, and maintaining a one-third ground alert force, SAC was now seeking to enhance the survival of the US deterrent by exploring the possibility of maintaining a continuous airborne alert force. A successful airborne alert test code-named 'Head Start I' was carried out from 15 September to 15 December 1958 by B-52s of the 42nd Bomb Wing operating out of Loring AFB, Maine. Airborne alert trials continued throughout 1959, and in November that year SAC and the Federal Aviation Agency (FAA) jointly announced that seven special air routes were to be established within the continental United States, so that the SAC bomber fleet could begin low-level training. Each corridor was to be about 500 miles long and 20 miles wide.

The emphasis on low-level training, brought about by the knowledge that Soviet surface-to-air missile technology and the growing sophistication of the USSR's air defences in general would soon make the high-level bomber extremely vulnerable, caused a whole series of problems and dilemmas. At the root of it all was a range of faulty strategic concepts which, formulated in the late 1940s, had failed to envisage the surface-to-air missile as a serious threat; the result was that bomber designs stemming from that period were not adapted to the stresses of prolonged low-level

flight. Some, like the B-52, could be adapted to it with the necessary modifications to strengthen the airframe; others, like the B-47, could not.

SAC had continued to test the airborne alert concept during 1959, and in connection with this, in March 1960, a new single sideband HF radio communications system was put into operation. Called 'Short Order', this consisted of four stations, one at HQ SAC and the others at three numbered air force headquarters in the CONUS. Its primary function was to provide a means of exercising positive control over SAC bombers which had been launched and which were *en route* to their targets. Under positive control procedures, bombers flew to a designated point outside hostile territory and then automatically returned to their bases unless they received authorisation – the 'Go Code' – to proceed to their targets.

On 1 July 1960, SAC began testing an airborne command post at Offutt AFB. During the remainder of the year, one of five specially modified KC-135s (EC-135As) of the 34th Air Division was placed on ground alert and periodically tested to ensure its ability to take off within 15 minutes. Once airborne, the EC-135A's primary role was to serve as an alternate command post, which would assume control over the SAC combat force should the underground facility at Offutt AFB and other command posts co-located with the numbered air force headquarters be destroyed by enemy attack. On each flight, the EC-135A carried a SAC general officer in addition to a team of controllers and communications experts. The airborne command

TOP & ABOVE: *Lockheed C-130E Hercules 63–7799 of the 313th Tactical Airlift Wing pictured at Lakenheath, September 1970.*
(Harry Holmes)

Lockheed C-130E 63–790 of the 47th Tactical Airlift Squadron, 313th Tactical Airlift Wing at Lakenheath, May 1971. (Harry Holmes)

post, or 'Looking Glass' as it was later called, became operational on 3 February 1961, beginning continuous operations that involved one EC-135A being airborne at all times, the aircraft working in eight-hour shifts. By this time, all combat-ready B-52 crews were participating in airborne alert training; more than 6,000 sorties flown during the trials period over the past two years had proved the feasibility of keeping a segment of the SAC bomber fleet constantly in the air.

Another important milestone in the US deterrent capability came on 1 February 1961, when the Ballistic Missile Early Warning (BMEWS) site at Thule in Greenland became operational. Other BMEWS sites subsequently became operational at Clear, Alaska, and Fylingdales in the UK. Operated by the North American Air Defense Command (NORAD), BMEWS was capable of detecting enemy ICBMs as they came up over the horizon, giving SAC valuable extra warning time in which to launch its retaliatory forces. The massive BMEWS radar scanners had a planned range of 5,000 miles, but under certain conditions it was much greater than that. On one occasion in the early days, BMEWS passed NORAD information that suggested a massive Soviet ICBM attack was coming in, except that the time lapse between the radar transmissions and the return echoes was far too great for this to be

possible. It turned out that the radars were bouncing echoes off the moon, a quarter of a million miles away. Equipment was later installed to filter out errors of this kind.

Following the shooting down of Gary Powers' U-2 on 1 May 1960, tension between East and West approached breaking strain. Only two months after the Powers incident there was another, this time involving an RB-47H Stratojet of the 55th SRW.

Long after the retirement of the RB-47E, the 55th SRW continued to use its mixture of RB-47H/Ks in the ELINT role, its operations conducted in strict secrecy on a global basis. Unlike the earlier RB-47Es, which had on occasions penetrated Soviet air space, the RB-47H/Ks confined themselves to operations around the periphery of the USSR and its allied countries, for which purpose it maintained permanent detachments in Alaska, the United Kingdom and Japan. The RB-47s were intercepted on numerous occasions by Russian, Chinese and North Korean fighters, and sometimes warning shots were fired, but the RB-47's ability to monitor radio and radar transmissions while standing off in international air space prevented any serious incidents resulting in the loss of an aircraft.

This record ended abruptly on 1 July 1960, when an RB-47H of the 38th SRS belonging to the 55th SRW's

Boeing KC-135A 61–274 making a slow flypast at Mildenhall in May 1971, boom fully extended. (Harry Holmes)

UK-based Detachment One took off from RAF Brize Norton to carry out an ELINT mission over the Barents Sea, with specific reference to Soviet naval facilities on the Kola Peninsula and the nuclear test facility on Novaya Zemlya. The aircraft carried a crew of six. High over the Barents Sea, north of Kola, the RB-47H was intercepted by a MiG-19 fighter of the Soviet 206th Air Division and, according to Russian sources, signalled to land in Soviet territory. The crew ignored the signals and the Stratojet was shot down. After ten days the Russians announced that they had picked up two survivors; a third crew member, the pilot, was found dead in his liferaft. The survivors were prosecuted by the Russians, imprisoned and later repatriated.

In March 1961, as part of his budget speech, President Kennedy called for half of SAC's fleet of B-52s and B-47s to be placed on 15-minute alert, and also directed the B-47 phase-out programme to be accelerated in order to provide, quickly, the trained crews that would be necessary to implement the new alert posture. The 50 per cent ground alert by the bombers and their associated tankers was attained in July 1961.

By now, America's nuclear deterrent was no longer the sole monopoly of Strategic Air Command. While SAC still controlled most of the USA's nuclear strength in 1960, substantial additional striking power was being provided by ballistic missile submarines and nuclear-armed missile and air units of the tactical forces deployed in forward areas overseas. This proliferation of nuclear strength brought with it the need for closer coordination of target planning within the US armed forces, and in August 1960 a Joint Strategic Target Planning Staff (JSTPS) was formed, with the C-in-C SAC as its director and its headquarters at Offutt AFB. Composed of representatives from all branches of the US Services, the JSTPS was charged with the task of preparing and maintaining a National Strategic Target List and a Single Integrated Operational Plan (SIOP) which would commit specific weapon systems to the various targets to be attacked in the event of war. The operational procedures of the United Kingdom Deterrent were also integrated into this new scheme, partly to avoid duplication of targets in the event of a global war and partly because the RAF's Medium Bomber Force would probably have formed part of the first retaliatory wave.

Crisis followed crisis. In April 1961 some 1,200 Cuban exiles, backed by the US Central Intelligence Agency, made an ill-conceived landing in Cuba; within days, most had been killed or captured. Then, in August, the building of the Berlin Wall brought renewed tension over that divided city and resulted in the B-47 phase-out programme being delayed in order to improve SAC's deterrent posture. Six Bomb Wings and their associated air refuelling squadrons were affected.

The most serious crisis, however, erupted in the

autumn of 1962. At 19.00 hours eastern standard time on 22 October, President Kennedy, in a televised speech lasting 17 minutes, announced to an unsuspecting American public the discovery of Russian missiles in Cuba and the immediate imposition of a naval blockade around the island. As the President began to speak, American forces worldwide were placed on a higher state of alert, with SAC moving to Defense Condition (DEFCON) Three. Battle staffs were placed on 24-hour alert duty, leaves cancelled and personnel recalled. B-47s were dispersed to several widely separated and pre-selected civilian and military airfields, additional bombers and tankers were placed on ground alert, and the B-52 airborne alert

TOP & ABOVE: *Lockheed T-33As 57–561 and 57–749 at Upper Heyford, June 1971. The T-33A was used by various Base Flights as a fast liaison aircraft until late in 1971. (Harry Holmes)*

indoctrination programme was immediately expanded into an actual airborne alert involving 24–hour sorties by armed aircraft and the immediate replacement in the air of each aircraft that landed. SAC's ICBM force, at that time numbering about 200 operational missiles, was brought into alert configuration.

As the crisis developed, the US intelligence agencies believed they had identified 24 SS-4 launchers, of which 20 were fully operational; the remaining four were expected to be operational early in November. The photographic interpreters had positively identified 33 SS-4 missiles at San Cristobal and Sagua la Grande, but were of the opinion that there were probably more, while a third site at Guanajay, north of San Cristobal, was apparently being readied to receive SS-5s. The first four SS-5 launchers were expected to be operational by 1 December, and the second and third SS-5 groups by the 15th. A fourth SS-5 group was clearly planned and construction of the site had begun. In fact, delivery of the last six SS-4s (of which there were actually 42 planned for deployment) and all 32 SS-5s was blocked by the naval quarantine. No MRBM or IRBM nuclear warheads were ever identified in Cuba, but a Soviet artillery battalion equipped with 'Frog' tactical rockets was present on the island, and it was revealed many years later that the missiles were nuclear-tipped and that its commander had the discretion to use them in the event of an American invasion.

Had war come, the spearhead of an attack on the Soviet facilities in Cuba would have been the Republic F-105 Thunderchiefs of Tactical Air Command's 4th Tactical Fighter Wing, which deployed to McCoy AFB on 21 October. The 4th TFW began a one-hour alert status at 04.00 the next day, and this was reduced to 15 minutes in the afternoon. But the F-105s were held back while international negotiations proceeded, and when they flew it was in the air defence role, patrolling the southern Florida peninsula on the lookout for Il-28 jet bombers. Nevertheless, TAC's RF-101 sorties made certain that the fighter-bombers' target folders were kept updated on a regular basis. In Europe, which would certainly have been the first to feel an armed Soviet backlash against any armed American action in Cuba, the nuclear alert force comprised USAF F-100 Super Sabre tactical fighter-bombers deployed on British bases, backed up by Thor IRBMs deployed with the RAF in the United Kingdom, and RAF Valiant bombers armed with Mk 28 nuclear weapons of American origin.

The commanding general of the United States Air Forces Europe, General Truman H. Landon, and his subordinate air force commanders (including Major-General R. W. Puryear, the Third Air Force's commander) were briefed on the Cuban situation by General Lauris Norstad, the Supreme Commander, Allied Powers Europe, at a hastily convened conference called at Orly Airfield, Paris, at 15.00 GMT on 22 October. Immediately afterwards, 'Covert Alert' was initiated at RAF Wethersfield and RAF Lakenheath, where the nuclear-capable F-100s of the 20th and 48th TFWs were based. This involved key personnel being contacted by radio telephone and ordered to report to their duty stations; it also involved the arming of some,

TOP: *Boeing B-52G 57–6505 of the 2nd Bomb Wing at RAF Marham, March 1976. (Harry Holmes)*
ABOVE: *Boeing KC-135A 59–1445 of the 55th ARS landing at Mildenhall, September 1975. (Harry Holmes)*

but not all, aircraft in the Theatre Tactical Nuclear Force.

A proportion of the TNF F-100s were coordinated with the RAF-manned Thor missiles, the idea being that an F-100 would attack first, the pilot aiming to deliver his bomb as accurately as possible. This attack would be followed almost immediately by a Thor strike, which would cause massive area damage. The purpose of the cross-targeting policy was to assure complete destruction of the target, and the overall strategy was to neutralise the Warsaw Pact's command and control structure. East Berlin, regarded as one of the Warsaw Pact's main command and control centres, was to be hit by two Thors, with a strike by a solitary F-100 in between.

As the crisis deepened, the tactical squadrons stepped up their state of alert. At the more critical points of the crisis, pilots adopted a cockpit alert posture, ground power units were engaged, all covers were removed from weapons and engines readied for an immediate start.

On 25 October 1962, RAF Bomber Command was

Lockheed C-130E 63–7820 of the 1611th ATW seen at RAF Leuchars, April 1976. (Harry Holmes)

informed that SAC had raised its alert status to DEFCON 2 in connection with the Cuban crisis. At this time the Command was carrying out a routine manoeuvre called Exercise 'Mick', which involved practising alert and arming procedures without dispersing the aircraft; a no-notice exercise, it required all bomber airfields to generate – in other words, prepare for war operations – all available aircraft, bringing together the three elements of each weapons system: aircraft, weapons and aircrew. ('Kinsman' was a squadron dispersal exercise and 'Mayflight' an exercise in which all aspects of the Bomber Command dispersal and readiness plan were practised; and 'Micky Finn' was a no-notice dispersal exercise that could happen at any time of the day or night.)

Generating and mobilising all available aircraft and crews of a V-Force Wing was a complex business, relying on up-to-date information on the movements and whereabouts of all personnel so that they could be called in, and the close control of all engineering activities so that aircraft and weapons could be quickly recovered and brought into the line. Some aircraft would inevitably be involved in major servicing or overseas deployment; nevertheless, most of the Wing's aircraft establishment – say, 16 or 18 aircraft – could be generated in 10 or 12 hours.

The fact that the Command was conducting such an exercise at that particular time may have been a coincidence, but it is far more likely that HQ Bomber Command had been advised by HQ SAC that something was about to happen. In any event, on 26 October the exercise was extended and the readiness state of the V-Force increased to Alert Condition 3 of the Bomber Command Alert and Readiness Procedures (Aircraft); all civilians employed on the bomber airfields were sent home, and armed patrols doubled on the airfield perimeters. Instead of generating all available aircraft, however, HQ Bomber Command ordered stations to double the number of aircraft on QRA (Quick Reaction Alert) so that most stations had six fully armed bombers at 15 minutes' readiness. The exception was RAF Waddington, where nine fully armed Vulcans were brought to 15 minutes' readiness. The decision to generate only part of the Medium Bomber Force was almost certainly political; generating the whole of the force might have persuaded the Russians that a pre-emptive nuclear strike was in the offing, with potentially disastrous consequences.

The Thor missile force, meanwhile – with 59 of its 60 IRBMs serviceable and generated – had been brought to Phase Two Alert, which meant that the missile shelters had been retracted, the missiles erected to their launch positions, and target data entered into the guidance system. This was the normal procedure adopted by the Thor missile squadrons in alert and readiness exercises; the Phase Two 'planned hold' alert state was followed by a simulated countdown to lift-off. According to some sources, however, the Thors of No. 97(SM) Squadron at RAF Hemswell were fully fuelled and brought up to Phase Four Alert, a technical hold of four minutes' readiness. This was achieved by increasing the length of the crews' shift periods from eight to 12 hours and constantly topping up the liquid oxygen fuel, which 'gassed off' freely.

The other UK-based component to be brought to a high-alert state during the Cuban crisis was the RAF Tactical Bomber Force, comprising three squadrons (Nos. 49, 148 and 207) armed with the Vickers Valiant, based on RAF Marham and assigned to SACEUR. The Valiants – 24 aircraft in all – could each carry two lightweight (1,900lb) Mk 28 bombs, weapons with a warhead variable in destructive power from 60 to 100 kilotons. Two aircraft of the Marham Wing were always kept in an armed condition inside a heavily guarded QRA compound, their crews on a 48-hour standby duty. The loading of the bombs was always supervised by American officers, and US Air Police also shared general guard duty at Marham with their RAF counterparts. By joint agreement, since the weapons were American-owned, release of an armed Valiant to the RAF could occur only after the American custodians had received an authenticated release message on dedicated US channels.

At some point during the crisis, RAF Marham received instructions via both American and British channels to arm all available Valiants at Marham. During this process, it became apparent that the American custodial officers were physically unable to maintain control of all the weapons, as they were only established with sufficient manpower to monitor the QRA compound and the nuclear weapons storage area. It was clearly an unacceptable situation, so at the discretion of the commanding general, USAFE, control of the weapons was handed over to the station commander at Marham – yet another example of the trust, born of the knowledge of each other's capability, that characterised the relationship between USAF and RAF.

The first major break in the crisis came on 28 October, when Russia agreed to move its IRBMs from Cuba, subject to verification by the United Nations. During the next few days, SAC aircraft maintained close aerial surveillance while the missiles were dismantled, loaded on to ships, and sent back through the quarantine. The quarantine was maintained until 20 November, when the Russians also agreed to remove their Il-28 light bombers from the island. SAC then began running down its high-alert state: the B-47s returned to their home bases, the ground alert force dropped back to its normal 50 per cent standard, and the B-52 Wings resumed their routine airborne alert training. In the United Kingdom, weapons were offloaded from all aircraft except those on QRA.

One crisis had been defused, but there was another in the offing. It would seriously affect the Third Air Force's posture in the UK, and it had nothing to do with any renewal of East–West tension.

Lockheed C-141A 65–217 of the 437th Military Airlift Wing at Greenham Common, August 1976. (Harry Holmes)

CHAPTER TWELVE

Withdrawal from France

For a time, in the latter part of the 1950s, the United States Government had considered the possibility of deploying IRBMs to France, but by 1959 this was no longer even a vague policy. The redoubtable General Charles de Gaulle, newly elected President of the Fifth Republic, showed every sign of embarking on a defensive policy that was separate from that of NATO. He had already withdrawn the French fleet from NATO command and had crossed swords with SACEUR, General Lauris Norstad, over control of the tactical nuclear weapons deployed on USAF bases in France. In the summer of 1959, de Gaulle broke the stalemate by the simple expedient of ordering all US nuclear weapons out of the country.

An immediate consequence of President de Gaulle's veto on American nuclear weapons in France was the removal to England in August 1959 of the 10th Tactical Reconnaissance Wing from Spangdahlem in Germany, to make room for the French-based nuclear-capable fighter-bomber units that would have to be redeployed there. Two RB-66 tactical reconnaissance squadrons, the 1st and 30th, were relocated at Alconbury, while the 19th and 42nd went to Bruntingthorpe and Chelveston respectively. The reshuffle also involved the redeployment of three Tactical Fighter Wings, all armed with F-100 Super Sabres: the 49th TFW from Etain to Spangdahlem, the 50th from Toul-Rosières to Hahn and Ramstein, and the 48th to Lakenheath. The impending moves were announced by HQ USAFE at Wiesbaden on 29 December 1959, and the transfer of the flying units began during the first week of the new year.

The Super Sabres of the 48th TFW, which had been based at Chaumont, began arriving at Lakenheath on 5 January 1960. It was not a new association with England, for the unit had flown P-47 Thunderbolts from English airfields during the Second World War as the 48th Fighter-Bomber Group before being deactivated in November 1945; reactivated at Cahaumont in November 1952, it had graduated from the F-84G Thunderjet to the F-86F Sabre before rearming with the F-100.

While the 48th TFW was located in France, the people of Chaumont had petitioned to have the unit named the Statue of Liberty Wing in honour of all the Americans who had lost their lives in France during two world wars. The name became official in July 1954, making the 48th the only USAF unit with both a numerical and a descriptive designation. During this period the 48th Fighter-Bomber Group operated as an integral part of the 48th FBW, and when the Group was deactivated for a second time in 1957, with the streamlining of the USAF, its honours and lineage passed to the Wing. In July 1958 the latter was redesignated the 48th Tactical Fighter Wing, and has carried the title ever since.

The summer of 1962 saw the cessation of operational flying at three USAF bases following another change in operational requirements. At Sculthorpe, the 47th Bomb Wing deactivated on 22 June 1962 and the airfield became a standby base. Chelveston also became a reserve airfield in August with the departure of the RB-66s of the 42nd TRS, while Bruntingthorpe was abandoned in September. Another change involved the move late in 1962 of Third Air Force HQ from Ruislip to Mildenhall.

In the early weeks of 1963, following the news that the ageing B-47 Stratojet was to be phased out of the bomber role, there were rumours that the 7th Air Division's bomber bases in the UK were soon to close. This was denied by a 7th AD spokesman at High Wycombe in February, but the denial was quickly followed by a rumour that the B-47s were to be replaced by a radical new bomber, the Convair B-58 Hustler, the first supersonic bomber to enter service with the USAF. It had, in fact, been anticipated that the Hustler would replace the B-47 in SAC's medium bomber force, but in the event only enough aircraft were built to equip six squadrons in two wings, the 43rd and 305th.

Individual B-58s did visit Brize Norton and Greenham Common from October 1963; before that, B-58s had visited Britain briefly in the course of record-breaking flights. On 16 October 1962, for example, one aircraft flew non-stop across the North Pole from Tokyo in eight hours and thirty-five minutes at an average speed of 938 mph, being refuelled in flight five times. But the Hustler's operational career was relatively short-lived, and the type was withdrawn from service in 1968.

Despite conflicting rumours, it was becoming increasingly clear that Strategic Air Command's mission in the United Kingdom was coming to an end. This was confirmed by 7th Air Division in April, although it was emphasised that there would be no closure of the SAC bases at Greenham Common, Fairford, Upper Heyford and Brize Norton until 1964.

On 17 April 1963 General Truman H. Landon, Commanding General of USAFE, announced that the command structure of USAFE was being realigned to reduce manpower. The Tactical Fighter Wings that had been withdrawn from France in 1960, and which had remained under the operational control of the Seventeenth Air Force in Germany, would now come under the command of the Third Air Force, though the change, which was to be completed by October 1963, was purely administrative and would not involve the movement of aircraft or personnel. Third Air Force was also to assume operational control of the tactical and reconnaissance units still in France, leaving Seventeenth Air Force responsible for Germany.

In October 1963 the USAF and US Army participated jointly in a massive exercise called 'Big Lift', which involved airlifting the entire Second Armored Division from Fort Hood, Texas, to Germany in 60 hours. Troops began to board C-124s and C-135s in Texas on 22 October, while other Military Air Transport Service aircraft began collecting their support equipment and

The Convair B-58 Hustler, the world's first operational supersonic jet bomber. (Phil Jarrett)

that of four USAF fighter squadrons involved in the exercise. The long-range transports flew directly to Germany, while smaller aircraft staged via Bermuda, Greenland and the Azores, and all 15,000 men and 450 tons of equipment were delivered to Rhein-Main AFB, Sembach AFB and Ramstein AFB and were in action within the planned 60 hours.

This exercise preceded an announcement later that month that substantial cuts were to be made in the USAF establishment in Britain over the following two years. The Tactical Air Division's bases were to be handed back to the Ministry of Defence in the summer of 1964, and the reductions would involve about 10 per cent of the USAF personnel then stationed in Britain, or about 2,500 men. On 8 November it was confirmed that the SAC bases to be affected would be Fairford and Greenham Common. Their closure would involve the withdrawal of 19 B-47s and 22 supporting tanker aircraft, most of them based at Sculthorpe with the 420th ARS. Fairford was returned to MoD control

in June 1964 and subsequently became the home of C Flight of the RAF Central Flying School until September 1966, when it was taken over by Transport Command. Greenham Common reverted to MoD control on 1 July 1964.

The remaining Reflex Action B-47 detachments, with their supporting tankers, were now concentrated on Brize Norton and Upper Heyford, but in the spring of 1965 Strategic Air Command terminated all its bomber operations in Britain and Brize Norton was taken over by the MoD on 1 April. The last Stratojet to leave Britain was a B-47E of the 380th BW, which took off from Brize Norton on 3 April. Upper Heyford, however, remained under American control as a Dispersed Operating Base under the care of the 7514th Combat Support Group.

Not long afterwards, American defence policy within the framework of European NATO was turned upside-down by a sudden, but hardly unexpected, move by the French Government. Ever since 1958

TOP: *Convair B-58 Hustler of the 305th BW touching down at London Airport after its record-breaking flight from Tokyo on 16 October 1962.*
(Phil Jarrett)
ABOVE: *B-58 59–2440 on a visit to Mildenhall, May 1969. (Phil Jarrett)*

Boeing RC-135V 64–14844 of the 55th SRW at Mildenhall in November 1976. (Harry Holmes)

President de Gaulle had been steadily reducing France's commitment to NATO, and by early 1966 the US Ambassador in Paris was aware that the French Government was preparing a request for changes in the various Franco-American agreements on US bases and troops in France. De Gaulle took a deliberately misleading line, telling the US Ambassador that there would be no precipitate action on France's part, but on 22 February he warned that he would like all NATO headquarters and foreign troops out of France by the end of the twenty-first period of the NATO treaty, in other words by April 1969.

A fortnight later, on 7 March, de Gaulle delivered his bombshell in a letter to President Lyndon Johnson and the heads of government of Britain, Canada, Federal Germany and Italy. Its text was as follows:

> In three years the Atlantic Alliance will complete its first term. I am anxious to tell you that France appreciates the extent to which the solidarity of defence thus established between fifteen free peoples of the West contributes to assuring their security, and especially what essential role the United States plays in this respect. Accordingly France intends from now on to remain party to the treaty signed at Washington on 4 April 1949. This means that, except in the event of developments which might occur in the course of the next three years to change the fundamental factors of East–West relations, she will be, in 1969 and thereafter, determined, even as today, to fight at the side of her allies in case one of them will be the object of unprovoked aggression.
>
> However, France considers the changes which have taken place or are in the process of occurring since 1949 in Europe, Asia and elsewhere, as well as the evolution of her own situation and her own forces, no longer justify insofar as that concerns her the arrangements of a military nature adopted after the conclusion of the alliance, whether in common under the form of multilateral conventions or whether by special agreement between the French Government and the American Government.
>
> It is for this reason that France proposes to recover the entire exercise of her sovereignty over her territory, presently impaired by the permanent presence of allied military elements or by constant utilization which is made of her air space, to terminate her participation in the 'integrated' commands and no longer places her forces at the disposal of NATO ...

De Gaulle's message was quite clear. Athough France was to remain a member of the Atlantic Alliance, and would adhere to the original articles of the North Atlantic Treaty of 1949, her forces would no longer be a part of the integrated NATO command structure. It was a situation that had been building ever since France, having made astonishing technological advances in the years after the Second World War, exploded her first crude nuclear device in the Sahara in 1960. The test was by way of an exclamation mark, informing the superpowers that a new France under the leadership of President Charles de Gaulle no longer adhered to the static, defensive 'Maginot Line' philosophy that had contributed to her collapse in 1940; from now on, French strategy would be mobile and offensive, aimed at keeping a hostile power clear of her frontiers.

91

De Gaulle's intention was to arm France with a triad of nuclear weapons delivery systems – bombers, land-based missiles and submarine-launched missiles – similar to the structure employed by the superpowers, although on a much smaller scale. In fact, de Gaulle inherited the basis for this plan, for a requirement for a long-range strategic bomber capable of delivering a nuclear weapon had already been issued by the French Chiefs of Staff in 1956. In broad outline, the requirement called for an aircraft with an unrefuelled combat radius of about 1,000 miles, including a high-speed dash into the target area and a minimum escape speed of 1.7M. The aircraft also had to be able to operate from the type of airfield used by the F-84F Thunderstreak fighter-bomber, then in service with the French Air Force.

There were two contenders: Sud Aviation, who offered a design based on their Vautour light bomber, and GAMD Marcel Dassault, who proposed a scaled-up version of their delta-wing Mirage III fighter, then under development. The Dassault proposal, designated Mirage IVA in its definitive form, received final approval in the summer of 1959, a proposal for a still larger version – the Mirage IVB – having meanwhile been rejected.

The prototype Mirage IV-01 made its first flight in June 1959, while the merits of the two rival designs were still being considered, and in September an order was placed for three pre-production aircraft. The first of these flew in October 1961 and was later used for armament trials, dropping replicas of the operational version of the French free-falling atomic bomb. The second pre-production machine was used mainly for flight refuelling trials, first with converted Vautours and later with Boeing KC-135s on loan from the USAF, and the last pre-production aircraft was a fully operational model.

The Mirage IVA entered service with the 91e Escadre de Bombardement in 1964 and ultimately armed three escadres, dispersed on airfields throughout metropolitan France and served by twelve KC-135 tankers. Each escadre was composed of three escadrons, each with four or five aircraft, and a centralised maintenance system ensured that at least 80 per cent of the Mirage IV strike force was operational at all times. One Mirage in each escadron was kept at fifteen-minute readiness, armed with a 70-kiloton atomic bomb (and later more advanced weapons) recessed into the underside of the fuselage.

The Mirage IV, 62 examples of which were delivered to the French Air Force, was powered by two SNECMA Atar 09K turbojets and carried a crew of two. It was extremely fast at high altitude, with a speed of over 1,500 mph at 40,000 feet. Service ceiling was around 65,000 feet and unrefuelled combat radius 800 miles.

The principal French deterrent eventually devolved on land-based and submarine-launched strategic missiles. Eighteen of the land-based version, the SSBS, were deployed in silos on the Plateau d'Albion, Haute Provence, in 1971–3; this was the S-2, with a range of 1,700 miles and armed with a 1.2-megaton warhead. The submarine-launched variant, the MSBS, had a similar range and carried a 500-kiloton warhead. Both types of missile and their warheads were progressively updated, but with the end of the Cold War the decision was taken to scrap the land-based SSBS, leaving the seaborne system as the only strategic component, deployed on six missile submarines.

The French never flinched from stating the action they would take in the event of a Soviet attack on their territory. As the military historian Hugh Faringdon put it, in his book *Confrontation: the Strategic Geography of NATO and the Warsaw Pact* (Routledge & Kegan Paul, London, 1986) at a time when East and West were still in confrontation:

> French Governments have never accepted the official NATO doctrine of Flexible Response. Rather they have made it clear that a threat to French 'vital interests' will be answered very smartly by a warning shot by tactical nuclear weapons, and that if these fail to produce the desired effect the use of strategic weapons will unfailingly follow. The 'vital interest' was once assumed to be the security of the Rhine, but by the 1980s it seemed to have marched a good way further east . . . An all-out nuclear exchange would certainly involve the destruction of France. However, the government hopes that the Soviets are persuaded that France would not go under before it had succeeded in 'tearing a limb off the Soviet Union'. Meanwhile the French independent nuclear deterrent sows a seed of doubt in the minds of Soviet planners. It might not be impossible for the Soviets to form a reasoned judgment about the nuclear responses of the Americans or the British, but it would be a foolhardy Russian who gambled on what the French might do if they were pushed too far.

The possible effect of France's nuclear 'wild card' on Soviet military planning became apparent only with hindsight. In the mid-1960s, the French withdrawal fron NATO's integrated command structure caused great consternation, not to mention a logistical nightmare as redeployments became necessary.

At the end of March 1966 the NATO Allies were informed that all French officers would be withdrawn from Supreme Headquarters Allied Powers Europe (SHAPE) and from other NATO commands too. On 1 April all French forces in Germany and elsewhere would cease to be under NATO command, and the Allies were given one year from that date to remove SHAPE and all other NATO headquarters, bases, troops and storage facilities from French territory.

At this time USAFE still had a considerable concentration of air power in northern France, with units based at Chaumont, Dreux, Evreux-Fauville, Laon, Etain, Chambley, Toul-Rosières, Phalsbourg and Châteauroux, although of course none of these was nuclear armed; the majority, in fact, were transport and reconnaissance units. With the launching of Operation 'FRELOC' – French Relocation of Assets – in the summer of 1966, these units were redeployed to bases in Britain, Federal Germany and the Netherlands. Britain's share in the reshuffle was two additional USAF Wings, the 513th Troop Carrier Wing from Evreux and the 66th Tactical Reconnaissance Wing from Laon. The latter, armed with McDonnell RF-101C Voodoos, was repositioned at Upper Heyford on 1 September 1966; the 513rd TCW, with C-130 transports, went to Mildenhall along with the EC-135s of Silk Purse Control, the European Command's

TOP: *F-100D Super Sabre of the 20th TFW, Wethersfield (A.A.B. Todd)*
ABOVE: *RF-4C Phantom of the 30th TRS, 10th TRW, Alconbury. (A.A.B. Todd)*

RF-4C Phantom of the 10th Tactical Reconnaissance Wing pictured over the hardened aircraft shelters at RAF Alconbury. (Philip Jarrett)

airborne command post facility. Another unit, the Military Airlift Command's 322nd Air Division HQ, was moved from Châteauroux to High Wycombe, but was later relocated at Rhein-Main Air Base in Germany.

Meanwhile, some of Third Air Force's resident units in the United Kingdom had benefited from a re-equipment programme

On 12 May 1965 two McDonnell RF-4C Phantoms touched down at Alconbury after a 5,750-mile non-stop flight lasting eight hours and forty minutes from North Carolina. The first of the two aircraft was piloted by Colonel deWitt S. Spain, commander of the 10th TRW, and its arrival at Alconbury heralded the beginning of the Wing's conversion to the new type.

The RF-4C Phantom was the first all-weather, day

and night tactical reconnaissance aircraft on the USAF's inventory. Carrying a crew of two – a pilot and systems operator – the aircraft was powered by two General Electric J79 turbojets developing over 34,000lb st with afterburning. Thanks to high-lift devices and boundary layer control it could fly at speeds as low as 150 mph, leading and trailing edge flaps providing increased lift at the high angles of attack required for sustained low-speed flying. At the other end of the scale, the R-4C had a typical low-level over-the-target dash speed of more than 600 mph and it could reach 50,000 feet in just over six minutes from the start of its take-off roll. Its maximum speed at altitude, clean, was around 1,500 mph.

For its reconnaissance mission the RF-4C carried

forward-looking radar (FLR) and optical and infra-red sensor systems. The optical sensors incorporated high- and low-altitude panoramic cameras, forward-, vertical- and side-mounted framing cameras and high-altitude mapping cameras. The infra-red sensors produced detailed maps from variable altitudes and in any weather conditions. The reconnaissance data gathered during operations, depending on the urgency attached to it, could be disseminated through air-to-ground high-frequency communication for the rapid deployment of tactical aircraft – known as direct reconnaissance reporting – or recorded on film for analysis on the ground. At the end of a mission the film shot by the RF-4C was rushed to the Photographic Processing and Interpretation Facility (PPIF), a self-

contained complex at Alconbury. The requirement called for the film to be processed within thirty minutes of engine shutdown and the aircrew's mission report (MISREP) confirmed by the imagery interpreter, who then made a detailed readout of the mission film. The completed reports, negatives, maps and prints had to be ready for forwarding to the user no later than four hours after engine shutdown. Reports were sent electronically, while the prints and negatives were forwarded by aircraft, and the information obtained from the interpreter reports could be used to determine priorities of targets, approaches to targets, bomb damage assessment, enemy resources and battle situations.

On 4 October 1965 the 81st TFW at Bentwaters also received its first Phantom. This was the F-4C version, developed for close support and ground attack with Tactical Air Command and able to carry a formidable load of up to 16,000lb of tactical nuclear or conventional stores. Conversion of the 81st TFW's squadrons at Bentwaters and Woodbridge was completed by April 1966; in April 1969 the 78th TFS at Woodbridge armed with the F-4D Phantom, basically an F-4C with improved avionics.

The news of the impending withdrawal from France came as a complete shock to many USAF personnel stationed there; the first most of them knew about the order was an announcement by Robert McNamara, the United States Defense Secretary. Once the news broke, however, they accepted it philosophically. Tactically, USAFE's NATO commitment was not hindered; some senior officers, in fact, believed that there would be an increase in efficiency following the move, since de Gaulle would cease to be a thorn in NATO's flesh. There were social benefits, too; as one US airman put it, 'It is sad that the French take this attitude. I think that most of us feel this way, but Britain is regarded as a better posting – I mean to say, you speak American, so it's easier'.

The move to Britain involved some 8,000 USAF personnel and their dependants. As things turned out, there were few problems; once the USAF's impressive logistics organisation got into full stride, Operation 'FRELOC' moved smoothly enough. The day after it began, Hercules transports of the 513th Troop Carrier Wing were already going about their NATO business from Mildenhall, and within a few days 18 of the Wing's aircraft had departed for an exercise in Greece.

By the late 1960s the USAF's offensive presence in the UK was entirely tactical in nature, its forces assigned to NATO and controlled by an airborne command post that was continuously airborne. The 55th SRW had now assumed responsibility for SAC's Looking Glass airborne command post operations as well as its normal strategic reconnaissance role, exchanging its Stratojets for RC-135s in 1967. The 338th SRS was reactivated briefly during this process to carry on with RB-47 operations while the rest of the wing converted, but it was deactivated again on 25 December. By the end of the year re-equipment with the RC-135 was complete, the last RB-47H (53-4296) having been flown from Offutt AFB to the storage facility at Davis-Monthan AFB on 29 December.

The 55th SRW received 18 RC-135s in all, 14 of them the RC-135V model. Manned by up to 21 linguists and

TOP: *Boeing RC-135V of the 55th SRW touching down at Mildenhall. Note the puff of smoke in the aircraft's wake. (Colin Lambert)*
ABOVE: *McDonnell F-4D Phantom 66–262 of the 48th TFW, Lakenheath, September 1975. (Harry Holmes)*

signals specialists from the USAF Electronic Security Command, the RC-135V was a true electronic reconnaissance platform, with an ability to fly 12-hour sorties using flight refuelling. The surveillance carried out by the RC-135s, under the code-name 'Rivet Joint', was worldwide, the aircraft rotating from Offutt AFB to Kadena on Okinawa, Mildenhall in the UK and Hellenikon in Greece, as well as operating from Shemya Island in the Aleutians and Eielson AFB in Alaska. The Kadena-based detachments covered the Kamchatka and Chukotski peninsulas, while those based on Okinawa covered Sakhalin. At the height of the Cold War the Mildenhall-based aircraft flew constant surveillance missions over the Baltic and the Barents Sea, while the RC-135s deployed to Greece covered the southern USSR and the Middle East. Other operations undertaken by the RC-135s included 'Cobra Ball', which involved monitoring

Soviet ICBM tests with two specially configured RC-135S aircraft carrying equipment to detect telemetry signals from test warheads, and 'Combat Sent', in which two RC-135U aircraft undertook random monitoring operations around the fringes of the Soviet Bloc.

On 1 April 1970 the 66th Tactical Reconnaissance Wing, by then operating a mixture of RF-101s and RF-4Cs, was deactivated at Upper Heyford, and in the months that followed the base underwent extensive modifications, turning it into the largest of its kind in Europe. The reason for all the activity became apparent when, following the arrival of the 20th Tactical Fighter Wing HQ for Wethersfield, two F-111E swing-wing fighter-bombers touched down at the Oxfordshire base on 12 September 1970 – the first of 72 aircraft which, by the following spring, would entirely replace the Wing's F-100s.

CHAPTER THIRTEEN

Interdictors and Aggressors

The arrival of the General Dynamics F-111 in Britain brought a completely new dimension to the Third Air Force's already considerable striking power. At last, the NATO air forces in Europe had an aircraft that was capable of delivering either nuclear or conventional weapons to targets deep inside Warsaw Pact territory at night and in all weathers; an aircraft whose advanced electronic systems and low-level penetration capability greatly enhanced its chances of survival in a hostile environment heavily defended by surface-to-air missiles and anti-aircraft artillery.

The development history of the F-111 began in 1962, when the General Dynamics Corporation, in association with Grumman Aircraft, was selected to develop a variable-geometry tactical fighter to meet the requirements of the USAF's TFX programme. An initial contract was placed for 23 development aircraft, including 18 F-111As for the USAF and five F-111Bs for the US Navy (in the event, the Navy cancelled the F-111 order). Powered by two Pratt & Whitney TF30–P-1 turbofan engines, the prototype F-111A flew for the first time on 21 December 1964, and during the second flight on 6 January 1965 the aircraft's wings were swept through the full range from 16 degrees to 72.5 degrees.

One hundred and sixty production F-111As were built, the first examples entering service with the 4480th Tactical Fighter Wing at Nellis AFB, Nevada, in October 1967. On 17 March the following year six aircraft from this unit flew to Takhli AFB in Thailand for operational evaluation in Vietnam (Operation 'Combat Lancer'), making their first sorties on 25 March. The operation ended unhappily when three of the aircraft were lost as a result of metal fatigue in a control rod, but the problem was rectified and in September 1972 the F-111As of the 429th and 430th Tactical Fighter Squadrons deployed to Takhli and performed very effective service in the closing air offensive of the war ('Linebacker II'), attacking targets in the Hanoi area at night and in all weathers through the heaviest anti-aircraft concentrations in the history of air warfare.

Years ahead of its time in technological terms, the F-111 incorporated many novel design features, such as a zero-speed, zero-altitude emergency escape module. The F-111's two-man crew (pilot and weapon systems operator) sat side by side in an air-conditioned and pressurised cabin that formed part of the module; the portion of the canopy over each seat was hinged over the aircraft centreline and opened upwards. The emergency escape procedure, which could also be initiated when the aircraft was under water, called for both crew members to remain in the module cabin section, which was boosted away from the aircraft by a 40,000lb thrust rocket motor and lowered to the

General Dynamics F-111A of the 474th TFW on a visit to RAF St Mawgan in April 1976. The first F-111As to visit the UK spent a week at Wethersfield in May 1967, bound for the Paris Air Show. (Harry Holmes)

TOP: *General Dynamics F-111F 71–890 of the 48th TFW approaching to land at Lakenheath in September 1979. The 48th TFW's aircraft formed a vital component of NATO's Theatre Nuclear Forces. (Harry Holmes)*
ABOVE: *A visitor from Holland: McDonnell Douglas F-15A Eagle of the 36th TFW, Soesterberg, pictured at Alconbury in May 1978. (Harry Holmes)*

ground by parachute. Air bags cushioned the impact on land and formed flotation gear in the event of an over-water escape, while the whole capsule formed a survival shelter.

The F-111E variant, which superseded the F-111A in service, featured modified air intakes to improve performance above 2.2M. Re-equipment of the 20th TFW (55th, 77th and 79th TFS) with its full complement of 72 aircraft was completed in the summer of 1971 and the unit, which became fully operational in November that year, was assigned the

war role of interdicting targets such as airfields, railway marshalling yards and junctions, vehicle parks and storage depots deep inside hostile territory as part of NATO's 2nd Allied Tactical Air Force.

In terms of performance, the F-111E was far removed from the F-100. Its maximum speed was in the region of 2.5M, and a red warning light instructed the pilot to throttle back if the aircraft approached the limiting Mach number, otherwise friction would heat the skin to a degree where structural failure might occur. With wings swept at 45 degrees the aircraft nosed through Mach 1 effortlessly, and maximum speed was reached with them swept at 72.5 degrees. The climb was spectacular too: under the combined 36,000lb thrust of its twin turbofans it was quite capable of reaching Mach 2 in the climb, which, for reasons of fuel conservation as well as to protect the ears of the citizens of Oxfordshire, nobody wished to see happen.

With the arrival of their first aircraft the crews of the 20th TFW, whose conversion course had been unusual in that it had taken place in the UK rather than in the USA, embarked on a series of intensive training courses, and soon the needle-nosed F-111Es became a familiar sight as they streaked along the low-level training routes that intersected the more remote areas of the British Isles.

To carry out its primary task of low-level penetration the F-111E had an astonishing array of electronic equipment. At the heart of it all was a CP-2A digital computer which processed all the information from the aircraft's systems and presented it to the crew in intelligible form. A General Electric APQ-113 J-band multi-mode radar provided accurate air-to-ground navigation, ranging and weapon delivery facilities; in the air-to-air mode it could track and scan hostile targets and control the aiming and launch of Sidewinder AAMs.

One of the most vital items of equipment was the Texas Instruments APQ-110 terrain-following radar (TFR), which was fully automatic and enabled the aircraft to follow the contours of the ground at a height of 200 feet without the pilot touching the controls. With TRF operating the F-111 could skim over the ground at 1.2M, its TF antenna nodding up and down to scan a narrow sector ahead of the aircraft, determining the height of the approaching terrain. This information was processed by the computer and transmitted to the aircraft flight control system, which raised or lowered the nose as necessary. The aircraft's track across the ground was determined by the navigational computers; all the pilot had to do was operate the throttles to compensate for any increase or decrease in speed and, in conjunction with the WSO, monitor the TFR constantly to make sure that everything was working properly. At such times the atmosphere on board could become very tense, especially over mountainous terrain at night, when all the F-111 crew could see was the dark grey of the inside of a cloud, punctuated by the red flashes of the aircraft's rotating beacon. It was small wonder that a qualified pilot needed a full year's training before he was fully conversant with the F-111's systems and could be declared combat-ready.

For an F-111 crew, a training sortie was a full day's work. First there was a lengthy briefing, involving such factors as selecting the best low-level route to the target, and even when the crew arrived at their aircraft they had to go through an extensive checklist, taking up another hour or so, before they were ready for take-off. Much of this time was spent checking out the WSO's equipment, which included a combined radar and projected map display, ground-mapping radar, stores management system for selecting which weapons were to be used and when, weapon-aiming mode selector, passive radar warning receiver and an active electronic countermeasures system. The aircraft's planned route was entered into the inertial navigation system by means of a computer keyboard; information included flight time to turning points, navigational checks *en route* (waypoints) and so on.

While the pilot monitored the TFR displaying the aircraft's low-level flight path, the WSO monitored the progress of the flight on his ground-mapping radar and carried out radar position fixes and weapon aiming;

General Dyanamics F-111E of the 20th TFW approaching to land at Upper Heyford. Note the large flap area. (Philip Jarrett)

Flight refuelling was an essential 'force multiplier' for the UK-based F-111 force. This photograph shows a 20th TFW aircraft topping up. (Philip Jarrett)

either crew member could update the present position stored in the central computer. Thanks to the stores management system, the navigator could assign weapons to a particular target before flight, and when a release signal was received from the main computer the stores management system automatically dropped the correct weapons.

The F-111's capabilities were well illustrated by its astonishing performance in Vietnam, once its technical problems had been sorted out. During the closing weeks of 1972, during Operation 'Linebacker II', F-111s of the 429th and 430th TFS, operating out of Takhli, hit their targets time after time in conditions when no other aircraft could fly. They entered the target area as low down as their TFR would permit, because the North Vietnamese defences were terrifying. Attacking crews had to fly through terrain that was stiff with surveillance radars on every piece of high ground, under a night sky bright with AAA fire and missile salvos; one F-111 crew reported 50 missile launches as they passed through the target area near Hanoi. But they succeeded in their mission, and usually the first indication the North Vietnamese had of an F-111 in the vicinity was when its bombs exploded, often in weather so bad that the enemy had believed no attack was possible.

In addition to the F-111's primary roles of strike, interdiction and counter-air attack, the UK-based F-111s had secondary roles of close air support, air defence suppression and maritime air support. For these missions the F-111 carried a formidable array of weapons, including two tactical nuclear bombs, two 2,000lb HE bombs or an M61 cannon in the internal weapons bay, or up to 14,000lb of bombs or missiles on its wing pylons.

During training in the UK, F-111 crews either flew at low level all the way to the target and back or, over longer distances, adopted the hi-lo-hi formula. A typical training sortie might involve an hour of high-level cruise, half an hour of low-level practice with 15 minutes or so spent in dropping practice bombs or illuminating targets by radar, and a high-level cruise back to base. For the crews, it was an exhilarating experience. As one crew member put it, 'Cruising at eight miles a minute, 500 feet off the ground is exciting and beautiful. You're low enough to get a really good look at the countryside, and in the United Kingdom that's rugged coastline, lakes, mountains and castles. After a while, 500 feet seems quite high – you can get quite comfortable there, at least in daylight.'

In parallel with the deployment of the F-111E in the UK, some subtle – and, for NATO, alarming – changes were beginning to take effect on the military balance between East and West. A decade earlier the doctrine of massive retaliation had lost its credibility in the face of a major Soviet nuclear build-up; NATO had therefore adopted its strategy of flexible response, which was designed to provide not just strategic nuclear retaliation in the event of aggression but a range of possible actions proportional to the challenge, including conventional defence, a range of theatre nuclear responses, and a general strategic nuclear option. Conventional forces, theatre forces, and strategic nuclear forces now constituted the triad on which NATO depended for deterrence. It was, however, a vulnerable triad.

The thinking behind flexible response was that a potential aggressor, unable to forecast the nature of NATO's response to an attack but certain that NATO had great flexibility in deciding how to respond or to escalate as necessary, would be deterred by the high risk associated with adventurism. It failed, however, to take into account the somewhat different approach of the Soviet Union's military planners.

As the 1970s progressed it became clear to the Russians that NATO might not use nuclear weapons from the outset of war, and that indeed NATO chiefs might be reluctant to authorise nuclear release at all because of the horrific consequences. The many peace movements advocating unilateral nuclear disarmament and the widespread publicity in the West accorded to the horrors of nuclear war, together with accompanying political arguments, all served in Soviet eyes to increase the pressure on NATO leaders to interpret flexible response as implying that NATO would initially only defend itself by means of conventional weapons, and would use nuclear weapons only as a last desperate measure to avoid total defeat.

During the era of US strategic superiority the size and character of Soviet long-range theatre nuclear forces were of less importance to NATO than was the case after the early 1970s, as the Russians could have expected any action taken by those forces in Europe to evoke a response from superior US intercontinental forces. With the emergence of parity in central strategic systems, however, the Russians came to believe – however incorrectly – that they could use or threaten to use their long-range theatre nuclear forces in the expectation that the US would be deterred from responding with its central strategic systems. Parity in central strategic systems therefore increased the importance of NATO's long-range theatre nuclear forces because the lack of a credible military response at this level created a serious gap in NATO's continuum of deterrence and defence.

Throughout much of the 1970s, NATO's long-range theatre nuclear force consisted of the 20th TFW's 72 F-111Es at Upper Heyford and 50-odd Vulcan B2 bombers of No. 1 Group, RAF Strike Command, distributed among six squadrons at RAF Scampton and RAF Waddington. Although long in the tooth, the Vulcan – which had relinquished its QRA role to the Polaris-armed nuclear submarines of the Royal Navy in the late 1960s – was still a viable weapons system, and was to remain so until the late 1970s when detachments of four aircraft from Waddington went to the United States to take part in 'Red Flag', the annual air warfare exercise held under realistic conditions in the Arizona desert. The Vulcans operated at night, and despite the fact that the ground was not ideal for terrain-following some good results were achieved, showing that the Vulcan still had the ability to penetrate sophisticated defence systems. Operationally, the Vulcan could be armed either with 21 1,000lb HE bombs or with the 950lb WE177B low-yield nuclear bomb, optimised for low-level delivery. And whatever the Vulcan could do, apart from carry a massive bomb-load, the F-111 could do better. Nevertheless, NATO's long-range theatre nuclear force remained static throughout the 1970s, and as Soviet defences improved its offensive capability – particularly that of the ageing Vulcan – became increasingly compromised.

The vulnerability of aircraft engaged in deep-penetration raids into heavily defended enemy territory, already exposed in the Vietnam War, was demonstrated again in the Yom Kippur War of October 1972, when Egypt and Syria attacked Israel on two fronts. The two surprising developments in the first few days of the war were the effectiveness of the Arab air defences and the deadly accuracy of Soviet-supplied anti-tank weapons. The air defence was based on a combination of the mobile SA-6 surface-to-air missile and the ZSU-23/4 Shilka radar-controlled mobile AAA system.

During the first three days of the war, which began on 6 October, the Israeli air and armoured forces suffered fearful losses; then the Syrians and Egyptians began to exhaust their supplies of missiles, enabling the Israelis to launch effective counter-attacks. Almost immediately the Russians, honouring a commitment made before the war, began to resupply their clients: the first shipload of supplies left Odessa on 7 October; by 10 October an airlift of equipment to Syria and Egypt was underway; and by 12 October they were making between 60 and 90 flights a day. On that same day, US President Richard Nixon ordered an immediate airlift to aid Israel. Skyhawks and Phantoms to replace aircraft lost by the Israeli Air Force were flown direct to Israel, while new tanks, self-propelled guns, helicopters, anti-tank missiles, ammunition and spare parts were also airlifted for the sake of speed. Between mid-October and mid-November Lockheed C-5 Galaxy and C-141 Starlifter aircraft delivered 22,400 tons of cargo in 566 separate flights.

By 16 October the Israelis had contained the Syrians and were able to concentrate on the Suez front. Pushing an armoured force across the Suez Canal, they began to roll up Egyptian SAM sites, making it possible for Israeli fighter-bombers to operate effectively in support of the ground forces, and the Egyptian Third Army found itself surrounded. On 24 October Egypt's President Sadat asked President Nixon and Russia's President Brezhnev to send a joint American-Soviet force to enforce a UN ceasefire; Brezhnev informed Nixon that if the US would not move in with them, the Russians would act independently.

The American response was a DEFCON 3 alert for all US forces worldwide, a drastic response based on intelligence reports that the Russians were about to fly several battalions of airborne troops to Egypt and the knowledge that the Soviet Naval Squadron in the Mediterranean, the 5th Eskadra, had been increased from 60 to 84 ships, outnumbering the US Sixth Fleet. The DEFCON 3 alert came as something of a surprise to Third Air Force personnel in Britain; married men stationed around the various US bases were sent home for their battle kit – CBW clothing and so on – and told to return immediately. From Mildenhall, Hercules transports of the 513th Tactical Airlift Wing ran a steady shuttle service, lifting spares and equipment to the fighter-bomber bases. The net result of the alert was a Soviet signal that no troops would be sent to the Middle East, and the Americans put pressure on the Israelis to cease offensive operations.

At the time of this latest Middle East crisis, the Order of Battle of the US Third Air Force was as follows. The 10th Tactical Reconnaissance Wing was still at Alconbury with RF-4C Phantoms; in 1965 its 19th and 42nd TRS had been reassigned to the newly activated 26th TRW, which came under the command of the Germany-based Seventeenth Air Force, and its assets now comprised the 1st, 30th and 32nd TRS. Bentwaters continued to host the 91st and 92nd Squadrons of the 81st TFW, with F-4D Phantoms; the

78th TFS was at Woodbridge, which was also the home of the HC-130 Hercules and HH-3E helicopters of the 67th Aerospace Rescue and Recovery Squadron. Greenham Common remained a standby base, adminstered by the 7551st Combat Support Group, and was used from time to time by transport aircraft engaged in 'Reforger' reinforcement exercises; in 1976 it was the temporary home for three months of the 20th TFW's F-111Es, which moved there while the Upper Heyford runways were being resurfaced.

The 48th TFW, with F-4D Phantoms, was at Lakenheath and awaiting eventual re-equipment with the F-111. Mildenhall, Third Air Force HQ, housed the C-130s of the 513th Tactical Airlift Wing, the EC-135s of the Airborne Command Post, the 435th Tactical Airlift Wing (a headquarters unit of Military Air Command responsible for handling C-130 Wings on TDY from the United States) and Detachment One of the 306th Strategic Wing, which operated the KC-135s of the European Tanker Task Force. The F-111s of the 20th TFW were at Upper Heyford, exercising their primary role of NATO theatre strike force.

At Alconbury, the 32nd and 30th TRS were inactivated on 1 January and 1 April 1976 respectively, and their RF-4Cs were reassigned to Air National Guard units. This was part of a reshuffle designed to make room for the activation at Alconbury on 1 April 1976 of a new and unique unit in USAFE: the 527th Tactical Fighter Training Aggressor Squadron. Its task was to provide combat tactics training for NATO air units in Europe, and for this purpose it was armed with the Northrop F-5E Tiger II, a highly manoeuvrable day/night fighter with a limited all-weather capability.

The first eight of the squadron's twenty F-5Es arrived at Alconbury on 21 May 1976 aboard a Lockheed C-5A Galaxy transport from the Air Logistics Centre at McClellan AFB, California, the aircraft packed in specially designed pallets with the wings and various other parts removed. After reassembly, engine testing and inspection, the first flight took place on 1 June 1976. Two more Galaxy flights arrived during June with the remainder of the squadron's aircraft, enabling the 527th to test and validate its training concepts and procedures before being declared fully operational on 1 January 1977.

First flown in August 1972, the F-5E Tiger II was an advanced version of the Northrop F-5 Freedom Fighter, which was widely exported. Powered by two General Electric J85 turbojets, each producing 5,000lb of thrust with afterburning, the F-5E could fly at 1,000 mph and reach an altitude of 50,000 feet. Built-in armament was two 20mm cannon in the nose, with 280 rounds per gun, and the aircraft could carry two AIM-9L Sidewinder AAMs on wingtip launchers and up to 7,000lb of mixed ordnance under the wings and fuselage.

Before the 527th Squadron was activated, the F-5E had already proved its value with the 4440th Aggressor Squadron in 'Red Flag' air warfare exercises at Nellis AFB in Nevada. With a wing span of only 26 feet and a length of just over 48 feet, the Tiger II was similar in both size and radar signature to the MiG-21, still the most common Warsaw Pact tactical aircraft in the mid-1970s, and to make things even more realistic the Aggressor F-5Es were painted in Warsaw Pact camouflage patterns. Their pilots specialised in Soviet fighter tactics.

The reason behind the formation of the Aggressor squadrons was that, at the beginning of the 1970s, the Soviet Frontovaya Aviatsiya (Tactical Air Force) was

A 10th TRW RF-4C lands at RAF Leuchars in 1984. (Philip Jarrett)

TOP & ABOVE: *These photographs clearly show the different camouflage schemes used by the Northrop F-5E 'Aggressors' of the 57th FWW at RAF Alconbury in the 1980s. (Philip Jarrett)*

TOP: *F-111F 71–0886 of the 492nd TFS, 48th TFW. Note the Paveway guided bombs. (A.A.B. Todd)*
ABOVE: *F-111F 72–1451, 494th TFS, showing the aircraft's large 'slab' tailplane. (A.A.B. Todd)*

equipped with aircraft which, across the board, were more manoeuvrable than most NATO types then in service. In providing what was known as DACT (Dissimilar Air Combat Tactics) training the 527th Squadron provided realistic opposition of the kind NATO pilots would encounter in an actual war situation, as well as providing academic instruction on all aspects of the Soviet/Warsaw Pact air defence system.

In March 1977 the 48th TFW at Lakenheath at last began to rearm with the F-111, eventually receiving 84 aircraft. It was assigned to 4 ATAF in its war role and had the ability to interdict targets as far away as the Adriatic. The 48th TFW was armed with the F-111F, a fighter-bomber variant combining the best features of the F-111E and the FB-111A (the strategic bomber version) and fitted with the more powerful TF30-F-100 engines. The 48th TFW's aircraft were equipped to carry two B43 nuclear stores internally, as well as a variety of ordnance under six wing hardpoints, and formed the core of NATO's theatre nuclear strike force.

In the conventional role, the F-111F's primary precision attack weapon system was the Pave Tack self-contained pod containing a laser designator, rangefinder and forward-looking infra-red (FLIR) equipment for use with laser-guided bombs like the 2,000lb Mk 82 Snakeye, the GBU-15 TV-guided bomb or the Maverick TV-guided missile. The Pave Tack pod was stowed inside the F-111's weapons bay in a special cradle, rotating through 180 degrees to expose the sensor head when the system was activated. The sensor head provided the platform for the FLIR seeker, the laser designator and rangefinder, so that the Weapons System Operator (WSO) was presented with a stabilised infra-red image, together with range information, on his display.

As the F-111 ran in at low level towards its target, the WSO's primary display showed a radar ground map which enabled major course corrections to be made. All the information from the aircraft's systems was processed by a CP-2A digital computer, which presented it to the crew in intelligible form. The aircraft's General Electric APQ-113 multi-mode radar operated in the J-band; as well as providing accurate air-to-ground navigation it also supplied ranging and weapon delivery facilities, and in the air-to-air role it could track and scan hostile targets and control the aiming and launch of defensive Sidewinder AAMs.

The WSO activated Pave Tack at a range of about four miles from the target. This provided more accurate steering information, and at the same time the infra-red image appeared on the display. After selecting the correct infra-red field of view the WSO centred a reticule on the target and fired the laser, which was kept in target by the F-111's inertial navigation system even when the aircraft was taking violent evasive action to avoid enemy defences. The WSO used a hand controller for the fine tuning of the laser line of sight. With the laser illuminating the target the F-111's CP-2A computer initiated a pull-up and automatically released the weapons at the optimum height for an accurate toss-delivery attack; as the aircraft turned away from the target Pave Tack's sensor head rotated so that it continued to illuminate the target until bomb impact. The pod was then retracted and the cleaned-up F-111, having pulled round hard and dived back to low level, accelerated to supersonic speed for its escape from the target area.

The combination of Pave Tack and F-111F provided an extremely viable weapons system. Within a decade, it would be put to the test operationally, under conditions far removed from any anticipated conflict on NATO's central front.

CHAPTER FOURTEEN

Tankers and Thunderbolts

In April 1977 HQ Third Air Force entered into preliminary and as yet informal discussions with the UK Ministry of Defence on the possibility of reactivating Greenham Common as a base for some twenty KC-135 tanker aircraft following a planned expansion of the European Tanker Task Force; Mildenhall was already overcrowded and Greenham Common had a great deal more to offer in the way of facilities than other standby bases such as Sculthorpe. This location, however, was rejected following a big public outcry centred on the fact that the KC-135 was an extremely noisy aircraft. Unlike the Boeing 707 airliner from which it was developed, it had no noise baffles on its engines, and with 26,000 gallons of fuel on board it required a lengthy take-off run followed by a shallow climb-out, which meant that its noise pattern would cover a wide area. According to the protestors, who had done a considerable amount of research, the area in the immediate vicinity of the airfield would be subjected to around 112 PNdB (perceived noise decibels), which was acknowledged to be close to the threshold of pain; the noise level within about six miles of a KC-135 starting its take-off roll would be twice that permitted at night (102 PNdB) four miles from that point at London-Heathrow; and by day the Greenham Common levels would be 40 per cent greater than those permitted at Heathrow (108 PNdB).

With the rejection of Greenham Common as a base for the KC-135s, the two most likely alternative locations were Fairford, which had been vacated by RAF Air Support Command in 1971 and so appeared the obvious choice, and Brize Norton, which housed the VC-10 long-range jet transports of No. 10 Squadron RAF and was still active. Protest movements developed at both locations and particularly at Fairford, which had a taste of the KC-135 in September 1978 when six aircraft were deployed there to take part in the annual series of NATO exercises code-named 'Autumn Forge'. The news that the MoD had agreed to the use of Fairford by the Strategic Air Command tankers had broken a few weeks earlier, so the arrival of the first two KC-135s on 5 September came as no real surprise.

These two aircraft carried out a series of noise tests, and later in the month the Cotswold District Council's Planning and Development Committee announced that it accepted that Fairford was 'the only suitable base in the short term' for the jet tankers. From then on, Fairford was to see regular visits by Stratotankers from the 34th Strategic Squadron at Zaragoza, Spain, and the 922nd Strategic Squadron at Hellenikon in Greece, both forming part of Strategic Air Command's 11th Strategic Group.

Meanwhile, at Bentwaters and Woodbridge, the 81st Tactical Fighter Wing had been moving steadily towards rearming with a dedicated close support aircraft, the Fairchild A-10A Thunderbolt II. The concept of the A-10 had arisen during the Vietnam War, when it became apparent to the Americans that they seriously lacked an aircraft designed specifically for ground attack and close support. The immediate result was a series of stopgap measures (which in practice worked quite well) involving the use of aircraft like

ABOVE & OPPOSITE: *KC-135RS of the 351st ARS, 100th ARW, Mildenhall. The 100th ARW assumed the responsibility for the European Tanker Task Force. (Colin Lambert)*

the North American T-28 trainer and the Douglas A-1 Skyraider. What NATO urgently needed, however, was a modern ground-attack aircraft for use in the European environment against a massive assault by Warsaw Pact armour, an aircraft that could destroy enemy tanks in all weathers and survive in an environment dominated by SAMs, fighters and the deadly ZSU 23/4 Shilka anti-aircraft artillery. Very heavy armour coupled with high manoeuvrability were the keypoints of the requirement.

In December 1970 Fairchild Republic and Northrop were each selected to build a prototype of a new close support aircraft for evaluation under the USAF's A-X programme, and in January 1973 it was announced that Fairchild Republic's contender, the A-10, had been selected. It was to prove one of the most remarkable – and certainly one of the ugliest – combat aircraft ever developed.

Fairchild met the armour requirement by seating the pilot in what was virtually a titanium 'bathtub',

The Fairchild A-10A Thunderbolt II, showing the seven-barrel nose cannon. (Colin Lambert)

resistant to most firepower except a direct hit from a heavy-calibre shell, and added to this a so-called redundant structure policy whereby the pilot could retain control even if the aircraft lost large portions of its airframe, including one of the two rear-mounted engines. The core of the A-10's built-in firepower was its massive GAU-8/A seven-barrel 30mm rotary cannon, which was mounted on the centreline under the forward fuselage. The gun fired up to 4,200 rounds per minute of armour-piercing ammunition with a non-radioactive uranium core for greater impact, and was quite capable of destroying a light tank or armoured personnel carrier. The aircraft also had eight underwing and three under-fuselage attachments for up to 16,000lb of bombs, missiles, gun pods and jammer pods, and carried the Pave Penny laser system pod for target designation. It was fitted with very advanced avionics including a central air data computer, an inertial navigation system and a head-up display.

The A-10 was designed to operate from short, unprepared strips less than 1,500 feet long. The operational tactics developed for the aircraft involved two A-10s giving one another mutual support, covering a swathe of ground two or three miles wide, so that an attack could be quickly mounted by the second aircraft once the first pilot had made his firing pass on the target. The optimum range for engaging a target was 4,000 feet, and the A-10's gunsight was calibrated for this distance. As the highly manoeuvrable A-10's turning circle was 4,000 feet, this meant that the pilot could engage the target without having to pass over it. A one-second burst of fire would place seventy rounds of 30mm shells on the target, and as a complete 360 degree turn took no more than sixteen seconds a pair of A-10s could bring almost continuous fire to bear. The 30mm ammunition drum carried enough rounds to make 10 to 15 firing passes.

In order to survive in a hostile environment dominated by radar controlled AAA, A-10 pilots trained to fly at 100 feet or lower, never remaining straight and level for more than four seconds. One of the aircraft's big advantages in approaching the combat zone was that its twin General Electric TF34–GE-100 turbofan engines were very quiet, so that it was able to achieve total surprise as it popped up over a contour of the land for weapons release. Attacks on targets covered by AAA involved close cooperation between the two A-10s; while one engaged the target the other stood off and engaged anti-aircraft installations with its TV-guided Maverick missiles, six of which were normally carried. The A-10 also had a considerable air-to-air capability, the tactic being for the pilot to turn towards an attacking fighter and use coarse rudder to spray it with 30mm shells.

The operation to replace the 81st TFW's Phantoms with the A-10 was code-named 'Ready Thunder'. By way of a preliminary, four A-10s of the 57th Fighter Weapons Wing, Nellis AFB, Nevada, visited Bentwaters on 21 February 1978; all were on their way back to the US after being involved in Maverick anti-tank missile trials in Germany. In the closing months of the year, pilots of the Bentwaters-based 92nd TFS began rotating to Davis-Monthan AFB in Arizona to begin conversion; this began with five conversion flights and a number of attack sorties using all the aircraft's combinations of weaponry, followed by more weapons-training flights under realistic tactical conditions, and then 12 sorties designed to familiarise them with the tactics employed by USAFE in battlefront operations.

The 81st TFW began to receive its A-10s in January 1979, and over the next seven months the type equipped the 78th, 91st and 510th TFS as well as the 92nd. The latter squadron, together with the 510th, moved to Sembach in Germany for operational training while the 78th went to Ahlhorn; the 91st stayed at Bentwaters, where it was joined in 1980 by the 509th and 511th TFS, bringing the total strength of the 81st TFW to six squadrons and 108 aircraft.

Operationally, from its main bases at Bentwaters and Woodbridge the 81st TFW deployed its aircraft, usually in clutches of eight or nine, to Forward Operating Locations (FOL) in West Germany. Each FOL had a computer link with Bentwaters, so that when spares were needed they could be quickly flown out, as could ground crews to undertake major servicing. This arrangement eliminated the need to maintain large stocks of spares and additional personnel in Germany, thereby easing logistics problems. Because the A-10 was designed to fly a very high sortie rate, servicing was made as simple as possible to cut down turnround time. Most of the aircraft's inspection panels could be reached by a man standing on the ground, and an automatic system facilitated rapid reloading of the 1,350–round GAU-8/A ammunition drum, which held enough rounds for up to fifteen firing passes. The fact that the 81st TFW was known to fly 86 sorties with 11 aircraft in one day was indicative of the Thunderbolt's capability; in fact, the limiting factor on sortie rate was pilot fatigue, which was high in the A-10, as operational sorties required a lot of high-g manoeuvring at low level.

The A-10 had a combat radius of 250 nautical miles, enough to reach a target area on the East German border from a FOL in central Germany and then move on to another target area in northern Germany. The aircraft had a three-and-a-half-hour loiter endurance, although operational war sorties in Europe would probably have lasted between one and two hours. In general, operations by the A-10s envisaged cooperation with US Army helicopters; the latter would hit the mobile SAM and AAA systems accompanying a Soviet armoured thrust, and with the enemy's defences at least temporarily stunned or degraded, the A-10s would be free to concentrate their fire on the tanks. Ten years later, these tactics would be used to deadly effect in the 1991 Gulf War.

An A-10 seen at RAF Coningsby in 1987.

TOP: *A-10A Thunderbolt II of the 81st TFW, RAF Bentwaters. (USAF)*
MIDDLE & ABOVE: *Lockheed C-141B Starlifter 66–0135 of the 437th Military Airlift Wing. (Colin Lambert)*

CHAPTER FIFTEEN

To the Brink of Nuclear War

By the mid-1970s NATO Intelligence had become aware that the Soviet Union was developing a new intermediate-range ballistic missile, which was given the NATO designation SS-X-20, simplified to SS-20 once it had reached operational status, to replace the weapons then deployed against western Europe. The new missile appeared to have an interesting development history. In 1965 the Soviet Union had publicly displayed what seemed to be its first solid-fuel ICBM, the SS-13, designed to be housed in underground silos and supposedly the equivalent of America's Minuteman. It entered service in 1968, but only about 60 were deployed before manufacture terminated in 1970. The Russians, it seemed, were concentrating on the development of a mobile version known to the West as the SS-16.

However, during SS-16 test flights, which were closely observed by the United States, the first of the

missile's three stages consistently failed to meet the specified performance, possibly because the Soviet chemical industry did not have the technology to produce solid-fuel rocket motors of the size and thrust required for the first stage of an ICBM. On the other hand, the second and third stages worked perfectly well and provided a ready-made basis for the development of a new IRBM. The result was the SS-20, deployment of which began in 1977.

Almost overnight, the SS-20 upset the whole East–West strategic balance – a balance that was already very fine, with the Soviet Strategic Rocket Forces having started to deploy extremely accurate ICBMs which were cold-launched from their silos by gas pressure before the rocket motors were ignited, allowing the silos to be reloaded. The first of the new-generation ICBMs was the SS-18 (Soviet designation RS-20), the largest ICBM in the world, which was first

TOP: *Boeing B-52H 61–0029 of the 93rd BS, 917th BW, making a fast pass with bomb doors open. (Colin Lambert)*
ABOVE: *Boeing B-52H 60–0062 of the 93rd BS, US AFRES, at Mildenhall in 1995. (Colin Lambert)*

TOP: *Boeing B-52H 61–0028 of the 96th BS, 2nd BW, rolling at RAF Mildenhall. (Colin Lambert)*
ABOVE: *Boeing B-52H 60–0017 of the 11th BS, 2nd BW, at RAF Fairford in 1996. (Colin Lambert)*

TOP: *Boeing B-52H 60–0023 of the 23rd BS, 5th BW, streams its brake parachute at Mildenhall in 1994. (Colin Lambert)*
ABOVE: *GD F-111F fighter-bomber of the 48th TFW taking off from Lakenheath. (Philip Jarrett)*

deployed in 1974. Its silos, which were later modified for the cold-launch technique, were specially hardened to withstand pressures of up to 6,000lb per square inch, making them virtually invulnerable to anything less than a direct hit by a thermonuclear warhead. The two-stage SS-18 could carry an immensely powerful warhead, or combination of warheads, over a range of 7,500 miles, and most of the 308 deployed were fitted with ten 500-kiloton MIRVs targeted on the US Minuteman missile fields.

Because of the ability of its silos to withstand a missile attack, the SS-18 practically demolished the West's deterrent credibility in the mid-1970s. Moreover, its deployment was followed by that of two more highly accurate ICBMs, the SS-17 (RS-16) and SS-19 (RS-18), both of which could carry up to six 500-kiloton MIRVs over a range of 6,200 miles. About 60 of the total 300 SS-19s deployed were assigned to

targets in western Europe.

Formidable though these weapons were, they were all fixed-site weapons subject to constant satellite surveillance, their locations known and targeted by Strategic Air Command. With the deployment of the SS-20, however, the Soviet Union was provided with a missile system whose mobility made it virtually impossible to counter. Moreover, the missile's estimated range of 4,600 miles with a 50-kiloton warhead (or 2,500 miles with three 150-kiloton MIRVs) meant that it threatened all the European NATO nations from bases inside Soviet territory.

NATO had nothing to compare with the SS-20. The only counter to it within the European theatre was the UK-based strike force of F-111s at Upper Heyford and Lakenheath, and the deployment of the SS-20 made their bases highly vulnerable. What was needed to counter the new threat was another mobile missile

system, easy to disperse and carrying a nuclear warhead, which would release aircraft such as the F-111 from the need to be held nuclear-ready to counter a Sovet in-theatre missile attack and free them for conventional operations.

The underlying need was to restore credibility to NATO's policy of flexible response, which required a full complement of effective weapons at four distinct levels: conventional, battlefield nuclear, theatre nuclear and strategic warfare. If the level of response at any of the first three stages became seriously weakened, a Soviet attack on Europe would almost certainly lead to a global nuclear exchange. Another factor was the growing ability of the Soviet Union to destroy NATO air bases, particularly those in the United Kingdom, using Backfire and Fencer bombers armed with long-range stand-off weapons, which would leave NATO devoid of a theatre nuclear response.

The choice, then, was stark. If NATO's theatre nuclear forces were knocked out at an early stage in any future conflict, the Alliance would either have to

ABOVE: *Lockheed C-5B Galaxy 87–0027 of the 436th Military Airlift Wing pictured at Mildenhall in 1997. (Colin Lambert)*
RIGHT: *Lockheed C-5B 87–0031 of the 436th MAW approaching to land at Mildenhall. (Colin Lambert)*

rely on its conventional forces to stem a Soviet assault – with an almost inevitable escalation to battlefield nuclear weapons, given the Soviet Union's vast conventional superiority – or resort to submarine-launched ballistic missiles. In either event a swift move up the ladder of escalation would be the likely outcome. By the beginning of 1979, with the deployment of SS-20 well underway, the situation was regarded as becoming dangerously unstable.

The result was that a special meeting of NATO foreign and defence ministers on 12 December 1979 decided to embark on a programme of long-range theatre nuclear force modernisation. Briefly, the decision involved the replacement of existing Pershing 1A tactical missiles in the Federal Republic of Germany with 108 longer-range Pershing IIs, and the

LEFT: *C-5B 87–7027 demonstrates its massive front loading door. (Colin Lambert)*
ABOVE: *The C-5B's massive cargo bay. (Colin Lambert)*

deployment of 464 ground-launched cruise missiles GLCMs on the territory of a number of the European Allies. Germany, Britain, Italy, the Netherlands and Belgium agreed in principle to host these weapons, although the Dutch and Belgians delayed their final acceptance. While some of the costs of the deployments would be borne by NATO's infrastructure programme, all the new missiles would be American-owned; however, as with all other US nuclear weapons deployed in Europe, they would be subject to well-understood NATO controls and guidelines. Each of the new missiles would have a single warhead, and as well as replacing 572 existing warheads they would enable a further 1,000 theatre nuclear warheads to be withdrawn from Europe.

The decision to introduce new long-range weapons into NATO's nuclear arsenal was only one element, albeit a controversial one, in a pattern of theatre nuclear force modernisation that had been going on for many years. From the very beginning of its existence the theatre nuclear stockpile available to NATO had been subject to change, with old systems withdrawn as new ones were introduced, and while its overall size had remained relatively static since the late 1960s, there had been significant changes in its character and composition. In the first place, greater attention had been given to the physical security of the weapons and to insuring against their seizure or unauthorised use; at the same time, new weapons had emphasised greater accuracy coupled with lower-yield

warheads in order to reduce the risk of undesirable collateral damage.

The decision to modernise the long-range theatre nuclear force, however, represented a major change of emphasis; the withdrawal of 1,000 nuclear warheads would ultimately result in a substantial reduction in the overall size of the stockpile, but the introduction of the new missiles would shift its balance towards longer-range systems. The really significant consequence of the new deployments was that they increased the ability of the Alliance to deliver warheads on Soviet territory from bases in western Europe. This in turn thrust the whole issue of what were termed 'forward based systems' by the Russians into renewed prominence.

Another factor in the proposed deployment of modernised LRTNF – although this did not really emerge until after the NATO decision to deploy the weapons had been taken – was a revision of the American strategic posture. The new US 'countervailing strategy' stemmed from a major review of targeting policy and of requirements for continued credible deterrence, and instructions for its implementation were issued on 25 September 1980 in the form of Presidential Directive 59. Basically, the object was to increase the flexibility of American strategic forces by increasing the range of targeting options available in the hope of reinforcing deterrence against less than all-out attacks on either the United States or its allies, and thereby reinforcing the

117

credibility of extended deterrence. American spokesmen stressed that the countervailing strategy was not new, but that it had evolved from established strategic concepts and policies. However, it did reflect a recognition on the part of the American policy-makers that a posture of assured destruction alone was an inadequate basis for the American strategic commitment to Europe. What the revised posture sought to do, in effect, was to reinforce the link between strategic and theatre nuclear forces by providing for more flexible options at the strategic level. Within such a strategic posture, the function of modernised long-range theatre nuclear forces was to close the gap between strategic weapons and the shorter-range tactical systems.

Before examining the deployment of cruise missiles in Britain, and the consequent involvement of the US Third Air Force, it is useful at this point to take a look at the nuclear capability of Britain herself in the early 1980s. In 1980 Britain had possessed her own nuclear weapons for 25 years, and it had been the policy of successive governments to align the UK nuclear forces ever more closely with NATO. All British nuclear forces therefore were (and are) without exception assigned to the Alliance and included in the plans of the Supreme Allied Command Europe (SACEUR) and the Supreme Allied Command Atlantic (SACLANT).

In comparison with those of the United States, Britain's nuclear forces were small, although in certain areas they were numerically important. For example, Britain made a significant proportion of the longer-range aircraft available to SACEUR for nuclear missions, and provided the bulk of the theatre nuclear forces in the eastern Atlantic. Their value, however, lay not so much in their numerical addition to NATO's strength, but rather in the fact that while fully NATO-committed they came under separate control, giving the Russians two nuclear powers to worry about, inevitably complicating both their judgement and their planning and increasing the risks and uncertainties they would face as a consequence of any aggression against NATO. This explained why the Soviet Union always insisted on the UK nuclear forces being weighed in the balance during strategic arms limitation talks.

When the Conservative Party took power in May 1979 they inherited a nuclear deterrent comprising four nuclear-powered submarines, each carrying 16 Polaris missiles. Already underway was a £1,000 million programme to give Polaris a new payload, with decoys and other penetration aids which would ensure that the six warheads fitted to each missile reached their targets despite improvements in Soviet ballistic missile defences. This system, called Chevaline, was designed, managed and paid for by the United Kingdom, with the full cooperation of the United States, and consisted of six 40-kiloton warheads; the payload could be manoeuvred in space, with a maximum spacing of 40 miles between individual warhead impact points, and was designed to keep Polaris viable until the planned Trident submarine fleet became operational in the 1990s.

In addition to the Polaris missile force, the United Kingdom also made a contribution to NATO's short-range theatre nuclear forces, deploying a number of systems equipped with American nuclear weapons and operated on a dual key basis. These included a regiment of Lance tactical surface-to-surface missiles (range 75 miles with a nuclear warhead or 45 miles with a conventional payload) and four regiments of artillery equipped with 8in and 155mm howitzers. All munitions for these systems were held under US custody at Special Ammunition Storage Sites.

In the maritime area the UK in 1980 had four squadrons of Nimrod long-range patrol aircraft capable of delivering American nuclear depth bombs. In addition, two squadrons of nuclear-capable Buccaneer strike/attack aircraft were assigned to SACLANT, along with Royal Navy helicopters – five squadrons of Sea Kings, two flights of Wessex, 25 flights of Wasps and 18 flights of Lynx – all of which were capable of delivering British-designed nuclear depth bombs, providing the bulk of ready theatre – nuclear forces in the EASTLANT area. Although final weapon release decisions rested with the UK Government, all the above systems were committed to NATO.

In all, the United Kingdom had at its disposal several hundred strike aircraft and helicopters capable of delivering tactical nuclear weapons, plus the Polaris strategic missiles, but a viable long-range theatre nuclear strike force simply did not exist. The Vulcan force was being progressively run down, the aircraft's operational career having been extended far beyond its planned life, and while the RAF's other nuclear-capable aircraft, such as the Buccaneer (which in 1980 equipped three UK-based squadrons in the maritime attack role and two more in Germany) and the Tornado, which was just coming into service, offered an attack capability that extended from the Murmansk Peninsula southwards to cover much of the Warsaw Pact's territory west of the Soviet border, they were in no sense long-range aircraft, even though their combat radius could be extended by in-flight refuelling.

It was against this background that the UK Government agreed to the deployment of Pershing IIs and GLCMs in Europe, and in June 1980 it was confirmed that the GLCMs to be based in the United Kingdom would be deployed at Greenham Common and Molesworth, with six flights housed at Greenham and four at the Cambridgeshire base. The missiles would be stored in special bunkers which would be grass-covered to blend in with the countryside, and no live missiles or warheads would leave the base for the practice deployments that would take place two or three times a month. Such deployments would usually be within a 100–mile radius of the home base, but in time of real war alert there would be no operational reason to limit the area of deployment. As part of the security arrangements, the UK government agreed to contribute 220 British personnel, probably drawn from the Parachute Regiment or the Royal Air Force Regiment, towards the guard force for the bases and the deployment dispersals. (In the event, an agreement was reached whereby one half of each GLCM flight's security force, or about 33 personnel, would be provided by the RAF Regiment. Under this arrangement, either a USAF or RAF Regiment officer could command a deployed GLCM flight.)

The Ground-Launched Cruise Missile, manufactured by General Dynamics and officially designated BGM-109G, was similar in configuration to the other members of the Tomahawk family, but had a range of 1,550 miles and was armed with a 200-kiloton W-80 nuclear warhead, although other warheads ranging in yield from ten to 50-kiloton could be fitted depending on operational requirements. All variants were subsonic, with a speed of 0.7M (530 mph) at sea level. The GLCM flights were housed in concrete shelters hardened to withstand a direct hit from precision-guided weapons with conventional warheads. Each shelter was divided into three cells, each containing two launch vehicles, and when a GLCM flight was deployed to its war station it travelled as two separate elements, each comprising two launchers and a control centre, and the vehicles themselves were armoured against small-arms fire. This was a necessary precaution, for in time of war cruise missile sites and launch vehicles *en route* would almost certainly come under attack by agents of Spetsnaz, the Soviet Special Forces.

The training programme for GLCM crews took place at Davis-Monthan AFB, Arizona, where the USAF activated the 868th Tactical Missile Training Squadron (TMTS) in July 1982. The first class of students entered in February 1983 and graduated on schedule on 26 April that year. Meanwhile, site activation work had begun at Greenham Common in mid-1981 with the arrival of various engineering and support detachments, and on 1 July 1982 the 501st Tactical Missile Wing (TMW), the organisation that would exercise operational control over the GLCMs, was activated. It had to negotiate many obstacles, not the least of which was that no formal mission statement or organisational directives existed. HQ USAFE at Ramstein AFB, Germany, provided a rough mission outline, but it was rudimentary, and it was left to the 501st TMW staff to put together their own plan; the wing was to 'maintain a capability to destroy or neutralize enemy offensive nuclear aircraft, fixed surface-to-surface missiles, nuclear storage areas, headquarters, command and control centres, and offensive and defensive air forces'. The first of 96 GLCMs destined for Greenham Common arrived on 14 November 1983 aboard a C-141B Starlifter, which was placed under heavy guard by USAF and RAF police and by RAF Regiment personnel while the rounds were offloaded and transported to their shelters.

The cruise missile's transporter/erector/launcher was a 78,000lb cross-country vehicle comprising a semi-trailer with an elevating armoured launcher containing four GLCM rounds towed by a MAN tractor. The launch control centre was a similar cross-country vehicle with a semi-trailer mounting an armoured shelter and generators. Each GLCM flight had a primary and back-up control centre linked by fibre-optic, electromagnetic pulse-resistant cable. (EMP is the massive burst of energy released by a nuclear explosion; it can cause severe damage to communications, radars and so forth.)

In the event of a war alert the 501st TMW's cruise missiles could be deployed to pre-surveyed sites almost anywhere in southern England, and as far west as the Welsh border. Once the missiles were on site, planning for their nuclear mission took about an hour, during which time the weapons remained vulnerable to Spetsnaz commandos. The Theatre Mission planning

system allowed the operator to select appropriate waypoints and Terrain Contour Matching (TERCOM) maps, which enabled the missile to avoid enemy defences en route to its target. The TERCOM system would not have been possible without years of satellite reconnaissance, which produced highly accurate, detailed and constantly updated maps of both friendly and potentially hostile territory. The information from the satellite imagery was digitised and stored in the cruise missile's computer.

Once the cruise missile was launched, it was guided by inertial navigation, updated at intervals to eliminate drift errors by means of the missile's radar altimeter, a part of the guidance system which enabled the missile to maintain smooth, terrain-hugging flight at altitudes down to 200 feet. The continuous stream of height data supplied by the radar altimeter was used to produce a profile of the ground over which the missile was flying and, by comparing this with stored data, to update the inertial platform. TERCOM maps were composed of matrices of spot heights drawn by the US Defense Mapping Agency and loaded into a missile's memory before launch. As the missile flew over a TERCOM field its altimeter mapped the ground directly below and the data was compared with that in the stored matrix. The flight path was identified and checked against the pre-planned route, and commands to rectify any errors were transmitted to the autopilot. By comparing three consecutive TERCOM fixes within the field, the possibility of the flight path being wrongly updated was eliminated.

As the flight progressed the TERCOM maps became smaller and more detailed until the final terminal matrix was reached just before the target, when final adjustments were made to the missile's flight path. Each potential target was surrounded by several terminal matrices, allowing the launch controller to choose the direction of attack and, if necessary, to arrange for several missiles to converge on the target from different directions.

The missile's memory contained up to 20 TERCOM maps. Between the TERCOM fields the GLCM navigated by means of pre-programmed, time-related waypoints, flying between them in straight lines at speeds and altitudes determined before launch. The pre-designated route took advantage of local terrain for concealment, avoided known defences and was designed to disguise its true destination. Suppose, for example, that a GLCM launched from southern England had as its target the big Soviet naval base of Kronshtadt, at the eastern end of the Gulf of Finland. Its route might take it out over the North Sea to make landfall on the Norwegian coast near Bergen, where its inertial navigation system would set it on course to the first TERCOM field, on the border between Norway and Sweden; from there it might turn south to fly through the Swedish valleys to a second TERCOM field at Lake Vanern, cruising on at 200 feet to cross the Swedish coast near Norrköping and enter the Baltic Sea, before continuing between the islands of Oland and Gotland to another TERCOM field on the Gulf of Danzig.

From then on the GLCM would be over enemy territory, manoeuvring to avoid known air defence sites and swinging north across Poland and Lithuania to pass well to the landwardside of the Gulf of Riga and enter its final TERCOM fields. As well as SAM and AAA sites it would now have to run the gauntlet of early-warning aircraft and interceptors armed with snap-down missiles, but being made of materials with a low radar signature it would be extremely difficult to detect, and the odds would be on it reaching its objective. To increase its chances of survival the missile would probably be launched at night, when its radar guidance would be unaffected, but enemy air activity would be greatly reduced.

The hypothetical GLCM flight described above would have involved it entering the neutral air space of Sweden, but nuclear wars are no respecters of neutrality and such a route would have been quite probable. In fact, likely routes might have been plotted anywhere from Norway in the north to the Swiss border in the south, and would have taken cruise missiles as far south as Odessa and as far north as Murmansk. The missile would be programmed to pop up at the end of its approach before diving on its target in a manoeuvre designed to circumvent any barriers, such as cables or high earthworks, that might be emplaced to protect important targets against horizontal attack.

To escape annihilation by surprise attack, GLCMs would have had to be deployed to their war stations at a very early stage in any serious rise in international tension. They would also have had to be used first, because in no sense is the cruise missile a retaliatory weapon. But neither were the NATO tactical nuclear weapons that preceded them; the option to use them first had always existed as part of the flexible response doctrine. In this respect the deployment of GLCMs in Britain and elsewhere in Europe did not deviate at all from previous NATO policy; rather, it bridged the crucial gap opened up in the 1970s by the deployment of new Soviet weaponry, no more and no less.

It was only after the end of the Cold War, when the GLCMs had been withdrawn from Europe following the signing of an Intermediate-Range Nuclear Forces (INF) Treaty in 1988, that the full extent of Soviet paranoia regarding cruise missiles became apparent. Here, for the first time, was a weapon apparently capable of emasculating the Soviet Union's offensive capability by means of a massive first strike; a weapon that could be launched from land, sea or air, and whose penetration might not be detected until it was too late. Also, there was the massive funding being poured into the US Strategic Defense Initiative, the so-called 'Star Wars' programme whose ultimate goal was to make the continental United States invulnerable to

ICBM attack. And thirdly, there was a major increase in Strategic Air Command's alert posture, culminating each year in a massive exercise called 'Global Shield'.

In this exercise, SAC practised its Emergency War Order procedures in a no-notice drill involving the whole of the Command, with more than 100,000 SAC personnel in the CONUS and on Guam responding to a simulated escalation in Cold War tensions by dispersing more than 120 bombers and tankers to 30 secure locations, while other unarmed bombers flew airborne alert missions along the low-level routes over Colorado, New Mexico, Kansas and Texas. Phase two of the exercise involved a simulated attack on the United States, and shortly before this some 400 SAC bombers and tankers conducted positive-control launches from about 70 locations in the CONUS. These were minimum-interval take-off operations in which aircraft at each location launched at 12- to 30-second intervals, using common runways, a procedure that ensured the entire Command would become airborne within minutes.

With President Ronald Reagan's administration adopting an increasingly aggressive stance, the Russians could not afford to ignore the possibility that America might be planning some form of pre-emptive action against the USSR. Documents uncovered in the former German Democratic Republic after the collapse of the communist bloc reveal that in the early 1980s the Soviet military leadership drew up a revised war plan for a surprise attack on the West. It envisaged a rapid advance on five fronts, with the aim of eliminating West Germany in thirteen to fifteen days before driving on through Denmark, the Netherlands and Belgium. All offensive resources were to be used, including chemical, biological and tactical nuclear weapons. The plan was complete down to the last detail, even to the issue of a currency to be used in the newly occupied territories.

It remained only a plan, because a realistic Soviet assessment showed that it would never succeed. But a key part of it included the elimination of the cruise missile bases in the UK, either by nuclear attack or by Spetsnaz operations. NATO Intelligence was aware of it, and in the mid-1980s great emphasis was placed on the formation of territorial and reserve units, in the UK and elsewhere, to defend key points against Soviet infiltration.

Luckily for the world, the threat of a major war that would have left Europe in ruins was replaced by President Mikhail Gorbachev's policies of *glasnost* and *perestroika*, leading to the demise of the old Soviet brand of communism and the integration of former potential enemies into a newly structured NATO.

Crisis Response:
Operation 'El Dorado Canyon'

At 21.00 hours eastern standard time on 14 April 1986, US President Ronald Reagan announced on national television that:

> At seven o'clock this evening . . . air and naval forces of the United States launched a series of strikes against the headquarters, terrorist facilities, and military assets that support Muammar Qaddafi's subversive activities. The attacks were concentrated and carefully targeted to minimize casualties among the Libyan people, with whom we have no quarrel . . . From initial reports, our forces have succeeded in their mission.

The attacks were the culmination of an escalating confrontation between the United States and Libya which had begun in October 1973, when the Libyan President, Colonel Qaddafi, had declared the Gulf of Sirte - which was indisputably international water - to be Libyan territorial waters south of latitude 32°20´ North. The Gulf, which covered an area of 3,200 square miles, was part of the US Sixth Fleet's operational area, and although American warships had continued to defy Qaddafi's edict, forays into the disputed area had been vetoed by President Jimmy Carter in November 1979, following the seizure of the US Embassy in Tehran and the taking of 66 American hostages by militant Islamic students.

On 17 August 1981, following the release of the hostages, the US Navy despatched the aircraft carriers USS *Forrestal* and *Nimitz*, with their associated battle

TOP & ABOVE : *Lockheed U-2R approaching to land at RAF Alconbury. U-2s were used for extensive surveillance of Libya and other Middle East areas. (Colin Lambert)*

groups, into the Gulf of Sirte for exercises. Libyan aircraft were detected in the vicinity of the exercise area during the next two days, and on the 19th two Sukhoi Su-22 'Fitters' closed with the US fleet. They were intercepted by two Grumman F-14 Tomcats of VF-41 from the *Nimitz*, and both Libyan fighters were shot down after they had launched two Atoll AAMs, which missed.

Following this incident, Qaddafi redoubled his efforts to hit back at the Americans by means of international terrorism. Libya – and also Syria – provided sanctuary, finance and training facilities for terrorist groups, and attacks on American lives and property intensified. Airliners carrying American passengers were hijacked, American citizens were seized as hostages, diplomatic outposts were bombed,

TOP & ABOVE: *KC-10A Extender 82–0191 of the 60th Military Airlift Wing. (Colin Lambert)*

and in Beirut 200 US marines were killed when a huge explosive device demolished their barracks in Beirut.

In October 1985, four Palestinian terrorists hijacked the 24,000-ton Italian cruise liner *Achille Lauro* and murdered an elderly, wheelchair-bound American passenger. The hijackers were given safe passage out of Egypt and, on 10 October, they took off from an air base near Cairo in an Egyptian Boeing 737. As it headed for Tunis, the airliner was intercepted by six Tomcats from the USS *Saratoga* and forced to land at Sigonella NATO air base in Sicily, where the gunmen were arrested.

There was no decrease in terrorist activity. In December 1985, terrorist bomb attacks at Rome and Vienna airports killed 20 people, including five Americans. The Americans decided it was time to act.

The build-up to the operation, code-named 'El Dorado Canyon', began in earnest on 11 April 1986, when the US Third Air Force and USAFE were placed on alert to carry out an air strike on selected military targets in Libya. This was to be a concerted action with air elements of the United States Sixth Fleet, which was then on station between Sicily and the Gulf of Sirte. Within the next 12 hours the USAF's tanker task force in Britain was reinforced by the arrival of 24 McDonnell Douglas KC-10 Extenders, 16 of which went to Mildenhall and the remainder to Fairford. Mildenhall's complement of 14 KC-135 tankers was also increased to 20 aircraft, including a single KC-135Q; this variant, two of which were already located at Mildenhall, was used to refuel the Lockheed SR-71A strategic reconnaissance aircraft, deployed to the United Kingdom by the 9th Strategic Reconnaissance Wing, whose Detachment 4 was at Mildenhall.

The USAF's explanation for the tanker deployments was that they were in connection with a NATO exercise, 'Salty Nation', but as the weekend of 12–13 April progressed the level of USAF activity made it increasingly clear that a war operation was being prepared. At Lakenheath, the engines of a proportion

of the 48th Tactical Fighter Wing's F-111Fs were being ground-run all through Saturday, and between 02.00 and 10.00 on Sunday eight more KC-10 tankers landed at Mildenhall, breaking the air base's long-standing ban on Sunday flying. The arrival of a large number of KC-10s was significant because, unlike the KC-135, they were equipped with both boom and probe-and-drogue refuelling systems, allowing them to refuel both USAF and US Navy aircraft. It was a sure indication that a combined operation was about to be mounted.

The operation itself was launched at 17.00 hours GMT on Monday, 14 April, when the first of 28 aircraft of the tanker force departed from Mildenhall and Fairford to position themselves at intervals along the F-111s' route. The original plan had envisaged a flight of around 1,600 nautical miles directly across continental Europe, but since the French, Spanish and Italian Governments had all refused permission for the strike force to overfly their territories, the route had to be rescheduled so that it crossed only international waters.

At 17.35 GMT on 14 April fifteen F-111Fs of the 48th TFW also began taking off from RAF Lakenheath and were joined by three EF-111 Raven electronic warfare aircraft from the 42nd Electronic Combat Squadron, RAF Upper Heyford. The total length of the flight, which now included a series of dog-legs to take it clear of France and Spain, was some 2,800nm, and as the F-111's combat radius with a 6,000lb warload was about 1,000nm the outbound flight required three refuelling contacts. The first of these was made off the Cherbourg Peninsula, the F-111s subsequently continuing on a south-westerly heading out into the Atlantic before turning south to fly parallel with the Atlantic coasts of Spain and Portugal. The second refuelling contact was made west of Lisbon and the strike force then continued south before swinging east to pass through the Strait of Gibraltar. The flight thus far had been made at high level, but the F-111s now descended to medium level for their third refuelling contact over the Mediterranean, off the Algerian coast.

Lockheed SR-71A of the 9th SRW streams its braking parachute. (Philip Jarrett)

RC-135V 64–14842 of the 55th SRW at Mildenhall on TDY from Offutt AFB, Nebraska. RC-135s undertook stand-off surveillance of Libya's air defences. (Colin Lambert)

With their tanks full again, the F-111 strike force now descended to low level, turning south at a point to the west of Sicily and bypassing the island of Lampedusa as they headed towards their assigned Libyan targets. There were three of these: the side of Tripoli Airport occupied by the Libyan Arab Air Force, the Al Azziziyah barracks in Tripoli, and the Sidi Bilal port facility ten miles west of Tripoli, where the Libyan Navy based its Nanuchka-class missile corvettes and La Combattante-class missile patrol boats.

The F-111 formation split into three waves. Those aircraft tasked with the strike on the airfield and port facility were armed with Mk 20 Rockeye laser-guided cluster bombs, while those assigned to the attack on the Tripoli barracks area and its associated command centre carried Mk 82 laser-guided bombs for greater effect against hardened targets. At the same time, 15 Grumman A-6 Intruders and Vought A-7 Corsairs from the Sixth Fleet carriers USS *America* and *Coral Sea*, also armed with 500lb and 2,000lb laser-guided weapons, headed in across the Gulf of Sirte to hit two targets near Benghazi: the Al Jumahiraya Barracks, which according to US Intelligence was a back-up command centre to the one at Tripoli, and the military airfield at Benina.

As the strike force made its final run towards the coast, top cover was provided by Sixth Fleet Grumman F-14 Tomcats and McDonnell Douglas F-18 Hornets as insurance against possible activity by the Libyan Arab Air Force's MiG-23 and Mirage fighter force, but in the event there was none. The F-111s made single passes through the target areas at 550 knots, using their Pave Tack equipment; Libyan defences were effectively jammed by the EF-111 Ravens and also by US Navy Grumman EA-6 Prowlers. The attack was carried out by twelve F-111Fs – two having aborted prior to reaching Libya and four more in the target area – through moderate and very inaccurate AAA and SAM fire, and of these four actually hit their targets accurately. One F-111, piloted by Captain Fernando Ribas-Dominicci, with Captain Paul Lorence as his weapons systems officer, crashed into the Mediterranean some 20 miles north of Tripoli, both crew being killed. The remainder began landing at Lakenheath at 04.45 GMT.

The 'El Dorado Canyon' operation, the first occasion on which US Third Air Force units had been used in anger from the United Kingdom, initially provoked a mixed response from the British public. The initial reaction was one of surprise that US forces in Britain, ostensibly committed to NATO, could apparently be used for unilateral action. The second was shock, bordering on anger, that Margaret Thatcher's Government had approved the use of British bases for the raid. Thirdly, there was the realisation that US bases in Britain, and the communities around them, were now potential targets for terrorist attack.

British anti-nuclear groups, primarily the Campaign for Nuclear Disarmament which had enjoyed some resurgence following the UK deployment of cruise missiles, seized their chance and organised large demonstrations at Lakenheath, Mildenhall, Upper Heyford and Fairford, but by 22 April, a week after the raid, the demonstrations had died down and the media, which had made much capital out of the affair, moved on to other stories. The assessment of HQ Third Air Force, which was that the public outcry against the raid would continue for several weeks and then gradually wane, proved to be correct; and when the Air Fête 1986, held at Mildenhall in May, passed without incident, the attention that the Libya raid had received in the media quickly dissipated.

In the short term, the attack on Libya – which had lasted just eight minutes and which at best could only be judged a partial success, even though Colonel Qaddafi went very quiet for some time afterwards – produced an unfavourable reaction among between 60 and 80 per cent of the British public. However, there was no escaping the fact that consultation between the US and British Governments had taken place before the raid, in full accordance with the 1952 Churchill–Truman protocol for joint consultation on the use of British-based US forces. And within five years the whole affair would be forgotten as the Americans and British formed the spearhead of a NATO-led coalition that would go into action against a far more dangerous dictator in Iraq.

Not Quite the Final Curtain

On 2 August 1990 Iraqi forces invaded Kuwait, and within a week USAF movements through Mildenhall were showing a dramatic increase as transport and tanker aircraft staged through *en route* to various Middle East destinations. Mildenhall's own Tanker Task Force's KC-135s departed and were replaced by others drawn from the ANG and AFRES. Fairford was reactivated and preparations made to receive B-52 bombers, and on 25 August, 18 48th TFW F-111Fs took off from Lakenheath, bound for Taif in Saudi Arabia. Eventually, 64 of the 48th TFW's aircraft were to be moved to the Middle East during the 'Desert Shield' military build-up period, a deployment that would not have been possible prior to the East–West rapprochement.

Four of the 42nd Electronic Combat Squadron's EF-111As also arrived at Taif from Upper Heyford on 21 December 1990, others being deployed to Incirlik in Turkey. Some F-111Es of the 20th TFW were already there on an exercise, and this deployment was later increased to around 20 aircraft as part of Operation 'Proven Force', an insurance against possible Iraqi incursions into Turkish territory. Completing the USAF deployment from UK bases was a move on 27 December 1990 by 18 A-10As of the 511th TFS, Alconbury, which went to King Fahd International Airport, Saudi Arabia, and the positioning of some

Woodbridge-based 39th SOW HC-130s and MJ-53Js to Turkey for aircrew rescue and special operations.

Early in 1991 the 806th Bomb Wing (Provisional) was activated at RAF Fairford to operate the incoming B-52 force, the first of ten aircraft arriving on 1 February, a fortnight after the start of the air offensive phase of Operation 'Desert Storm'. The first B-52 raid from Britain was carried out on 9 February and the last on the 25th, and between those dates the big bombers flew 60 effective sorties and dropped 1,158 tons of bombs, their principal targets being Iraqi Republican Guard armoured formations dug in around the perimeter of Kuwait. Its task completed, the 806th BW was deactivated on 6 March 1991.

The 48th TFW's record in the Gulf War was impressive, the F-111Fs flying 2,200 effective sorties out of 2,417 despatched, using Pave Tack and laser-guided bombs on most of them. Over 5,570 bombs were dropped, the type varying according to the selected target: 410 were GBU-10s, 2,542 GBU-12s, and 212 CBU-89s, the rest being a mixture of GBU-15s and large 4,700lb GBU-28s, the latter developed in just 17 days for attacks on deep Iraqi bunkers and command posts. The 48th TFW was credited with the destruction of 160 bridges, 113 bunkers and 920 armoured vehicles; in addition, 245 hardened aircraft shelters were heavily damaged. No aircraft was lost. The 20th

Rockwell B-1B 86–0126 of the 28th BS, 7th BW, seen at Mildenhall in 1996. USAF airfields in Britain are geared up to operate the B-1B, but to date no operational deployments have been required. (Colin Lambert)

Lockheed MC-130P of the 67th SOS, 352nd SOG, refuelling an MH-53J of the 21st SOS. (Colin Lambert)

TFW, meanwhile, flew 1,181 sorties, also without loss.

In April 1991, in the immediate aftermath of the Gulf War, the United Nations initiated Operation 'Provide Comfort', its aim to protect the Kurds of northern Iraq from attack by Saddam Hussein's forces. Initially, patrols over the threatened area were flown by A-10As of the 78th TFS, 81st TFW, which remained at Incirlik for three months until they were replaced by aircraft of the 92nd TFS. From then until the end of 1992 the 81st TFW kept eight A-10As on standby at Incirlik to deal with any possible threat to the Kurds, the whole operation supported by three EF-111As of the 42nd ECS from Upper Heyford, the latter returning to the UK in June 1992.

Meanwhile, the F-111Es of the 20th TFW had returned to Upper Heyford in March 1991, the 48th TFW's F-111Fs were back at Lakenheath by the middle of May, and the 10th TFW's A-10As were in position at Alconbury by 8 June, together with TR-1As of the 17th Reconnaissance Wing which had also been deployed to the Middle East. In July the 17th RW was downgraded and, redesignated the 95th Reconnaissance Squadron, was assigned to the 9th Strategic Reconnaissance Wing. The 95th RS, with four TR-1As, remained at Alconbury for operations over the former Yugoslavia until 15 September 1993, when it deactivated.

In October 1991 the squadrons of the 10th TFW began to leave Alconbury for the USA, beginning with the 509th TFS; the last aircraft departed on 30 March 1992. Alconbury now came under the control of the 10th Air Base Wing, USAFE, which administered the 352nd Special Operations Group. This unit was formed from the 39th Special Operations Wing, which moved

from Woodbridge to Alconbury on 15 January 1992 with the 7th SOS (Lockheed MC-130Es and Hs), 21st SOS (Sikorsky MJ-53Js) and the 67th SOS (HC-130s). The 352nd SOG came under the orders of the Commander, Special Operations Command Europe.

Changes at Mildenhall in 1992 included the departure, in January, of the Silk Purse EC-135Hs of the 10th ACCS, which had stood continuous airborne alert from 1962 until July 1990. On 1 April 1992, the 100th Air Refueling Squadron (later redesignated 351st ARS) was activated at Mildenhall within the 100th Air Refueling Wing, which became the European Tanker Task Force and operated in support of NATO air deployments throughout the theatre.

At Upper Heyford, the 42nd ECS deactivated on 10 July 1992 and its EF-111As returned to the USA in August. At the same time, as part of the overall drawdown of US forces in Britain, the 81st TFW's A-10As began returning to the USA from Bentwaters, with the exception of 28 aircraft reassigned to the 510th FS at Spangdahlem. The last aircraft departed in March 1993.

At Lakenheath, the 48th TFW had begun to rearm with the McDonnell Douglas F-15E Strike Eagle in February 1992, the aircraft going to the 492nd and 494th FS. The F-15E Strike Eagle played a major role in the Gulf War and proved what the F-111 had already demonstrated six years earlier, that modern combat aircraft can deliver precision-guided weapons on to heavily defended point targets. One of the F-15E's primary tasks in Operation 'Desert Storm' was to seek out and destroy Iraqi Scud missiles at night, working in conjunction with the Boeing E-8 Joint Surveillance Target Attack Radar System (JSTARS). Developed from

TOP: *Lockheed MC-130H of the 7th SOS, 352nd SOG. (Colin Lambert)*
ABOVE: *Sikorsky MH-53J 69–5784 of the 21st Special Operations Squadron, 352nd Special Operations Group, Alconbury. (Colin Lambert)*

TOP: *A dramatic climb-out from Mildenhall by B-1B 83–0065. (Colin Lambert)*
ABOVE: *Strike Eagle duo: F-15Es of the 493rd and 494th FS, 48th FW. (Colin Lambert)*

TOP: *F-15E of the 493rd FS, 48th FW, on the approach to land. Note the large air brake. (Colin Lambert)*
ABOVE: *Cockpit canopy detail of the F-15E Strike Eagle. (Colin Lambert)*

Shape of the future: Douglas C-17A 92–3291 of the 17th ACS, 437th MAW. (Colin Lambert)

the Boeing 707 airliner, the E-8 carried very advanced surveillance systems to detect second echelon ground concentrations deep behind enemy lines. The aircraft's computers then broadcast target information to both ground and air forces, directing tactical and strike aircraft, missile strikes or artillery fire as required. Once the E-8 had located an objective, the F-15E's WSO would use the aircraft's Low-Altitude Navigation and Targeting Infra-red for Night (LANTIRN) sensor to pinpoint the missile and its launcher and destroy them.

Developed by Martin Marietta, LANTIRN comprised two pods, one for navigation, the other for targeting. The AAQ-13 navigation pod contained a forward-looking infra-red (FLIR) sensor and a terrain-following radar, while the AAQ-14 targeting pod housed a steerable FLIR, laser designator and missile boresight correlator. The navigation FLIR enabled the crew to maintain high speeds at night and at low altitude, beaneath bad weather. Infra-red images of the terrain ahead of the aircraft were projected on to the pilot's Kaiser wide-angle HUD; compared with the F-15C's HUD, the F-15E display had a wider field of view – twenty degrees in elevation by thirty degrees in azimuth – made possible by holographic optics.

The navigation pod's Ku-band terrain-following radar enabled the crew to avoid obstacles while flying at high speeds and low altitudes. The pilot could manually follow commands displayed on the HUD or alternatively couple LANTIRN to the digital automatic flight control system for 'hands-off' terrain-following at altitudes down to 200 feet and speeds up to 520 knots. The companion targeting pod contained a high-resolution, stabilised, steerable FLIR for target acquisition and tracking at ranges over 8nm (18km). A laser boresighted to the FLIR designated targets for precision-guided weapons. Alternatively, a missile boresight correlator could hand off targets to imaging-infra-red Maverick missiles. The F-15E/LANTIRN system was tested and evaluated during 'Desert Storm' and produced some spectacular results. Although the primary targets were Scuds, command and control links, armour, airfields, roads and chemical, biological

and nuclear storage areas were also attacked in the course of over 2,200 sorties; only two of the 48 F-15Es deployed were lost. While flying night-time anti-Scud patrols, the aircraft usually flew in two- or four-ship elements, covering a large patrol area.

The F-15E concept arose out of a USAF requirement, identified in 1982, for a new long-range interdiction aircraft, and the first of 200 production examples flew for the first time in December 1986. The F-15E is powered by two Pratt & Whitney F100-229 engines producing 29,000lb of thrust, enough power to enable it to dogfight with types like the MiG-29 and Su-27. The aircraft is stressed to withstand 9g at combat gross weight and the weapon system can be reconfigured from air-to-ground to air-to-air mode by the flick of a switch. For air combat the F-15E can carry four AIM-7F/M Sparrow radar-guided AAMs and four AIM-9L/M Sidewinders, or up to eight AIM-20 AMRAAMs; a 20mm M61A1 six-barrel Gatling gun is mounted in the starboard wing root with a 512–round magazine. The F-15E can also carry a wide variety of 'smart' weapons, including GBU-10, -12 and -24 laser-guided bombs, BBU-15 glide bombs, GBU-28 laser-guided penetration bombs and AGM-65 Maverick missiles.

The F-15E's radar is the Hughes APG-70, a development of the APG-63 installed in earlier-model F-15s. While retaining the APG-63's air-to-air capability, the APG-70 has a synthetic-aperture high-resolution mapping mode. Terrain maps of near-photographic resolution are 'drawn' during rapid radar sweeps up to 45 degrees either side of the flight path, and these can be 'frozen' on the cockpit displays for navigation and targeting purposes, minimising the risk of radar emissions being detected. The aircraft can lift a maximum warload of 24,500lb and has a maximum range of 2,400nm; maximum combat radius is 685nm.

On 15 December 1993 RAF Upper Heyford closed, the last F-111Es of the 20th TFW having departed a week earlier. On 1 January 1994 the 20th's identity was transferred to the 363rd Fighter Wing at Shaw AFB, South Carolina, so maintaining the lineage of a unit that stood at the forefront of the USAF's battle line in Britain during most of the Cold War era.

Appendix

Main USAF Bases in Britain, 1948–98

ALCONBURY (Huntingdon)

After being relinquished by the RAF on 26 November 1945, Alconbury remained inactive until 1 June 1953, when it was reactivated by the USAF. The first unit to move in was the 7523rd Air Base Squadron, which set about extending the existing installations to receive the first combat squadrons. The work received fresh impetus in 1954 when the main runway was lengthened, and in March 1955 the 7560th Air Base Group moved in to pave the way for the arrival, on 15 September 1955, of the 85th Bomb Squadron from Sculthorpe with its B-45 Tornados. The 85th, which later rearmed with Douglas B-66Bs, remained at Alconbury until August 1959, when it was replaced by the 1st and 30th Squadrons of the 10th Tactical Reconnaissance Wing from Spangdahlem, Germany. Shortly before the 85th's departure, the airfield was occupied briefly, from May to August 1959, by the WB-50Ds of the 53rd Weather Squadron. The 10th TRW operated RB-66s out of Alconbury until May 1965, when the Wing began to rearm with RF-4C Phantoms.

The 30th TRS was deactivated on 1 April 1976, and on the same date the 527th Tactical Fighter Training Aggressor Squadron formed to provide target facilities for NATO air forces, receiving its first Northrop F-5E Tiger IIs in May. The squadron became fully operational on 1 January 1977. The 527th Squadron remained at Alconbury until June 1988, when it moved to Bentwaters.

The 1st TRS was inactivated on 29 May 1987, and on 20 August that year the 10th TRW was redesignated the 10th Tactical Fighter Wing, rearming with the A-10A Thunderbolt II. This unit began returning to the USA in October 1991, the withdrawal being completed in March 1992. Alconbury was also used by the 17th Reconnaissance Wing, activated on 1 October 1982 and operating Lockheed U-2R/TR-1 reconnaissance and battlefield surveillance aircraft, and by the US Army for helicopter operations.

On 15 January 1992 the 39th Special Operations Wing moved to Alconbury from Woodbridge and was joined there by the 7th Special Operations Squadron's MC-130Es, subsequently replaced by MC130Hs. In May 1992 the MJ-53J Pave Low III helicopters of the 21st SOS and the Combat Shadow HC-130s of the 67th SOS were also transferred from Woodbridge to Alconbury. In December 1992 the 39th SOW was downgraded and emerged as the 352nd Special Operations Group, with three flying squadrons, a maintenance squadron, a special tactical squadron and a supply squadron.

BASSINGBOURN (Cambridgeshire)

In the years following the Second World War Bassingbourn was used by RAF Transport Command, but on 25 August 1950, as a result of increased international tension following the outbreak of the Korean War, the B-29 Superfortresses of the 353rd Bomb Squadron, 301st Bomb Group, were deployed there on overseas detachment. Because of the international situation this unit remained at Bassingbourn until January 1951, when it was replaced by the RB-50Bs of the 38th Squadron, 55th Strategic Reconnaissance Wing. These stayed until May 1951, when they were in turn replaced on a rotational basis by the B-50Ds of the 97th Bomb Group. With the departure of the 97th in September 1951 Bassingbourn reverted to RAF control.

BENTWATERS (Suffolk)

Having been an RAF jet fighter station in the years immediately after the war, Bentwaters was inactive from 1 September 1949 until 1 July 1950, when it was placed

Lockheed MC-130H of the 7th Special Operations Squadron, 352nd Special Operations Group, RAF Alconbury. (Colin Lambert)

under Care and Maintenance and eventually transferred to the USAF on 16 March 1951. Six months later, on 3 September 1951, the 91st Squadron of the 81st Fighter Interceptor Group arrived with its F-86A Sabres, the first aircraft of this type to be based in Europe. On 1 April 1954 the Group was redesignated the 81st Fighter Bomber Wing and began to replace its Sabres with F-84F Thunderstreaks, re-equipment being completed by January 1955. On 8 July 1958 the unit was redesignated the 81st Tactical Fighter Wing, and shortly afterwards it received the first examples of a potent new tactical fighter, the McDonnell F-101 Voodoo. By the end of the year the Wing had received its full complement of these aircraft and its 41 F-84Fs were then transferred to the Federal German Luftwaffe. The 81st TFW now comprised the 91st and 92nd Squadrons, the latter having redeployed from Manston in April.

In October 1965 the Wing received the first examples of the F-4C Phantom, and by April 1966 was fully equipped with these aircraft. The Wing's third squadron, the 78th TFS, at Woodbridge, rearmed with F-4D Phantoms in the summer of 1969, and the 91st and 92nd Squadrons at Bentwaters also received F-4Ds in September 1973. In the autumn of 1978 the 81st TFW's Phantoms began to be replaced by A-10 Thunderbolt IIs, these aircraft being deployed from Bentwaters and Woodbridge in clutches of eight to forward operating locations (FOL) on the continent. Tactical fighter squadrons based at Bentwaters with the A-10A were the 92nd, 509th, 510th and 511th.

In June 1988 the 527th Aggressor Squadron moved to Bentwaters from Alconbury, replacing its F-5Es with F-16Cs. The 527th deactivated in January 1990, and on 21 May 1993 the 81st TFW also deactivated, the last of its A-10s having departed on 23 March.

BOVINGDON (Hertfordshire)

Bovingdon, an important USAAF bomber base during the Second World War, was subsequently used by BOAC and BEA for a period of five years, after which it was returned to American use on 25 May 1951, the USAF unit involved being the 7531st Air Base Squadron operating C-47 transports. Bovingdon remained in American hands until 1962, serving as a communications base for the US 3rd Air Division HQ at South Ruislip, and a wide variety of American aircraft types visited the base during this period. They included most types of transports on the USAF inventory, as well as occasional visitors such as the B-29, B-50 and B-26. After the departure of the Americans, Bovingdon passed under the control of the RAF's Southern Communications Squadron.

BRIZE NORTON (Oxfordshire)

For fifteen years Brize Norton was one of the most important USAF bases in Britain. After reconstruction of the runways and airfield installations the base was officially handed over to the USAF on 16 April 1951, and the first American bombers were deployed there on 27 June 1952 in the form of 21 B-36Ds and B-36Fs of the 11th Bomb Wing (Heavy), Carswell AFB. The deployment was only temporary, as they flew out again a fortnight later. Regular deployments to Brize Norton by Strategic Air Command units under the control of the 7503rd Strategic Wing began in December 1952 with the arrival of B-29s of the 301st Bomb Wing; this unit remained until March 1953 when it was replaced by the B-50As of the 65th Squadron, 43rd Bomb Wing.

The deployment of the 301st BW to Brize Norton and also to Fairford, Greenham Common and Upper Heyford, was a stop-gap measure pending the arrival of the first B-47 Stratojets. These arrived in September 1953 with two squadrons of the 305th Bomb Wing from Limestone AFB, Maine. B-47 detachments during the months that followed were from the 22nd BW, the 320th BW, and the 43rd BW, and to extend the periods of continuous airborne alert flown by the Stratojets, the KC-97Gs of the 321st Air Refueling Squadron arrived in December 1954, followed by similar aircraft of the 310th ARS.

SAC detachments continued until September 1955, when Brize Norton closed for six months to undergo runway repairs, and the next SAC unit to move in was the 307th BW, again with B-47s, followed in January 1957 by the 384th BW. The sixteenth of that month saw the arrival in Britain of the first B-52B Stratofortress, an aircraft of the 93rd BW, which touched down after a flight from Castle AFB in California. The next SAC unit to arrive, in April 1957, was the 380th BW with B-47Es, and its departure was followed by another period of airfield closure for runway repair. B-47 units deployed to Brize Norton early in 1958 included the 68th Bomb Wing and a squadron of the 100th BW. From March 1958 the KC-97G tankers which had accompanied the SAC detachments began to be replaced by KC-135s.

In April 1958 six B-52Ds of the 92nd BW deployed to Brize Norton to take part in the annual Bomber Command Bombing Competition, and B-52s continued to visit the airfield at irregular intervals. By this time Strategic Air Command's policy of sending its bombers overseas on three-month deployments had changed, small groups of aircraft now being deployed on Reflex Action alert which rendered the overseas bases less crowded and vulnerable. During this period RB-47s of the 55th and 98th SRWs also visited Brize Norton, together with the occasional U-2 *en route* to or from clandestine missions over the USSR. The airfield was also occasionally visited by B-58 Hustlers from January 1964, but the days of Brize Norton as a USAF base were numbered. The last SAC bomber, a B-47E of the 330th BW, flew out on 3 April 1965 and the airfield subsequently reverted to RAF use.

BRUNTINGTHORPE (Leicestershire)

Bruntingthorpe's career as a USAF base was brief. Although it was allocated to USAF use in November 1953, it reverted to Air Ministry control at the end of that year and was not reallocated to the USAF until February 1957. A new runway, suitable for high-performance jets, was built and Bruntingthorpe was designated as a satellite field for RAF Alconbury, the first unit to move in being the 3912th Air Base Squadron. January 1959 saw the start of a 90-day rotation period by the B-47s of SAC's 100th BW; these were followed in August by the RB-66s of the 19th TRS, 10th TRW, which remained until the autumn of 1962. Bruntingthorpe, which featured regular SAC deployments until that time, then closed as an airfield.

BURTONWOOD (Cheshire)

Burtonwood, an important USAAF supply and maintenance base during the Second World War, was reopened for USAF use in 1948 as a supply depot for SAC units on detachment to the United Kingdom. During the Berlin Airlift Burtonwood was responsible for the inspection and overhaul of C-54 transport aircraft, and afterwards the base retained its responsibility for the maintenance of aircraft and the supply of materiel to USAF airfields in Britain, being designated the Northern Air Materiel Area on 1 September 1953. Burtonwood's resident unit was the 53rd Weather

Reconnaissance Squadron, with WB-50s, but the base was visited by almost every aircraft type in USAF service from time to time, including, in 1956, a detachment of B-36 bombers. Up to 1958 Burtonwood had been the main terminal for the Military Air Transport Service in the United Kingdom, but this now moved to Mildenhall and the WB-50s of the 53rd WRS went to Alconbury. With the departure of the United States forces from France, Burtonwood became a massive storage complex; together with Caerwent in South Wales, it was the main storage facility for US weaponry in the UK. Burtonwood was progressively run down after 1976, although there remained a small American presence until 1992.

CHELVESTON (Northamptonshire)

Chelveston, from where USAAF B-17s had operated from 1942 to 1945, returned to American control in December 1952 with the arrival of the 3914th Air Base Group, Strategic Air Command. For the next few years Chelveston was the scene of frequent SAC deployments, but the only resident flying unit was the 42nd Tactical Reconnaissance Squadron, 10th TRW, which arrived from Spangdahlem in August 1959 with its RB-66s and remained until August 1962. Chelveston subsequently became a reserve airfield and the site of the USAF communications and storage centre.

FAIRFORD (Gloucestershire)

Work on enlarging Fairford and extending its facilities began with American help in the summer of 1950, and on 1 July 1951 the base came under the control of the 7th Air Division, Strategic Air Command. During the next 18 months the airfield was visited by detachments of B-29s and B-50s, and on 7 February 1953 17 B-36 bombers arrived from Carswell AFB, Texas. A few weeks later, on 7 April, two B-47s landed at Fairford; this was a preliminary to the arrival, on 2 June, of the 367th, 368th and 369th Squadrons of the 306th

TOP: *Lockheed EC-130E ELINT Hercules of the Missouri ANG, seen at RAF Fairford in 1994. (Colin Lambert)*
ABOVE: *Rockwell B-1B 85-0072 of the 96th B.W. (Philip Jarrett)*

TOP & ABOVE: *Lockheed F-117A 85–0835 of the 9th FS, 49th FW, approaching to land at Fairford in 1997. Had the Cold War continued, F-117A units might have been deployed to the UK on a regular basis. (Colin Lambert)*
BELOW: *F-117A 85–0834 of the 8th FS, 49th FW, at Mildenhall in 1997. The tail in the background belongs to a MiG-29 'Fulcrum'. (Colin Lambert)*

BW, whose B-47Bs stayed until 4 September 1953. In addition to the regular B-47 detachments that arrived at Fairford during the succeeding months, usually in the form of a single squadron, the base also saw deployments by the RB-47Es of the 68th Strategic Reconnaissance Wing and the RB-36Fs of the 5th SRW, both of which occupied Fairford for some weeks in 1954. The use of Fairford by SAC continued until the early 1960s, although on a much reduced scale, and the airfield reverted to RAF use in June 1964. In 1979 the 7020th Air Base Group was activated to administer tanker operations by the KC-135s of the 34th and 922nd Strategic Squadrons of the 11th Strategic Group, SAC. In 1991 Fairford was used by B-52s engaged in bombing operations against Iraqi forces, and in 1999 it was used as an operational base for B-52s and B-1s engaged in NATO air attacks on Serbia.

GREENHAM COMMON (Berkshire)

Greenham Common's long association with the USAF began in April 1951, when an extensive airfield rebuilding programme was begun by the 804th Engineer Aviation Battalion, the base's administration being taken over by the 7501st Air Base Squadron. Wartime installations were destroyed and a new 10,000-foot east–west runway was laid. The airfield was formally handed over from nominal Air Ministry control to the 7th Air Division, Third Air Force, in June 1951, but reconstruction work was not completed until September 1953, when the base was declared operationally ready to receive B-47 Stratojets.

The first operational SAC deployment to Greenham Common took place in March 1954 and involved a detachment of the 303rd BW's B-47s. Their stay, however, was short, for the runway showed signs of breaking up and the 303rd had to move to Fairford to complete its deployment. In April 1956, following extensive runway repairs, Greenham Common passed under the control of the 3909th Air Base Group and shortly afterwards the 97th Air Refueling Squadron arrived with KC-97G tankers. In October 1956 the 310th BW arrived with 45 B-47s, whose operations caused a considerable outcry among the local population, and public opposition to the use of Greenham intensified in March 1958 when a B-47 was forced to jettison its underwing tanks following engine failure on take-off; one tank exploded inside a hangar and the other hit a parked B-47, causing a fire that raged for several hours and destroyed another B-47 that was parked close by.

In April 1958 the 90-day deployments came to an end and were replaced by three-week Reflex Action rotations, which considerably reduced the noise factor. In the early 1960s Greenham Common was the scene of periodic visits by B-52 Stratofortress bombers, and on one occasion, in October 1963, by a B-58 Hustler, but the only regular visitors continued to be SAC B-47s on Reflex Action deployments. These deployments continued until April 1964, when a change in USAF policy resulted in the airfield being handed back to RAF control three months later.

In the late 1960s Greenham Common was designated a NATO standby base under the control of the 7551st Combat Support Group and was subsequently used as the terminal for a number of rapid reinforcement exercises. In March 1976 the 20th Tactical Fighter Wing's F-111Es moved in from Upper Heyford for three months while that airfield's runways were resurfaced. Later plans to use Greenham Common as a base for KC-135A tankers were never implemented, largely due to local opposition, and although an American presence remained there in the form of the

7273rd Air Base Group from 1979 the airfield passed briefly out of the news.

Then came a renewed outcry. In June 1980 it was announced that Greenham Common was to be one of two sites in Britain where US cruise missiles were to be deployed. The first of these weapons, operated by the 11th Tactical Missile Squadron of the 501st Tactical Missile Wing, arrived at Greenham in May 1983 aboard C-5A Galaxy aircraft. The 501st TMW attained IOC (Initial Operational Capability) on 30 December 1983 and was inactivated in 1989 following the signing of the INF Treaty eliminating intermediate-range theatre nuclear forces.

LAKENHEATH (Suffolk)

Lakenheath has remained one of the most important USAF bases in Britain for five decades. The initial post-war American presence here involved B-29s of the 2nd Bomb Group, which arrived in July 1948 in response to growing international tension over the Russian blockade of Berlin. During the next 10 years the base was visited by more than 30 Strategic Air Command units on 90-day temporary deployments, the B-29s giving way in August 1949 to B-50As supported by their KB-29M tankers.

The first B-50A unit to visit Lakenheath was the 65th Bomb Squadron, 43rd Bomb Group, and from January 1951 SAC deployments also involved B-36Ds supported by C-125 Globemasters carrying spares and ground crew. During the next few months Lakenheath became the principal base for USAF strategic reconnaissance operations from the United Kingdom and was frequently used by RB-36s and RB-50s. The first B-47s visited Lakenheath in April 1953 but operational deployments by these aircraft did not begin until June the following year, when supporting KC-97 tankers were also based there. In 1956 there was much local speculation when a mysterious jet aircraft with long glider-like wings was seen slipping into and out of Lakenheath; it was subsequently identified as a Lockheed U-2. Later that year the base was vacated by the Americans, but they returned in January 1960 with the redeployment of the 48th Tactical Fighter Wing from France. The unit successively operated F-100D Super Sabres, F-4D Phantoms, F-111Fs and F-15E Strike Eagles, which were Lakenheath's tenants in 1998.

MANSTON (Kent)

Manston's position made it an important base for fighter escort operations during the Second World War, and in the summer of 1950 it was decided to transfer the airfield to the US 3rd Air Division. The first USAF unit to move in, in July 1950, was the 7512th Air Base Group, although American units subsequently based there came under the operational control of No. 11 Group, RAF Fighter Command. The first operational unit to arrive at Manston, in July 1950, was the 20th Fighter-Bomber Wing with Republic F-84E Thunderjets, and this was followed in January 1951 by the 31st Fighter Escort Wing, which in turn was replaced by the 12th Fighter Escort Wing in June. A permanent USAF search-and-rescue facility was also set up at Manston from April 1951 with the arrival of the 9th Air Rescue Squadron, operating SA-16 Albatross and SB-29 aircraft.

Strategic Air Command relinquished control of Manston in November 1951, whereupon the base was taken over by the Third Air Force, USAFE. For the next few months Manston was the home of the 123rd FBW of the Kentucky Air Guard, operating F-84Es; this was one of the units mobilised as a result of the Korean War, but it was deactivated in July 1952

ABOVE & RIGHT: *F-15E of the 48th TFW, Lakenheath, approaching to land and rolling after touchdown. (Colin Lambert)*

and its aircraft were used to re-form the 512th, 513th and 514th Fighter-Bomber Squadrons of the 406th FBW. In November 1953 this unit became the first to arm with the F-86 Sabre and its designation was changed to Fighter Interceptor Wing; at the same time the 9th Air Rescue Squadron detachment was expanded and redesignated the 66th ARS. In November 1954 the 512th FIS moved to Soesterberg in Holland and its place at Manston was taken four months later by the 92nd Fighter Squadron from Bentwaters. The 406th FIW remained at Manston until it was deactivated in May 1958, after which the airfield reverted to RAF control.

Low and fast : a Rockwell B-1B streaks across a desert landscape in its intended low-level penetration role. B-1Bs were deployed to RAF Fairford in the UK for operations in the Balkans, (Philip Jarrett)

MARHAM (Norfolk)

Marham's post-war association with the USAF began in the spring of 1946, when seven B-17 Flying Fortresses and three B-29 Superfortresses were based there for Project 'Ruby', which involved deep-penetration bombing trials. In June 1947 Marham was visited by nine B-29s of the 97th BG, and later that year three B-29s were based at Marham for bombing trials against the U-boat pens at Farge. From July 1948 the airfield was used by SAC for B-29 units on TDY, including the 307th BG (370th and 371st BS) from July to October 1948, and the 97th BG (340th and 341st BS) from November 1948 to February 1949, after which the base reverted to RAF control.

MILDENHALL (Suffolk)

Mildenhall became an important SAC base in July 1950 when, as a result of the Korean War emergency, the 93rd BG's 329th BS arrived with B-50Ds. It stayed until February 1951 when it was replaced by the 509th BG, the unit that had been specially formed to drop the atomic bombs on Japan six years earlier; other bomb groups on TDY at Mildenhall in 1951 were the 2nd and 22nd. In August 1953 Mildenhall became a primary flight refuelling base with the arrival of KC-97E tankers, and in 1959 it assumed Burtonwood's role as the principal Military Air Transport Service transatlantic terminal under the control of the 322nd Air Division. During this period B-47s also used Mildenhall at intervals on Reflex Action deployments. In 1966 the 513rd Troop Carrier Wing arrived from Evreux, France, together with Silk Purse Control, which was the European Command's airborne command post facility. In July 1968 the controlling unit was redesignated 513th Tactical Airlift Wing, which assumed responsibility for all base functions including aircraft maintenance and the upkeep of the airborne command posts for EC-135s.

Over the years Mildenhall has seen transport aircraft movements on a massive scale in its role as the main terminus for transatlantic flights to and from Britain and Germany. C-130 Wings rotated there on a regular basis, coming under the control of the 435th Tactical Airlift Group. Mildenhall is also the base of the European Tanker Task Force, which was controlled by Detachment I, 306th

Afterburners blazing, streaming wingtip contrails, B-1B 83–0065 of the 9th BS steep-turns over Mildenhall. (Colin Lambert

B-1B 86–0130 of the 28th BS, 7th BW, at Mildenhall in 1995. (Colin Lambert)

Strategic Wing and later by the 100th Air Refueling Squadron. Mildenhall is also used by Lockheed U-2R and TR-1 reconnaissance aircraft and by Rivet Joint electronic surveillance RC-135s of the 55th SRW.

MOLESWORTH (Cambridgeshire)

The second of the USAF's cruise missile bases in the UK, Molesworth's association with the Americans began in July 1951, when a new runway was laid down and other airfield modifications were carried out. Operations began in February 1954 with the arrival of the 582nd Air Resupply Group with twelve B-29As, four SA-16A Albatross amphibians, three C-119Cs and a C-47. The primary role of this unit was to provide search-and-rescue facilities for crews of reconnaissance aircraft which might be forced down in hostile territory. The B-29s remained operational until October 1956 when the 582nd ARG was redesignated the 42nd Troop Carrier Squadron (Medium) under the control of USAFE. More C-119Cs were added to the strength, as well as some C-54s. Other visitors to Molesworth in the 1950s included some B-45s of the 47th BW and WB-50 weather reconnaissance aircraft. The airfield was deactivated in December 1957 but returned to operational use in the 1980s as a cruise missile complex, the first GLCM flight being activated in 1987 and deactivated two years later following the signing of the INF treaty.

PRESTWICK (Ayrshire)

As the terminal of the North Atlantic ferry route Prestwick was extensively used by USAF and US Navy transport aircraft in the late 1940s, but it was not until 1951 that the wartime USAF base there was reactivated to provide support facilities for the Military Air Transport Service and also to give air-sea rescue coverage over the eastern Atlantic. The resident air-sea rescue unit was the 67th ARS, which left for Spain in 1966.

SCAMPTON (Lincolnshire)

During the period of the Berlin Airlift Scampton was one of the RAF bases made available to the US Government, and 30 B-29s of the 28th BG were based there between July and October 1948. This unit was replaced by the 301st BG, which returned to the USA in January 1949 following the relaxation of international tension. Scampton subsequently returned to RAF control, although the 3930th Air Base Squadron was based there for a brief period in 1952.

SCULTHORPE (Norfolk)

The first American unit to operate from Sculthorpe post-war was the 92nd BG, which arrived in February 1949 with its B-29s. In August that year the base became the home of the first B-50As to be stationed in Britain, those of the 63rd Squadron of the 43rd BG. During the years that followed many SAC bomb groups rotated through Sculthorpe on TDY, among them the 2nd, 22nd, 97th and 301st. Until January 1951 Sculthorpe had been under RAF control, but it then came under USAF administration and on 31 May 1952 B-45 Tornado jet bombers of the 84th and 85th BS, 47th BG, flew in to become permanent residents. A third squadron, the 86th, formed there in March 1954. In May that year Sculthorpe received another resident unit, the 19th Tactical Reconnaissance Squadron, whose RB-45Cs were tasked with night radar reconnaissance, while another permanent unit to arrive in 1954 was the 8554th Tow Target Flight with TB-26B Invader target tugs and L-5 Sentinels.

As well as the front-line units Sculthorpe housed the HQ

of the 49th Air Division, whose C-119s, C-47s, L-20s and T-33s provided transport and communications support for the USAF's tactical forces in Britain. In January 1958 the RB-45Cs of the 19th Squadron were replaced by RB-66s, and soon afterwards B-66s also replaced the Tornados of the 47th Wing. A support tanker force was provided by KB-50D and KB-50J aircraft, which remained operational at Sculthorpe until March 1954. In June 1962 the 47th BW was deactivated but Sculthorpe was retained by the USAF as a Dispersed Operating Base. In the 1980s Detachment One of the 48th TFW was based there.

SHEPHERD'S GROVE (Suffolk)

In August 1951, soon after it was reactivated as a USAF base, Shepherd's Grove received the first F-86A Sabres to be based in Britain. These aircraft belonged to the 116th Squadron of the 81st FIW, and they were joined shortly afterwards by aircraft of the 92nd FIS. It was the first time that foreign aircraft had been assigned to the air defence of Great Britain, the aircraft coming under the control of No. 12 Group, Fighter Command. In November 1952 the 116th FIS was redesignated 78th FS, and in April 1954 its identity changed yet again to the 78th FBS, the reason for the change becoming apparent when the squadron began to receive F-84F Thunderstreaks later in the year. The 78th moved to Woodbridge in December 1958 and soon afterwards work began on the building of a Thor IRBM site for RAF Bomber Command. No. 82(SM) Squadron was based there from July 1959 to July 1963, after which the airfield reverted to civilian use.

UPPER HEYFORD (Oxfordshire)

Upper Heyford's long association with the USAF began in June 1950, when various support units moved in to prepare the base for eventual use by Strategic Air Command. The airfield was formally handed over to the USAF in May 1951 when it passed under the administrative control of the 7509th Air Base Squadron.

Alterations to the main runway were completed by the end of 1951, when the KB-29Ps of the 93rd Air Refueling Squadron arrived at the start of a 90-day TDY. For the next two years Upper Heyford remained primarily a flight refuelling base, used by the KB-29 and KB-50 tankers that were responsible for flight refuelling the 2nd, 97th, 301st and 509th Bomb Groups on TDY to British bases.

The airfield was used by B-47 and RB-47 Stratojets from June 1953, and these aircraft remained Upper Heyford's principal users until March 1965 when, together with other British bases, it was transferred from SAC to USAFE. For just over a year it was maintained as a Dispersed Operating Base by the 7514th Combat Support Group, which was deactivated on the arrival of the 66th Tactical Reconnaissance Wing from France in September 1966. This unit operated RF-101C Voodoos and RF-4C Phantoms until April 1970, when it too was deactivated. Upper Heyford subsequently became the home of the 20th Tactical Fighter Wing (55th, 77th and 79th TFW) with F-111Es. The 20th TFW deactivated in December 1993 (its identity passing to the 363rd FW a year later) and Upper Heyford then closed.

WETHERSFIELD (Essex)

After five years on Care and Maintenance, Wethersfield was taken over by the Americans in the early 1950s and the main runway was lengthened. In June 1952 the 20th Fighter Group flew in with its Republic F-84G Thunderjets after a transatlantic crossing. In February 1955 the unit's designation changed to the 20th Fighter-Bomber Wing and later in the year the Thunderjets began to be replaced by F-84F Thunderstreaks. These were followed in the summer of 1957 by F-100 Super Sabres, and in 1958 the unit was renamed the 20th Tactical Fighter Wing. Another resident unit at this time was the 23rd Helicopter Squadron with its H-21Bs for rescue and fire fighting.

The 20th TFW left Wethersfield early in 1970 to rearm with F-111s at Upper Heyford, and in April 1970 Wethersfield was taken over by the 66th Combat Support Group. In August 1976, after being successively designated the 66th Combat Support Squadron and then Operation Location A, 10th Tactical Reconnaissance Wing, the former 66th CSG became Detachment One, 10th TRW. Its principal role was support and administration, and it was later joined by the 819th Civil Engineering Squadron and the USAF Rapid Engineer Deployable and Heavy Operations Repair Squadron Engineer (Red Horse), whose task was to undertake runway repairs in Third Air Force's area.

WOODBRIDGE (Suffolk)

Woodbridge passed under American control in June 1952 and subsequently became the home of the 79th Fighter-Bomber Squadron of the 20th Fighter-Bomber Wing, operating first F-84Gs and later (from 1957) F-100s. In July 1958 the 81st TFW assumed operational control of Woodbridge and after necessary runway repairs the 78th TFS flew in from Shepherd's Grove with its F-84F Thunderstreaks. These were soon replaced by F-101 Voodoos which the 81st operated until it began to receive F-4 Phantoms in March 1966. Late in 1969 the 79th TFS moved to Upper Heyford, leaving the 78th TFS at Woodbridge with F-4D Phantoms. The move made room for the arrival of the 67th Aerospace Rescue and Recovery Squadron from Moron AB in Spain with HC-130 Hercules and HH-3E helicopters. This unit was later redesignated the 67th Special Operations Squadron, and together with the 7th and 21st SOS came under the command of the 39th Special Operations Wing, which moved to Woodbridge from Germany in 1990. All units vacated Woodbridge for Alconbury in May 1992.

Bibliography

Bowyer, Michael J. F. *Force for Freedom* (Patrick Stephens Ltd, 1994). Note: a very useful reference work, providing a record of USAF units deployed to the UK from 1948, with aircraft serials etc.

Burrows, William E., *Deep Black* (Bantam, 1988)

Cochran, Thomas B., William M. Arkin, Robert S. Norris, and Jeffrey I. Sands (eds), *Soviet Nuclear Weapons* (Nuclear Weapons Databook Vol. IV, Harper & Row, 1989; prepared by the Natural Resources Defense Council, Inc.)

Crampton, Sqn Ldr John, 'RB-45 Operations' paper delivered at an Air Intelligence Symposium, RAF Bracknell, and reproduced in the proceedings of the Royal Air Force Historical Society, 1997

The Development of Strategic Air Command 1946-1986, (Office of the Historian, HQ SAC, Offutt AFB, September 1986)

Faringdon, Hugh, *Confrontation: the Strategic Geography of NATO and the Warsaw Pact* (Routledge & Kegan Paul, 1986)

Futrell, Robert F., *The United States Air Force in Korea 1950-53* (Duell, Sloan and Pearce, 1961)

Gowing, Margaret, assisted by Lorna Arnold, *Independence and Deterrence: Britain and Atomic Energy 1939-1952* (Vol. I: Policy Making, Macmillan, 1974)

Gunston, Bill, *General Dynamics F-111* (Ian Allan, 1978)
——, *Illustrated Encyclopaedia of the World's Rockets* and *Missiles* (Leisure Books, 1979)

Jackson, Robert, *Avro Vulcan* (Patrick Stephens, 1984)
——, *The Berlin Airlift* (Patrick Stephens Ltd, 1988)
——, *Combat Aircraft Prototypes Since 1945* (Airlife, 1985)
——, *V-Bombers* (Ian Allan, 1981)
——, *World Military Aircraft Since 1945* (Ian Allan Ltd, 1979)

Jacobsen, Meyers K. and Ray Wagner, *B-36 in Action* (Squadron/Signal Publications, Carrollton, Texas, 1980)

Joy, Admiral C. Turner, *How Communists Negotiate* (The Macmillan Company, New York, 1955)

Nemecek, Vaclav, *The History of Soviet Aircraft from 1918* (Willow Books, 1986)

Norris, R. S. 'Questions on the British H-Bomb' (Nuclear Weapons Databook working paper, National Resources Defense Council, 1992)

Peacock, Lindsay, *Boeing B-47 Stratojet* (Osprey, 1987)
——, 'SAC's Fighters' (articles in *Aviation News*, 24 April to 7 May 1981).
Rowlands, Air Marshal Sir John, 'The Origins and Development of the British Strategic Nuclear Deterrent Forces, 1945-1960. (Proceedings No. 7, Royal Air Force Historical Society, paper delivered on 23 October 1989)

Schroeder, Sgt C.M., *A History of the Third Air Force 1940-1988* (ed. MSgt V. L. Briley, 3rd AF Historical Pamphlet, 1988)

Wagner, Ray, *The North American Sabre* (Macdonald, 1963)

Welzenbach, Donald E. 'Overflying the Soviet Union' (paper delivered at a symposium on Anglo-American air power cooperation during the Cold War, reproduced in the proceedings, *Seeing off the Bear*, ed. Roger G. Miller, (1995)

Whiting, Kenneth R. *The Development of the Soviet Armed Forces, 1917-1977* (Air War College, Maxwell AFB, Alabama, 1978)

Wynn, Humphrey, *RAF Nuclear Deterrent Forces* (HMSO, 1994)

Index